REACHING & TEACHING

KIDS WHO DON'T FIT IN THE BOX

MAKING SCHOOL WORK FOR EVERY STUDENT

PETE HALL

Solution Tree | Press
a division of Solution Tree

555 North Morton Street
Bloomington, IN 47404
800.733.6786 (toll free) / 812.336.7700
FAX: 812.336.7790

email: info@SolutionTree.com
SolutionTree.com

Visit **go.SolutionTree.com/studentengagement** to download the free reproducibles in this book.

Printed in the United States of America

FSC
www.fsc.org
MIX
Paper | Supporting responsible forestry
FSC® C008955

LCCN: 2026009512

Solution Tree
Cameron L. Rains, CEO
Edmund M. Ackerman, President

Solution Tree Press
Publisher: Kendra Slayton
Associate Publisher: Todd Brakke
Acquisitions Director: Hilary Goff
Editorial Director: Laurel Hecker
Art Director: Rian Anderson
Managing Editor: Sarah Ludwig
Copy Chief: Jessi Finn
Senior Production Editor: Miranda Addonizio
Copy Editor: Jessica Starr
Proofreader: Sarah Ludwig
Text and Cover Designer: Abigail Bowen
Content Development Specialist: Amy Rubenstein
Associate Editor: Elijah Oates
Editorial Assistant: Madison Chartier

To Mindy Hall, my wife and ballast:
You know when to lift me up a
notch or knock me down a peg, and
I appreciate it. I love you.
You're the greatest teacher I've ever known.

ACKNOWLEDGMENTS

THIS BOOK IS for educators. As such, I feel it's important to offer a nod to the educators I've known who set the bar higher than I could have imagined—for themselves, for me, for their kids, and for the profession.

When I was in sixth grade, Mrs. Andrews captured my heart and brain, and my life was never the same. Uncle Nelson, my first and only basketball coach, taught me about the power of being part of a team, both on and off the court. Coupled with my first teachers, my parents—Cliff and Gay, Alice and Guy—set me on a path to success from an early age.

Professionally, I cannot say enough about the power and collective impact of these folks on the lives of thousands and thousands of kids, as I witnessed it firsthand: Thelma Fones, Debbie Cylke, Frank C. Garrity, Mark Niemeyer, Lisa Ramburado, Kathy Ludwig, Sandy Anderson, Ethel Kellogg, Lori Houck, Taj Jensen, Michelle Wolfe, Ann Kaluza, Batman Meisfjord, Slash Caldwell, Ashley Gotta, Collette McIntyre, Katie Gurule, Amanda Romey, TC Imes, Tammy Campbell, Kipton Solmonson . . . the list could go on and on. For word count's sake, I cannot include everyone. Just know you're in my heart.

Special shoutouts to the teachers who impacted the trajectory of my kids' lives: the triad of sixth-grade teachers who inspired Daniel (Derek Cordell, Dennis Dyer, and Kim Price), the kindergarten teacher who launched Indy's journey (Denise Fitzpatrick), and the Spanish teacher who captivated Peja (Shasta Bell). With the utmost respect and admiration, I tip my cap to you.

A book only becomes a book because a special collection of people found the ideas preceding it to be worthy enough for publication. Enter the team at Solution Tree Press. Only by the dogged determination of Douglas Rife and the indomitable spirit of Claudia Wheatley did this particular book find its way through the channels to exist in the first place. To the editorial team, especially Amy Rubenstein and Miranda Addonizio, I owe a particular debt of gratitude for shaping and cleaning these ideas, stories, and tools in what ended up being a palatable resource that I'm extraordinarily proud of.

Decades ago, the late Rick and Becky DuFour, the architects of the ideas that provide the foundation of Solution Tree, invited me to be a part of their team. The circumstances weren't right at the time; alas, our partnership never materialized. But look at where we are now! Better late than never, I say. I hope this book amplifies the spirit of your eternal work.

And to you, my readers, I thank you a million times over. Without you, where would we be? I appreciate your interest in shaking things up and doing right by kids—whether it's in school, in the community, or anywhere else. Cheers!

Solution Tree Press would like to thank the following reviewers:

Chris L. Bennett
Executive Director of Middle Schools and Accountability
Cleveland County Schools
Shelby, North Carolina

Jami Burr
Principal
Connect Academy
West End, North Carolina

Timothy Carlson
Principal
Calgary, Alberta, Canada

Jody Dendewicz
Partners in Education Inclusive Education Teacher
qathet School District No. 47
Powell River, British Columbia, Canada

Tara Hagood
Assistant Principal
Kenneth Cooper Middle School
Oklahoma City, Oklahoma

Ian Landy
Regional Principal
qathet School District No. 47
Powell River, British Columbia, Canada

Bill Rounis
Secondary Mathematics Teacher
Wellington Secondary School
Nanaimo, British Columbia, Canada

Calen VanNess
Assistant Principal
Daniel Webster Elementary School
Marshfield, Missouri

Jacqueline Yu
Student Services Coordinator
Christ the Redeemer Catholic Schools
Calgary, Alberta, Canada

TABLE OF CONTENTS

Reproducibles are in italics.

Visit **go.SolutionTree.com**
/studentengagement
to download the free
reproducibles in this book.

ABOUT THE AUTHOR

PETE HALL is a retired educator and currently provides professional learning experiences through his position as president and CEO of EducationHall. After a teaching career that spanned grades preK–8 in three states, Hall served twelve years as a principal in three schools: Anderson Elementary in the Washoe County School District (Reno, Nevada) and Sheridan Elementary and Shaw Middle in the Spokane Public Schools (Washington). Under his leadership, each of the schools received awards for academic performance, growth, and student achievement.

With numerous honors and accolades for his leadership on the local, national, and international stage, including ASCD's Outstanding Young Educator Award and Nevada's Martin Luther King, Jr. Award, Hall also served on the Nevada Governor's Commission on Excellence in Education and the National Education Association's Great Public Schools Indicators project. He is author or coauthor of fifteen books, including several bestsellers, and has spoken or presented to hundreds of audiences internationally. His down-to-earth personality, real-life application, and practical tools have helped educators, leaders, and systems accelerate their growth for over twenty years. His topics of expertise include leadership, coaching and mentoring, positive learning environments, solid core instruction, high-leverage interventions, and creating personal balance to fuel unmitigated success—in work, at home, and everywhere in between. Hall provides coaching and mentoring support to school leaders, business executives, professional athletes, stand-up comedians, custodians, and more.

Hall received a bachelor's degree in communication from the University of California at Davis, a master's degree in education from Boston University, and an education specialist degree in educational leadership from the University of Nevada. He and his family live in Coeur d'Alene, Idaho.

To learn more about Hall's work, visit www.EducationHall.com or www.linkedin.com/in/petehallstrivesuccesssolutions.

INTRODUCTION

"I DON'T TAKE phone calls during the school day."

"Yes, I know," my office manager, Sandra Joy, replied. "They're unpredictable, and you want to leave as little to chance as possible."

It was my third year as principal of Anderson Elementary School in Reno—a school that just two years prior had been the lowest-performing school in the State of Nevada. We were climbing the proverbial mountain, and there was a lot of work left in front of us. I didn't have the luxury of time, so here I was on this nondescript morning, scrambling about my office, doing the things I prioritized as a principal: analyzing spreadsheets of student performance data, aligning and realigning my vision board, preparing to visit classrooms with my instructional coach, rehearsing my feedback language, and so on.

"You know me all too well." I busied myself with my laptop.

"Yet here we are," she said, pointing at the blinking light on my office phone.

I looked at her. She looked back with that double-raised-eyebrow look of a mom who's had enough of her kid's shenanigans when it is time to clean up. I didn't really want to trifle with her, since she'd been the office manager for over a hundred years (or so she told me on many occasions), plus she was tethered to her oxygen tank and rarely strayed from behind her desk, so this call must have been important for her to venture all the way to my doorway.

I reached for the phone.

It took a second as some secure lines clicked in, and I heard, "Hello, Mr. Hall. This is Secretary Rod Paige calling from the White House. I hear things are going quite well at Anderson Elementary."

After swallowing my gum, I told the education secretary, "We're on our way, that's for sure."

"The only Title I-funded school in the entire state of Nevada to earn a High Achieving designation, and just two years after the school was placed on the Needs Improvement list. You must be very proud."

"Yes, I am, sir, thank you," I responded.

He continued, "We are, too. And the president would like to recognize you and the incredible work you've done as champions for kids there at Anderson. He'd like to reference it in the upcoming State of the Union address. Can you be there?"

I was flabbergasted, to say the least. My gut response, however, was to step slowly back into the hedges. Maybe it was my mild case of social anxiety—I really didn't enjoy large crowds, and I certainly wasn't interested in a round of applause in a spotlight, especially because our school hadn't arrived. We were a work in progress. So, I responded, "That's a very gracious offer, thank you. I have a school to run here in Reno, so I feel I must respectfully decline."

After a momentary pause, Secretary Paige said, "Understood. We can appreciate that. And we want to commend you for being a beacon of light for the kids in your school community; your dedication is admirable."

I sat silently, thinking of the hundreds—nay, thousands—of kids who had passed through our doors and struggled because of a subpar education over the years. The tide was turning, and their futures were brighter; yet, we still had a lot of work to do.

The final thing Secretary Paige said really stuck with me. It was like he had a conduit into my self-talk when he said, "When you do good work, it's not always recognized. I encourage you to stand up, tell your story, and let folks learn from it. It's not bragging; it's building a bridge. In fact, you'd be doing a disservice to the profession if you kept that story to yourself."

Only after hanging up, did I notice Sandra Joy, still standing in my office doorway, with a big smile on her face. She said, "Sometimes it's OK to break your own rules, isn't it?" And she returned to her desk.

She was right. In fact, sometimes it's OK to break *lots* of rules, or at least bend them. I daresay it was our willingness to step outside our comfort zone, get creative, and challenge the status quo that resulted in the school improvement that prompted Secretary Paige's phone call in the first place.

The way you break those rules will look a little different depending on whether you're a school leader, teacher, counselor, family member, or occupying any other role supporting kids. So, be prepared, keep your eyeballs peeled, and sharpen those axes.

The first set of rules I would like to place on the chopping block is the Box.

THE BOX

If you've spent any time in a classroom, or in a school at all, you know it doesn't take long to realize there's a way we do things in our school system. It's the right way. The proper way. Heretofore the only way. And smack-dab in the middle of all this is the Box: that defined space where traditional school success lives. It's not even nuanced; verily, it's overt and explicit. For kids to be successful in school, they've got to fit in the Box. And this Box, as I'll explain, has been around, in various forms, as it's been built, curated, and protected for generations.

You, no doubt, know—intuitively and from your own experiences as a student, an educator, and a member of our society—exactly what I'm talking about. You can likely picture the Box quite clearly in your head. You know which kids fit in the Box and which ones don't, and you know how that plays out in the classrooms, schoolyards, offices, detention rooms, and diploma lines at graduation.

The kids who fall in line tend to progress. The kids who fit the mold tend to excel. In kidspeak, the kids who fit in the Box tend to become known as the *good* kids. The *smart* kids. The *successful* kids.

Inside the Box rest the characteristics we, as an education system, value. The youngsters residing in the Box possess the traits that allow them to survive and thrive in school. They can play the game because they've learned the rules written by the authorities, and they know exactly where their boundaries reside.

What are these characteristics? You could probably list them faster than a search engine.

- Disciplined
- Obedient
- Respectful
- Attentive
- Docile

That collection of characteristics is displayed in the daily behaviors of successful students, and this list also won't surprise you (in fact, you might have seen or written them on a report card at some point).

- Follows directions
- Speaks when spoken to
- Works well with others
- Exhibits politeness and respect to adults
- Completes tasks on time
- Scores well on assignments
- Performs well on tests
- Boasts high grades
- Stays out of trouble
- Demonstrates responsibility
- Is eager to do as told

Think of the children you've known—from your childhood and your professional experiences—who have performed well in school. Most likely, you could tick almost all the boxes in the previous two lists. They've stayed on the adults' good sides, they've accumulated points and received good grades, they've followed the rules, they've colored inside the lines. . . . They've remained safely, squarely, and securely in the Box.

The schooling experiences we provide children are an endless parade of lessons, activities, courses, units, semesters, and years of reinforcing the Box. Students are required to comply, and are rewarded for complying, with the expectations of the adults in charge. To remain inside is to avoid trouble and increase the likelihood of personal success in school. To venture beyond the walls is to risk everything school-related and quite possibly land yourself in a steaming heap of trouble.

Like it or not, the Box is real. And it is the standard by which we assign value to students in our school system.

THE LIE

For generations, we've tethered kids' hopes and dreams for a productive, bountiful, fulfilling future to their ability to excel in the Box. We've told them one of these two versions of the Lie.

- **Version A:** If you can succeed in school, you'll be successful in life.
- **Version B:** If you want to be successful in life, you must be successful in school.

The only problem with the Lie is, well, it's a lie. Unless, of course, our collective goal in schooling isn't to ensure all children (and that means each and every child) are successful, which I'll touch on shortly. Fundamentally, the Lie doesn't hold water because of these two important human truths.

- **Truth 1:** There are a million definitions of "success" that guide our lifelong pursuits, not just the one to which school success leads.
- **Truth 2:** There are a million paths that lead to the various forms of life success, and school success is but one of those avenues.

A former principal of mine in Reno, Debbie Cylke, once told our teaching staff this story, and I believe it may resonate with you.

One afternoon, Debbie found herself at the bus loop, trying to usher hundreds of middle schoolers onto their big, yellow rides home. It was like herding cats, and to complicate matters, one of her students, Greg, was riding his bike in and out of the parking lot, weaving between buses and wreaking all sorts of havoc. Greg, that little bugger, had skipped school that day but for some reason made it a priority to return in time to disrupt dismissal and the bus lines.

After finally wrangling the last kid onto the final bus, Debbie waved Greg over. Reluctantly, the lad rode his bike over and faced his principal.

"What are you doing, Greg?" Debbie asked.

In typical teenage fashion, Greg responded, "Nothing."

"Exactly. You're doing nothing. Your grades are in the tank, you're skipping school and always getting in trouble, and you're not focused on school. You'd better pull yourself together," Debbie said, eyeing his bicycle, "because you're never going to make any money on that bike, Greg."

As it turned out, that mischievous middle schooler was none other than Greg LeMond, who would become a three-time winner of the Tour de France and a member of the United States Bicycling Hall of Fame, and he earned quite a bit of money on that bike.

Who are we to tell kids that their success in life will be determined solely by their ability to kowtow, to follow the crowd, to contort into widgets and cogs, and to squeeze and squish themselves into the Box?

We've become so enraptured with our singular focus of making sure kids are successful in school that we've forgotten our original goal. The bulkiness of the Lie has essentially eclipsed the truth: We want to make sure kids are successful in life.

I contend that if you can succeed in school, the only guarantee for future success—and it's only a partial guarantee (if you'll forgive the oxymoron)—is in an environment that replicates school. What fits that bill? Let's consider settings that value disciplined, obedient, respectful, attentive, and docile personnel: a career in education perhaps, as well as the military, a factory, or prison.

Go back to the lists of characteristics and behaviors I included earlier in this introduction. These seem awfully similar to the prized traits of a good teacher, a good soldier, a good line worker, or a good inmate, don't they?

We have compulsory education laws. Our society dictates that all our children attend formal schooling until a certain age, usually between sixteen and eighteen years old. And if these are the characteristics we prize and promote during our children's crucial developmental years, what does that tell us about our desire for the citizens that emerge from our schools years later? Somewhere along the way we've directed our priorities to value conformity and obedience. Why is that, and what is the purpose of the Box?

THE PREMISE

Let's start with the end in mind and ask this essential question: "What is the purpose of education?"

As educators reading this book, you probably operate with a belief system like mine. A moment ago, I shared what I deemed the truth: We want to make sure kids are successful in life. Does that resonate with you?

Further, education is the secret sauce that fuels the engine of personal and societal development. All things being equal, those with a solid education are better equipped to handle the curves and challenges life throws at us. Education can be an agent of upward social mobility, progressive change, limitless potential, and equality. Indeed, it is the most powerful engine to propel those efforts forth. The purpose of education, then, is to serve as the mechanism for strengthening and growing our collective society.

What is the purpose of education?

Perhaps this is a more apt question to ask: "What is the purpose of schooling?"

In a podcast discussing her book, *Raised to Obey: The Rise and Spread of Mass Education*, University of California at San Diego professor Agustina Paglayan states:

> The expansion of primary education in the west was driven not by democratic ideals but by the state's desire to control citizens and to control them by targeting children at an age when they are very young and susceptible to external influence, and to teach them at that young age that it's good to respect rules, that it's good to respect authority—with the idea in mind that if you learn to respect rules and authority from that young age, you're going to continue doing so for the rest of your life, and that's going to lead to political and social stability and, in particular, the stability of the status quo, from which these political elites who are using primary education benefit. (Demsas, 2025)

What if education was designed to keep folks in the Box? What if Paglayan's research summary is correct? American education has a track record of being reactive—and the United States is not unique in this approach, as my readers from other countries can attest. When things are going well, we leave it be; however, if something threatens the status quo, we jump into action.

What is the purpose of schooling?

In *Questioning Education*, Sean Slade (2022) offers this accurate analysis of our preoccupation with maintaining the status quo and elevating the Box:

> If there was ever a sector, or an industry, that should be at the cutting edge of innovation, it is education, whose whole raison d'être is preparing those soon to be living in the future for the future. Yet education for too long has appeared less the sails of a ship pushing it forward to new horizons and more of the anchor stuck to a sea floor and restricting its own progress. (pp. 1–2)

So, how are we doing, according to the metrics—standardized tests—we use to gauge our effectiveness, in educating the masses? In a word, miserably. Unless, of course, we're judging our status by the degree to which the anchor is doing its job.

Let's use the National Assessment of Educational Progress, a test that's been administered in various grades across the United States since 1969, as an illustrative example. According to the 2024 assessment, the Nation's Report Card shares the following takeaways (National Assessment Governing Board, n.d.).

- Across the United States, scores were lower in 2024 than in 2019 in all tested grades and subjects.
- Any progress in 2024 (compared to 2022) was attributed to higher-achieving students.
- The gap between higher-achieving and lower-achieving students widened between 2019 and 2024.
- No state showed gains in fourth- or eighth-grade reading scores in 2024, compared to 2022.
- One-third (33 percent) of eighth graders across the United States scored below Basic level in reading.
- Fourth-grade mathematics scores rose two points across the United States in 2024, compared to 2022 (though the achievement gap was responsible for the gains).
- Mathematics scores in eighth grade remained flat, even after a historic eight-point drop in 2022.

Certainly, attendance is a factor in student achievement, both at the local and international levels. Chronic absenteeism is a hot topic, and rightly so. According to data analyzed by FutureEd, the rate of chronic absenteeism in the United States—defined as a kid missing 10 percent or more of a given year—was 23 percent in the 2023–2024 school year. That's down from the pandemic-high 28 percent in 2021–2022, but significantly higher than the pre-pandemic 15 percent in 2018–2019 (DiMarco, 2025).

If kids aren't coming to school, they're going to struggle to measure up in any metric used to determine school success. That's just common sense—so we need our kids to come to school, right?

Well, what if they come to school and don't fit in the Box? In one way or another, they become disenfranchised and disconnected from school. Student discipline data paints a vivid and unambiguous picture of the results.

- Student suspension and expulsion rates have steadily climbed since the 1970s, though data is incomplete due to pandemic-related school shutdowns (Leung-Gagné, McCombs, Scott, & Losen, 2022).
- The school-to-prison pipeline is a well-documented blight in our system (Keefer, 2023).
- Discipline is disproportionately applied to certain subgroups, such as minorities in race, sex, language proficiency, and special education status (U.S. Department of Education, 2023).

- Exclusionary measures (for example, removal of students from class, isolation from peers during lunch and recess breaks, and loss of extracurricular and activity eligibility) still permeate after a sloppy, decades-long attempt to implement zero-tolerance policies (Axelrod & Hupp, 2024).
- Data on student engagement and enthusiasm about school is daunting: The longer kids stay in school, the less they're drawn to it (Patall, Vite, Lee, & Zambrano, 2024).

I got to see the issues around student discipline firsthand when I was appointed principal in a high-needs middle school. I convened the leadership team, and we scoured through our recent data. Immediately, we were struck by the inordinate number of disciplinary referrals (over four thousand) and suspensions (over seven hundred) that had been logged during the previous year.

Despite a population of just six hundred students, we had racked up a veritable mountain of exclusionary discipline data. Not surprisingly, academic performance suffered, attendance data was in the tank, and the vibe of the school was one of militaristic, toe-the-line, suffocating regulation. As we pored over the data, we noticed the most frequent rationale for disciplinary referrals was "defiance and disrespect."

As vague and subjective as those two words may be, their ultimate meaning was clear: Do what I say, and you can stay. If not, you're out. When kids don't fit nicely into the Box, for whatever reason, they're going to be forcibly excluded.

Our team and our staff set to work, and throughout this book, I'll share many of the approaches and strategies we implemented. We worked with experts, we examined our mindsets, and we scrutinized our policies and procedures. Three years hence, the metrics spoke for themselves. Referrals were down significantly, suspensions were slashed, attendance rates increased, academic performance skyrocketed, and one of the most powerful statistics of all glimmered: Staff attendance increased appreciably.

What does all this mean? We have a lot of kids who are struggling. Whether we're looking at attendance data, behavior referrals, academic proficiency, graduation rates, or any other metric, there's room for improvement. With higher-performing students excelling, and lower-performing students faltering, the gap is widening. The kids who fit in the Box thrive in the Box. And the kids who don't, for whatever reason . . . not so much.

We tend to think the students are the problem. They're lazy, distracted, entitled . . . why, just the other day I was out running with my dog, Bo, and I mused, "You know, kids these days are a mess. Children now love luxury; they have bad manners, contempt for authority; they show disrespect to their elders and love chatter in place of exercise . . . they contradict their parents and tyrannize their teachers."

Bo looked up at me, his little half Shih Tzu, half Pomeranian, Ewok-looking face askew as if to correct me: "That wasn't you; that was Plato."

All kidding aside, the ancient Greek philosopher Plato (ca. 380 B.C.E./2007) was quoting his teacher Socrates, lamenting the state of youth. For millennia, we've blamed the next generation for the downfall of society and the decay of our greatness. Our *juvenoia*—negative feelings of an older generation toward a younger one—induces a fear of how kids are and what they're like, and we dread the damage they'll do to the world we inherited and, according to our parents, screwed up.

The reality is we're evolving. Changing. We're different, and society is different, too. Our antiquated mindsets and ideas must likewise evolve.

Maybe it isn't the kids. Maybe, in the words of author Alexander den Heijer (2018), "When a flower doesn't bloom, you fix the environment in which it grows, not the flower" (p. 22).

Let us return to the essential question I posed at the beginning of the section: What is the purpose of education?

I'm an educator. I've met thousands of teachers, administrators, counselors, and superintendents who have used their positions and passions to influence educational outcomes in favor of students.

In that light, maybe the education system was created and refined along the way to truly meet each individual student's needs and educate the entire populace to create a thriving, booming society. If that's true, the data should rightly be setting off clanging alarms because we're struggling.

If another interpretation is accurate, that the education system was built to control and indoctrinate the masses into a subservient way of thinking and behaving, the data should be rightly setting off clanging alarms as well, because we have massive numbers of kids struggling. They're growing up and struggling as adults, and our society is struggling as a result.

Whichever interpretation you subscribe to, we can do better. We must do better. And it's up to us, as educators, to take the lead.

What's it going to take to shift those beliefs? It may be that we need some clarity in the goals and ideal outcomes of raising and developing kids. Maybe we need a better, clearer picture of the society we want and the adults we want to populate it. That'll cause us to reconsider schooling. Not school—schooling.

THE DREAM

With all that in mind, maybe it's time for a change. Maybe, instead of waiting for global events to occur and reacting to them to reinforce the Box, we ought to become proactive. And if the Box isn't serving the greater good, perhaps we can dismantle it, one student at a time.

According to research curated by Britannica (2026), virtually every ancient civilization prioritized the education and development of their youth. Generally speaking, I've observed that most followed this pattern: The community's elders shared traditions, culture, and stories, and the children learned skills, crafts, and duties in various forms of apprenticeship models, all the while engaged in the pursuit of new knowledge. It seemed to be less about competition and conformation and more an endeavor to answer these two questions: (1) What do we want for our society? and (2) How should we raise and develop our kids so they can help us create that type of society?

What do we want for our society? How should we raise and develop our kids so they can help us create that type of society?

The rate of change in technology, commerce, industry, information, and so on is remarkably fast—and accelerating. We need innovators, collaborators, divergent thinkers, and creators—folks who color outside the lines and bring new ideas and different perspectives to our complex challenges.

To maximize their collective impact, we, as educators, need to tap into the skills, strengths, passions, and interests of all our kids. Each and every one of them. Even—and one might say *especially*—the ones who don't fit in the Box. We'll need to help our young people meet and exceed their potential, to celebrate their unique contributions, and to find ways to keep them connected, engaged, and committed to themselves and our society.

In an *Education Week* special report, education researcher Kevin Bushweller unveils an uncomfortable truth: "The most meaningful learning happens outside school." And if you shuddered when you read the title of the article, "The Kids Are Right: School Is Boring," you ought to also note the publication date: January

2019. That's right, a year before COVID hit our streets, communities, and classrooms. This is not a pandemic-born issue. It's not new.

This makes me wonder: What are the characteristics we really want in our neighbors? What do we want the grown-up members of our society to be like? When I'm in the field working with educators and educational leaders, I often ask my colleagues and audiences those very questions. The following shows the results of my investigation into the virtues and values we tend to extol as an educational community.

- **Compassion:** Understanding and sharing the suffering of others; actively seeking to alleviate their pain
- **Courage:** Facing challenges and taking risks despite fear; standing up for what is right
- **Curiosity:** Desiring to learn and know more; seeking explanations for phenomena
- **Empathy:** Seeing things from another person's perspective and understanding their emotions
- **Fairness:** Treating everyone equally and justly; avoiding bias
- **Generosity:** Willingly sharing resources and time with others
- **Honesty:** Being truthful and transparent in all situations
- **Integrity:** Doing the right thing even when it's difficult; being truthful and consistent in actions and words
- **Kindness:** Showing genuine care and concern for others; performing acts of generosity without expecting anything in return
- **Perseverance:** Staying committed to goals despite obstacles and setbacks
- **Respect:** Valuing others and their opinions; treating everyone with courtesy
- **Responsibility:** Being accountable for one's actions and commitments; fulfilling obligations diligently

If you were to ask me, I'd love to live in a society that entirely comprises folks who demonstrate these characteristics.

Part of the problem is we often ask kids the wrong question. We've all been that teacher, or that family member—haven't we?—who has looked into a child's eyes and asked, "What do you want to be when you grow up?"

We've conflated our job with our identity.

The question we really want to be asking, in that context, is this: "What do you want to *do* when you grow up?"

I'm eagerly awaiting the first time I overhear a grown-up ask a child, "What do you want to be when you grow up?" and the child answers with, "Curious, generous, and kind."

Indeed, let's promote a view of education as a system for developing, nurturing, teaching, and raising young people to be productive, happy, uplifting grown-ups and neighbors in our communities. Perhaps we ought to focus on a more holistic version of success, one that goes beyond standardized test scores, percentile ranks, grade point averages, and other murky, subjective measures that schools are beholden to.

I propose we take a lesson from the aforementioned Plato, who suggested an education that balances mind, body, and spirit (or mind, body, and soul, if *spirit* blurs the line between religion and state in your interpretation). In *The Republic*, Plato (ca. 380 B.C.E./2007) espouses raising our children with a keen focus on grammar (which included civics, or the study of the rights and duties of a citizen in a society), gymnastics, and music. Grammar for the mind, gymnastics for the body, and music for the soul.

The result? Strong minds, strong bodies, and strong souls.

THE CHALLENGE

Who are the kids that don't fit in the Box? Why don't they fit in the Box? How can we help them realize success, joy, and impact, no matter where they are in relation to the Box? These are the intense, pressing, challenging questions we're going to tackle together.

Here, Secretary Paige's words ring in my ears: "I encourage you to stand up, tell your story, and let folks learn from it." That's why I've written this book—not because I've figured out the answers; rather, because these are the right questions to ask.

Because we don't often know our kids' stories, we simply see them as struggling students. They're not performing well on tests. Their grades are dreadful. Their attendance is suffering. Their behaviors exacerbate everything. And we treat them thus—with consequences, punishments, removal of privileges, lowering expectations, placement into more restrictive environments, ejections, suspensions, expulsions—until they begin to see themselves as failures. Rejects. Outcasts.

Remember, even if we expel them from our schools, they're not out of our communities. These are the kids who, as grown-ups, will change the oil in our cars; change the way we experience the world through their personalities, attitudes, knowledge, and technologies we haven't even imagined yet; and quite possibly change our diapers in the nursing home.

In a world where being consistent, almost robotic, is prized, we devalue the individual skills, talents, and interests of kids who survive and thrive outside the perimeter of the Box. It's up to us to start looking at them differently, and instead of seeing what they lack as students, we need to start seeing their gifts, their dreams, their potential, and what makes them amazing young human beings. That's our responsibility.

THE OPPORTUNITY

You're ready. The book is in your hands. Now what? You may want to read it from start to finish, or you might find yourself seeking answers to specific questions about a specific kid. In that case, use the chapter titles to hone your approach as you "choose your own adventure" in this professional learning journey. I've tried to make this as user-friendly and intuitive as possible to counteract the vexing complexity of the kids with whom we work. Here's how the resource is organized.

In chapter 1, I'll provide you access to a mental model that will usher you ever forward. The way we orient our brains and our reflective practices will determine how successful we are, and this work is too important to leave to chance. In that light, I'll also share four very handy, replicable templates and protocols that you can use repeatedly.

Then, over the following five chapters, you'll meet Jason (the kid who doesn't fit in), Skyla (the kid who lacks consistent support), Anthony (the kid who doesn't care), Mayra (the kid who's way behind), and Penelope (the kid who's struggling emotionally). They're all real kids in real situations that I've known personally in my career, though I've changed their names to honor their privacy. Each one, you'll notice, represents one of the five most common challenges that lead to kids finding themselves outside the Box at school.

Within each chapter, I'll follow a consistent pattern.

- **Meet the student at the center of each chapter:** Sharing a real-world anecdote from my own experiences as a teacher, assistant principal, and principal, I'll invite you to understand and empathize with the hero of each chapter's story. You'll likely draw parallels between a kid you're concerned about and the protagonist I describe.
- **What's really going on?** If we're going to paint an accurate picture of success for the kid, we must begin by scrubbing what we think we know and start with a fresh canvas. Our open minds will allow us to examine

the characteristics and attributes of that kid, unpacking some of the *why* behind the challenges. In this section, I'll hit the highlights of the research describing what you're seeing in a way that helps you view your kid's scenario through a different lens.

- **What do kids who don't fit in the Box need?** Rather than becoming stuck admiring the problem, we're going to shift our focus to the ideal outcomes for the young person in question. This short section includes a very clear statement of your collaborative goal to support your kid.
- **How do we do this?** You want tactics, approaches, and ideas for helping your kid meet the goal, right? That's precisely what this resource offers. I'll share a menu of practical, applicable, high-yield strategies—and clear, supportive tools—that provide you with options for addressing your kid's needs in a thoughtful, thorough way.
- **Back to the hero of the chapter:** Returning to the real-world anecdote that launched the chapter, I'll share the positive resolution of the hero's journey, connecting the dots between the strategies I, and my team, selected and the successful attainment of the kid's goal.
- **Conclusion:** By the end of each chapter, you will be able to reflect on your kid's challenge, clarify the collaborative goal, select a course of action that best meets their needs, don your hard hat and gloves, and get to work.

Understanding our kids' needs, clarifying the goal, and creating a plan are fantastic steps toward reaching and teaching the kid who's outside the Box. To multiply the likelihood you achieve success, I've added over two dozen tools, four of which are in chapter 1, while the rest await you in the appendix—all of them are available at **go.SolutionTree.com/studentengagement** as downloadable forms. See page 150 for a comprehensive list.

Along the way, you'll encounter text boxes that call your attention to additional stories or practices, pullout quotes that emphasize certain ideas or essential beliefs, and numerous reflective questions couched in Ponder This boxes for you to consider by yourself or with your colleagues. I encourage you to engage with the text. Read it. Question it. Discuss it with teammates. Bring it to team meetings. Write notes in the margins. Consider its applicability to your work and your life. Throw it across the room and pick it up again when you're ready. All the while, keep every kid front and center while you're reflecting and digesting it.

PONDER THIS

What is the challenge you're currently facing?

There's a reason you picked up this book, and that reason is still holding your hand as you've walked together through the introduction. What is it?

In a perfect world, how will you emerge differently after reading this text? What are you curious about? What ideas would you like to collect? What questions are pinging around your brain like an upended tennis ball cart? What change do you aspire to make? To support? To become?

Consider these questions with a trusted colleague, your team, an administrator or instructional coach, or your faithful canine companion while on a quiet walk through the park. Reflect on your purpose and your goals and then set yourself firmly with conviction and direction. Then proceed.

This book is designed to be a bridge between theory and practice. I'll share the research, the anecdotes, and the dispositions that'll stimulate your desire to act. Then, I'll point you to the tools that I've assembled to help you make this work real. A great book—like a great tool—is only as good as it is put into practice.

As you already know, kids are complex, and the unique situations they're in demand that we look at the entire human. Most of the conditions, driving forces, underlying causes, goals, strategies, and approaches will overlap. So, keep your eyes, mind, and heart wide open as you read the chapters and consider your particular kids' circumstances. It's quite possible—and likely—that a strategy you encounter in chapter 4 will match a kid's needs that you're exploring in chapter 2. And just about every tool you'll find in the appendix could be used to support kids from any chapter.

Are there wonderful, well-intentioned teachers who are already dismantling the Box and doing this work? Absolutely! Are there wonderful, well-intentioned teachers who are inadvertently promoting and reinforcing the Box? Absolutely.

This book is for all the wonderful, well-intentioned teachers out there. You want what's best for kids, and you're willing to do whatever it takes to help each one of them become successful. And success, as we've already discussed, totes with it a different definition for each individual young person under your care. Together, perhaps you can describe it, picture it, and work earnestly and boldly toward it.

You may not know exactly what to do to reach and teach the kids who don't fit in the Box; that's OK, and that's the challenge du jour. You may ask, "So, Pete, how do

I use this book?" Great question. No matter your role—teacher, administrator, counselor, support staff, or something else—my suggestion is the same: Use it together. We're at our best when we collaborate, pair up, work in concert, and link arms.

My intent is to provide you with a resource that will offer you the motivation, tools, confidence, and reminder to free your mind, liberate your heart, reset your expectations, align yourself with the goal, roll up your sleeves, buckle your helmet, and get to it.

1

STRUCTURAL PREPARATIONS

IF THERE'S ONE thing I've learned in my decades of teaching, principaling, working in schools, and supporting educators across the globe, it's this: If we're going to be successful, we'll need a structured way to organize our thoughts, our goals, our strategies, our analysis, and our modifications. We must go about this work with intentionality and tactical precision. Anything less amounts to *wingin' it*, and good luck to you if you're wingin' it.

Thus, consider the four protocols and templates I've provided in this chapter. They'll add an important element of consistency, provide bumper lanes to keep your navigation on course, and allow the requisite structure to move your conversations, your work, and your progress ever forward.

AS WE REFLECT, SO WE GO: THE REFLECTIVE CYCLE

What's the Reflective Cycle? In a nutshell, it's the mental model we follow when the outcomes matter to us. Not *a* mental model—*the* mental model. The *Reflective Cycle*, as Pete Hall and Alisa Simeral (2017) first define it in *Creating a Culture of Reflective Practice: Capacity-Building for Schoolwide Success*, is the "predictable pattern of thinking that we all pursue as we build our skills, develop expertise, and progress toward excellence" (p. 26).

The Reflective Cycle is a model you'll want to apply over and over again. Go ahead and place a sticky note on this page, dog-ear the corner, or write yourself a reminder in the margins to return here as you examine and address your plan to reach and teach every kid you encounter who's outside the Box.

> You may have noticed that I tend to eschew the word *student*, opting instead to use *kid*, unless the situation demands the former. In fact, up to this point, *kid* outscores *student* on your makeshift tally sheet, 74 to 27. There's a pointed reason for this, of course (because now you know I'm not wingin' it).
>
> It might even be a fun exercise for you to return to the introduction and note where *student* appears, sharpening the point of my rationale. To be clear, our young people are kids first and always; of the 157,680 hours they'll live by their eighteenth birthday, just under 9 percent of them (14,040 hours, assuming perfect attendance for the 13 years of kindergarten through high school) will be spent as students. And I'm not even counting leap days! That means about 91 percent of their childhood is enjoyed exclusively as kids, and since they don't leave their *kidness* at the door when they enter school, that 9 percent in the schoolhouse is a shared experience. They're kids first and always.

The Reflective Cycle follows four steps, in repeated succession, as depicted in figure 1.1.

I recommend using this model to structure your reflective focus as you process each scenario you encounter. With precision and intentionality, you (and your colleagues) will orient your mental energy in a continuous progression, following these steps.

Step 1: Build Awareness of Goals

The question that you'll wrestle with first, and which will drive everything that follows, is pretty straightforward: What is your goal for this kid?

What is your goal for this kid?

For each of the five scenarios you'll read in the chapters that follow, I've identified a clear, appropriate, authentic goal for that chapter's kid. Use that goal statement as a starting point for your kid and adjust it as necessary based on the situation, context, and timing of your work. Beyond the question listed in the pull quote, here are some additional prompts for you to consider.

- What are you trying to accomplish?
- What challenge do you want to overcome?

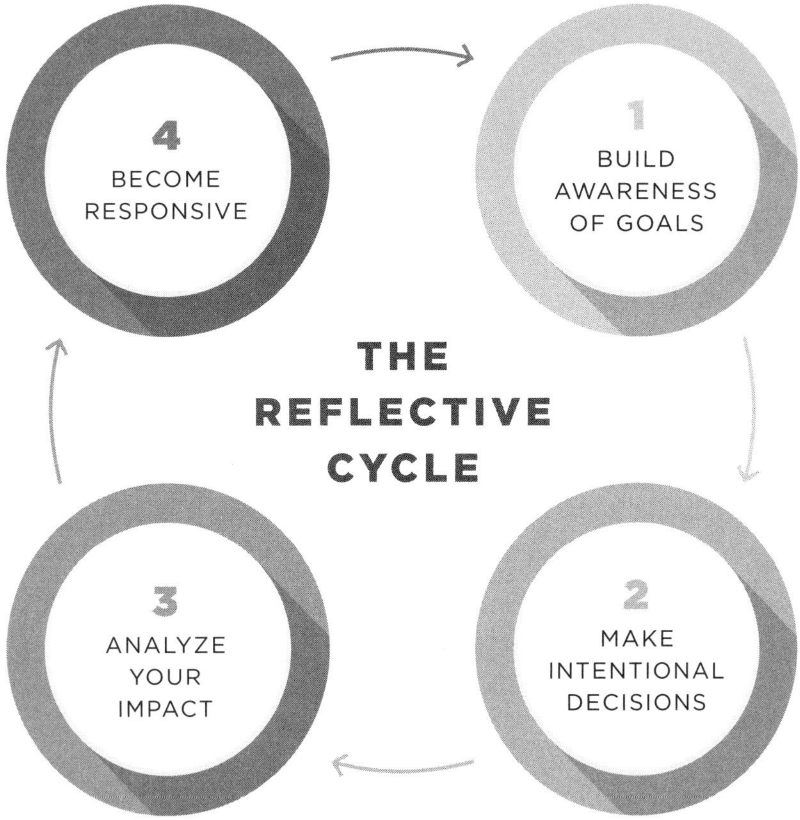

Source: Creating a Culture of Reflective Practice: Capacity-Building for Schoolwide Success, *by Pete Hall and Alisa Simeral, Arlington, VA: ASCD. © 2017 by ASCD. Adapted with permission. All rights reserved.*

Figure 1.1: *The Reflective Cycle.*

- What question do you seek to answer?
- What skills, habits, or abilities do you want your kid to learn?
- Where did this goal originate?
- Why is this goal important to you?
- Why does it matter if you address this?
- How will meeting this goal benefit your kid?
- Who played a role in identifying the goal?
- What data or evidence have you collected that supports this goal?
- Where on the pathway between *here* and *the goal* is the kid currently operating?
- If you could wave a magic wand and—*voila*—fix everything, what would be different for this kid?

Beginning with the end in mind ensures that all your efforts are aligned with the ultimate outcome. Sometimes, beyond the goal statement itself, it helps to have a clear, common, compelling vision of success beckoning you forth. At the onset of your work with any specific kid, it might be beneficial for you and your teammates to create that vision together because, in the words of a Disney imagineer, "Human beings are programmed to believe what they see" (The Imagineers, 2003, p. 73). The previous questions focus and sharpen your mind, with great clarity and precision, on the thing that matters most.

Record your team's responses, brainstorms, and collective vision of success as a succinct goal statement on the Priority Planning Template, which you can find in figure 1.2 and as a downloadable template at **go.SolutionTree.com/studentengagement**. As you proceed in your collaborative work to reach and teach this kid, use the Priority Planning Template as a living action-planning document that you reference, monitor, update, and celebrate frequently.

Step 2: Make Intentional Decisions

With a clear outcome in mind, the next question propelling your reflective focus is this: How will you select the optimal strategies to meet this goal?

If we're going to be successful, we need to know what that success will look like, smell like, feel like, taste like, sound like, and produce before we implement any strategies. We're so prone to looking for what's wrong that we often forget to look for what's right, and the research tells us we'll get more of what we focus on. For example, our bodies tend to follow the *heading direction* set by our gaze (Chow, Knöll, Madsen, & Spering, 2021), offering a scientific explanation of the law of attraction. So, let's focus on what's going to work by hitching our efforts to the optimism of a successful outcome.

How will you select the optimal strategies to meet this goal?

Review and dissect the strategies I offer throughout this book one at a time. With your team, identify a small selection of strategies (two or three is a good place to start) that you feel may yield positive results for your kid. Then, conduct a SWOT analysis of the strategies to determine which is most likely to produce the greatest positive outcomes.

What's a SWOT analysis, you ask? SWOT is an acronym for the four key elements of a plan that you can assess before enacting the plan to ensure its success.

PRIORITY PLANNING TEMPLATE

Purpose: This template provides educators with a clear focus on the goals that matter most. Oriented around the Reflective Cycle, it offers a real-time, tactical plan that leads to continuous growth.

Directions: With your team, discuss and complete the following template. Monitor progress, update the template, and revise strategies on a regular basis.

Today's date: ______________

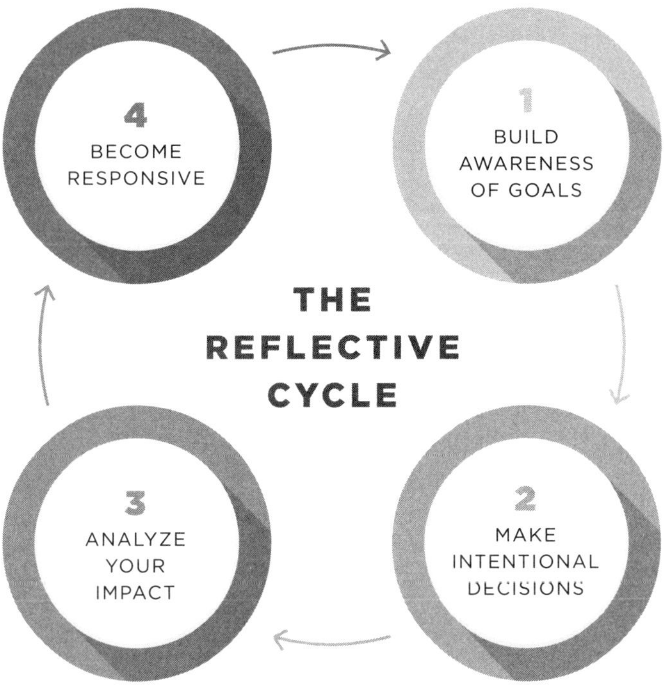

Team members:

Goal statement:

Rationale for this goal and description of current reality:

***Figure 1.2:** Priority planning template.*

continued →

List up to three action steps that you will take to move toward the goal. Be specific.	What support (and from whom) will you need to make progress?	How will you measure success and assess the impact of your actions?	When will you check in to modify and complete this step?

Other notes regarding this goal and priority plan (remember to remain focused on your self-reflective habits, as they drive your actions):

Source for cycle: Creating a Culture of Reflective Practice: Capacity-Building for Schoolwide Success, *by Pete Hall and Alisa Simeral, Arlington, VA: ASCD. © 2017 by ASCD. Adapted with permission. All rights reserved.*

Visit ***go.SolutionTree.com/studentengagement*** *for a free reproducible version of this figure.*

- ***S* is for strengths:** These are positive, internal factors that increase the likelihood of success. The following are some questions you might ask yourself and your teammates.
  - What specific strengths does the kid possess that we can tap into?
  - What aspects of the intervention plan play to those strengths?
  - What resources, supports, or staff expertise does our team already have in place?
  - How well does this plan align with school goals or existing systems?
  - How consistent and committed are the staff who will implement the plan?

- ***W* is for weaknesses:** These are negative, internal factors that might limit success. The following are some questions for you and your teammates to consider.
    - Where might there be gaps in data, communication, or follow-through?
    - What are the kid's skill or mindset barriers that this plan doesn't fully address?
    - Are there time, personnel, training, or other constraints that could weaken implementation?
    - How realistic are our expectations for the kid and our staff?
    - Have we clearly defined how we'll measure progress and adjust the plan, if needed?
- ***O* is for opportunities:** These are positive, external conditions that could enhance the plan's success. The following are some questions you and your teammates might discuss.
    - What new or existing supports (family, community, and partnerships) could strengthen this plan?
    - What school initiatives, grants, budgets, or programs align with this intervention?
    - How can we leverage upcoming transitions (new grading period, team meeting, or event) to reinforce progress?
    - What professional development or coaching could increase staff skill and commitment?
    - Where are the opportunities for student voice, choice, and ownership in refining the plan?
- ***T* is for threats:** These are negative, external conditions that could undermine success. The following are questions for you and your teammates to address.
    - What systemic barriers (schedule, staffing, policy, and budget) could interfere with implementation?
    - Are there competing priorities that might pull our attention away from the plan?
    - Could changes in the kid's life (home, peers, or attendance) affect consistency or engagement?

- Are there external pressures (academic, behavioral, and social) that might counteract the intervention?
- How might bias, assumptions, or miscommunication influence the application or impact of the plan?

Following this protocol allows you to streamline your decision-making process and raise the likelihood of success before even beginning implementation.

When you run a predictive analysis and compare your options side by side, which of the strategies you're considering will bring you—and your kid—closer to your goal? When you're ready to commit to an approach, be sure to use the information you gathered in the SWOT analysis to leverage the identified strengths, improve the areas of weakness, capitalize on the opportunities, and work around the threats. Then, add your selected strategies to the Priority Planning Template you began in step 1.

See the SWOT Analysis Protocol, which you can find in figure 1.3 and as a downloadable template at **go.SolutionTree.com/studentengagement**, for guidance on analyzing your choices and selecting the optimal strategy.

SWOT ANALYSIS PROTOCOL

Purpose: This protocol guides educators through analyzing factors that may influence an intervention plan's success.

Directions: With your team, the kid (as appropriate), and parents, brainstorm observations, evidence, and ideas relevant to the student and intervention plan for each of the four sections in step 1. Use the guiding questions to prompt your thinking. Then, using the questions in step 2 to guide your discussions, investigate ways to enhance the plan using the strengths, weaknesses, opportunities, and threats to your advantage.

Kid's Name: ____

Date: ______________________ Class/Grade: __________________________

Team members:

Step 1: Analysis

Proposed strategy:

Strengths (Internal, positive factors):

Guiding questions: What is the kid good at? What skills, behaviors, or supports already exist that will help the intervention succeed? What motivates or engages the kid?

Weaknesses (Internal, negative factors):

Guiding questions: What challenges does the kid face academically, behaviorally, or socially? What gaps in skills, knowledge, or support could hinder the intervention? Are there patterns of difficulty to consider?

Opportunities (External, positive factors):

Guiding questions: What resources, people, budgets, or strategies could support the intervention? Are there upcoming programs, mentors, or classroom activities that can be leveraged? What partnerships or supports exist?

Threats (External, negative factors):

Guiding questions: What obstacles or risks could impede success? Are there environmental, social, or institutional factors that may interfere? What limitations do we see? Are there competing demands on the kid's time or attention?

Note: It may help to represent this information in a 2×2 grid. If so, feel free to use the following template to facilitate this design.

Strengths *(Internal, positive factors)*	**Weaknesses** *(Internal, negative factors)*
Opportunities *(External, positive factors)*	**Threats** *(External, negative factors)*

Figure 1.3: *SWOT analysis protocol.*

continued →

Step 2: Application

Proposed strategy:

Leveraging strengths (Internal, positive factors):

Guiding questions: How might you use the identified strengths in this intervention plan? What are some ways that you could prioritize these positive, internal factors?

Improving weaknesses (Internal, negative factors):

Guiding questions: How could you schedule sessions to shore up weaknesses in this plan? What are some ways that you might remedy these negative, internal factors?

Capitalizing on opportunities (External, positive factors):

Guiding questions: How could you maximize the impact of the opportunities present in this plan? What are some ways that you might utilize these positive, external factors?

Working around threats (External, negative factors):

Guiding questions: How might you mitigate the threats to this plan? What are some ways that you could incorporate structure and safeguards from these negative, external factors?

Visit ***go.SolutionTree.com/studentengagement*** *for a free reproducible version of this figure.*

PONDER THIS

Do you believe you're the X factor?

When you experience a moment of success, to what do you attribute this triumph? If you're like most educators, you ascribe this to outward factors: The kids arrived ready to learn today, the curriculum was written just right, the stars were aligned . . . you've probably said or heard all that and then some, right?

How do you account for that collapse when things go sideways? Again, you usually attribute it to external factors: The kids were in a mood, the copier jammed, the Wi-Fi was down, it was a full moon last night . . . all of which was out of your control.

If the factors, *x*, that influence the outcomes, *y*, are all external, how could you possibly impact student learning? How could you make a difference? Following that logic, what difference would it make if you were an excellent teacher or a mediocre teacher if kids' performance is based entirely on powerful internet connections and the lunar cycle?

Do we, as a team, have collective efficacy?

Collective teacher efficacy is a fun term, isn't it? If you've read John Hattie's (2009) mega meta-analysis, *Visible Learning*, you know that it's the primary influence on student achievement, with a mean effect size (Cohen's *d*, for all my fellow statistics buffs out there) of 1.57—more than triple the effect of classroom management. But what, exactly, does *collective teacher efficacy* really mean?

In short, it's our collective belief that we, as a collaborative team of educators, can positively affect student learning outcomes. That we can make a difference. That we are the X factor. That even with poorly written curriculum, discordant stars, a *fanged dragon* full moon, a potholed playground, kids arriving jumbled and haywire, and broken-down technology, we can still ensure high levels of student learning, foster healthy development, and exceed the potential of each and every kid within our scope of influence.

So . . . do you believe you're the X factor? Do y'all have collective efficacy?

Step 3: Analyze Your Impact

When you've selected the high-promise strategy that you believe will be effective in achieving your clear, common, compelling goal, commit to it. Confidently implement the approach with consistency and intentionality and monitor the results by directing your attention to the following question: What result does this strategy yield?

What result does this strategy yield?

What you're looking for is a simple cause-and-effect relationship between your actions (and the related implementation of the plan) and the outcomes (however you've decided to measure progress toward achieving the goal). Now, when you read *simple* in the preceding sentence, that just means you're not going to apply statistical analyses, run regression discontinuity design, or incorporate a control group. You will, however, do your darnedest to isolate the independent (what you're doing) and dependent (the result you're measuring) variables and look for the linear chains: When we did *x*, the result was *y*.

To record data and monitor progress, I suggest a plain form like the Double-Ledger Data Template, which you can find in figure 1.4 and as a downloadable template at **go.SolutionTree.com/studentengagement**. The second column includes implementation notes (frequency, time, and method) of the independent variable, *x*, while the third column allows space for recordkeeping on the outcomes (the kid's response, changes in behavior, and results) of the dependent variable, *y*.

As you collect and compile the data from your trials and summarize your progress along the way, use the keyword *because* to highlight the cause-and-effect relationship. Think of it like this: "*Because* we did *x*, the result was *y*." Or, looking at it from a different angle, you can think of it as, "We observed *y because* we did *x*." Consider the following examples.

- "*Because* I introduced a class mantra in a whole-class setting, [kid] became shy and retreated, and he really struggled with contributing to class discussions. I plan to adapt this strategy by using it behind the scenes in one-on-one or small-group settings instead of the whole class."
- "[Kid] began contributing to class discussions *because* I introduced a class mantra that he and his classmates recited before starting their worktime. This became something that his classmates would say to him when he got stuck, and he would repeat it again before taking another crack at the content. I will continue to use this strategy."

Using the term *because* empowers you, as the adult, to have some impact on the outcomes. If you don't own the input, you can't own the output, and you can only make savvy, informed modifications to a plan (see step 4) if you understand the cause-and-effect relationship between your actions and their products. You have

DOUBLE-LEDGER DATA TEMPLATE

Purpose: This template assists educators in monitoring the cause-and-effect relationship between actions and outcomes.

Directions: As you implement an action plan, record the steps and strategies you take in the first column. Provide ample detail as appropriate and possible in the second column (for example, What specific question did you ask? What tone of voice did you use? Where were you standing in relation to the kid?). Then, in the third column, record what happened as a result of your action. Again, provide sufficient details to aid in analyzing the plan's implementation. Add notes as necessary.

Date: ______________________

Action Taken	Detailed Explanation and Notes	Result of the Action and Notes

Figure 1.4: *Double-ledger data template.*

Visit ***go.SolutionTree.com/studentengagement*** *for a free reproducible version of this figure.*

to believe that what you do matters, and that you're the X factor in the classroom. If you're struggling with this concept, using the word *because* will help.

You can only make savvy, informed modifications to a plan if you understand the cause-and-effect relationship between your actions and their products.

Step 4: Become Responsive

With a clear goal in mind, selected promising strategies, and a trove of data analyzed for causal relationships, you're ready to complete one revolution of the Reflective Cycle to position yourself, your team, and your kid for continued success. In this fourth step, you'll address the responsiveness question: How will you adapt and revise your strategies to improve outcomes?

You may have a protocol for analyzing data that is well established on your team or in your district. If you have one that you're familiar and comfortable with, please use it. This process is no different from dissecting the results of a unit test, scrutinizing a kid's essay alongside a performance rubric, or any other data analysis method you use with students' academic work. What separates the Data-Driven Decision-Making Protocol is the depth of the questions, the emphasis on reflective practice, and the direct, explicit link along the Reflective Cycle from the goal to selecting strategies and their causal impact and now to the "So, what are we gonna do about it?" step.

How will you adapt and revise your strategies to improve outcomes?

See the Data-Driven Decision-Making Protocol, which you can find in figure 1.5 and as a downloadable template at **go.SolutionTree.com/studentengagement**, for guidance on adapting and adjusting your approaches in response to the data.

DATA-DRIVEN DECISION-MAKING PROTOCOL

Purpose: This protocol guides educators through analyzing a situation, condition, cache of information, or set of data. It leads educators to continue, refine, or abandon elements of an action plan.

Directions: With your team, gather the data in question and follow these five steps.

Step 1: Predict. Before viewing the data, ask yourself and your teammates, "What are some predictions we might make about how the data will look? Why do we think so?" Record your predictions individually, then share aloud within small groups or as a team.

Step 2: Investigate. Dig into the data, unpack the information, and examine the situation. Remember to center your guiding questions or problem of practice to keep all participants focused. To the extent possible, take a clinical viewpoint and remove emotional reactions to data. Keep in mind this expression: *Just the facts*. Data, by itself, is benign. It only carries value when we assign that value. For now, ask questions such as the following to move the investigation forward with clear eyes and an open mind.

- What do you notice?
- Are there any patterns that emerge?
- Do the results change or remain consistent over time?
- How do certain groups or individuals perform?
- Are there outliers?
- What do you *not* notice? What's absent?

Step 3: Explain. In this step, all participants have an opportunity to hypothesize the cause-and-effect relationship (or correlative relationships) between actions and inputs and the data itself. Handy questions to pose to analyze the data directly may include the following.

- Why does this data look the way it does?
- What might have contributed to these results? Why do you think so?
- Why might these differences and similarities exist?
- What inferences might you make about the factors that impacted this data? Why do you say so?
- How might this data look differently if conditions were to change? Why do you think so?

Step 4: Decide. Data analyses only help us if we're willing to act. Now, we must respond to our data and adapt and adjust our work to improve the outcomes. Questions like these can help you refine your next steps.

- What actions can you take immediately to strengthen your plan? Why do you think so?
- What elements of your plan can you amend to impact the outcomes? Why might these work?
- What other steps can you take to improve the results of your efforts? Why could those be successful?

Step 5: Update the strategic, focused action plan with the revised, adapted steps determined by the team through this process.

Figure 1.5: *Data-driven decision-making protocol.*

Visit ***go.SolutionTree.com/studentengagement*** *for a free reproducible version of this figure.*

Once you have identified your adaptations, you'll find yourself at the beginning of a new Reflective Cycle. Around and around you go, each time with greater frequency, accuracy, and depth of reflections to aid in the evolution, refinement, and advancement of your efforts.

SUCCESS IS 90 PERCENT PREPARATION

Amazing things happen when you orient your brain toward an outcome that matters to you. Engaging in regular self-reflection, using tools like the ones I've included in this chapter, can have powerful effects on the bottom line. To wit, consider the following.

- Maintaining awareness and clarity of your goals streamlines and enhances the neurophysiological and behavioral process of decision making, leading to greater success (Balconi, Angioletti, & Acconito, 2023).
- Prioritizing self-reflection on a regular basis has a direct relationship to achieving your goals (Lanaj, Foulk, & Jennings, 2022).
- Incorporating self-reflective practices positively impacts knowledge acquisition, efficacy, and confidence (Hoang, Hepburn, Morawska, & Sanders, 2025).
- The habit of self-reflection may well be the basis of the skills that separate extraordinary performers from their mediocre counterparts (Bailey & Rehman, 2022).

If extraordinary performance, to spur the never-ending growth and success of the kids you serve, is on your to-do list, you're in the right place. You've got a mental model—strike that, remember it's *the* mental model—that orients your brainpower toward realizing your goals. You've got a couple of templates and protocols in your pocket, ready to roll. You're undoubtedly enthusiastic and optimistic about the journey ahead. There's a spring in your step.

Yes, success is 90 percent preparation, and you're prepared. The other 10 percent is a mix of perspiration, the right soundtrack, and really good coffee.

Look, there are kids out there who don't fit in the Box. Amazing, creative, dynamic, extraordinary kids with tons of untapped potential. So, to reconfigure a quote from Elinor Smith (1981), "People of consequence rarely sat back and let things happen to them; they went out and happened to things," as an imperative: Let's go out and happen to things.

2

JASON

THE KID WHO DOESN'T FIT IN

WE'RE GOING TO launch our journey with a discussion of the kids who don't fit in. This might seem self-evident, since the very title of the book includes "kids who don't fit in"; however, with this first batch, there's a little more to it.

Some kids, for a variety of reasons, just don't fit in with other kids. They stand out.

That's why they don't fit in the Box.

In a setting that values uniformity, standing out can create tension. This chapter's kid is a kid who's different, and it's these differences that peers, teachers, and other adults tend to notice first. The differences dominate what others see, and the kid becomes known for—and defined by—these differences.

What ensues, not surprisingly, is that they struggle. Whether that means having difficulties establishing friendships, interacting in social settings, participating in activities, or engaging in discussions, the common element is this: They struggle being with other kids.

MEET JASON

It was my first year of teaching second grade, and I had no idea what I was doing. In all honesty, that feeling never fully went away over the course of my career. In education, everything's in flux, and no matter what you've experienced, a lot of it feels like walking through a swamp blindfolded. Nevertheless, my eyes were wide open, and I was committed to making a difference, one kid at a time.

As I taught and did fun voices during my read-alouds, assigned group projects, led small-group instruction while praying the rest of the class would behave, hung up our guided-writing anchor charts, played soccer on the field during recess, and did all the other things teachers are supposed to do, I really became attached to this crew of eight-year-olds. And that included Jason.

Jason had a hard time at school. He was almost always alone. In class, he'd work by himself. On the playground, he stood off to the side in the breezeway, mostly just watching his classmates play. In the cafeteria, he sat at a table and ate in solitude, with nary an interaction with others.

As I got to know him better and watched him more closely, I realized there was an undercurrent of fraught social dynamics at play. I overheard some unkind comments about Jason's weight, saw an eyeroll that may or may not have been directed at his contribution to a class discussion, and listened to Jason use, more than once, negative self-talk to describe his intelligence, his appearance, and his popularity.

"I suck at everything," Jason muttered to me one day when I asked him to join a game of wall ball during recess. Despite my encouragement, he simply slumped his shoulders and walked away.

I didn't know what to do. I'd been trying to create a warm, inviting environment in my classroom in which we respected and appreciated each other, and for the most part, it was working well. But for Jason . . . not so much.

At some point in late fall, my principal shared the details and schedule of the upcoming parent-teacher conference week. We were going to hold classes in the morning and release our students after lunch, thereby opening the afternoons for the parents to come to school to meet with their kid's teacher.

Dutifully, I emailed invitations that included several options to try to meet everyone's schedule. I was so excited to meet my kids' parents and learn more about the kids' goals and dreams and, of course, share their progress and the parts of their learning that need more attention.

Unfortunately, my enthusiasm clattered on the linoleum classroom floor when the RSVPs started arriving in my inbox. I had a couple confirmations, a few requests for schedule changes, and an email from Jason's mom.

She had sent a very direct, simple response: "None of the above, thank you."

When I asked Jason about it while we were cleaning up the mathematics manipulatives during recess that morning, he said, "My mom doesn't want to come to school ever again."

Yikes. "Doesn't she want to meet me? She must want to talk about you a little bit," I asked, playfully bouncing my eyebrows at him.

Jason responded flatly, "Maybe."

Later that day in the staff lounge, I overheard a couple of my colleagues discussing the pros and cons of conducting home visits instead of hosting in-school conferences.

"That's how you build relationships with families."

"You want parents coming to your house? They don't want you there either."

"That's how I got all those parent volunteers last year."

"From that neighborhood? I wouldn't go there alone."

Home visits, huh? I thought. This would be an opportunity to see the kids in their natural habitats, to open a window just a crack to view their worlds outside the classroom—to truly understand them as the kids they are, rather than just as my students in class.

Immediately, I thought of Jason. Maybe this was an option for his mom? I called her. Would she be willing to host me during a home visit? I could bring Jason's schoolwork, and we could talk in the comfort of their living room, kitchen, wherever. She agreed, and we scheduled it for a late afternoon that very week—two weeks before the official parent-teacher conference week.

My principal wasn't a big fan of this idea—or perhaps he didn't like that I committed to it without getting his permission first—but, to his credit, he didn't get in the way, either. When the day came, I drove to the apartment complex where Jason and his mom lived. I'd never been there before, and I was struck by the number of kids playing in the dirt and gravel courtyard, smiles and grime all over their faces.

Jason and his mom opened the door together after I knocked. The first thing I noticed wasn't the piecemeal furniture, the cracked shades, or the stained carpet—it was the smell. It was like nothing I'd ever smelled before.

I must have given away my observation, because Jason's mom said, "Come in, we made cookies. Do you like chocolate chip?"

Boy, do I, and, boy, were they delicious! As we devoured the homemade cookies, Jason gave me a tour of the cramped apartment, and the first thing he did was show off his pride and joy: an old, rickety telescope pointed out his bedroom window. "Can you see the moon with that?" I asked.

He scoffed. "The moon has over 100,000 craters."

"Whoa. Can you see them all?"

The eight-year-old scoffed again. "Synchronous rotation. We can only see one side of the moon from Earth."

We continued the tour, and I helped Jason clean off a section of a living room table so it could be dedicated to homework. Over the next hour and a half, I sat with Jason and his mom and learned quite a bit about him, his interests (besides astronomy, he loved flowers and gardening, though he only had one windowsill to put that passion into action), his insecurities (they didn't have money for a haircut or new shoes, so he considered himself ugly and fat "from head to toe"), and his family history.

It turned out his mom had pretty rotten school experiences. She didn't fit in either, and she'd been telling her stories to Jason. The theme was "It's OK if you don't fit in; who needs them?" and "I wasn't a good student and dropped out after my fifth-grade teacher told me I was a loser, so don't worry about it. School's not for everyone." That's why she didn't want to come to school for parent-teacher conferences.

I didn't blame her. Or him. I felt for them, and I wanted to help make a difference.

We didn't solve all the world's problems or come up with a life-altering strategy during that home visit, but—in addition to sharing some pretty darn good chocolate chip cookies—we sure as heck built a bridge and laid the foundation for some profound changes that were soon to come.

WHAT'S REALLY GOING ON?

When we see kids like Jason in our schools, hallways, and cafeterias, they catch our attention. There's something about this kid that's different—something that stands out. Maybe there's something about their physical appearance, clothing, behaviors, or mannerisms that's unusual. Maybe the way their minds work—and their associated behaviors and mannerisms—catches our attention. We'll dig into these maybes in just a moment.

Whatever it is, that bit of quirky, atypical *je ne sais quoi* causes a reaction. Their peers reject them. Adults worry about them. They question themselves. They don't fit in, so they opt out. We may even push them out, then we often leave them out. It's not kind, and it's usually unintentional, yet it happens more often than we'd like to admit.

Because of our attraction to the Box, we formulate appraisals, conclusions, and judgments about the Jasons we meet, and those can set us down the wrong path.

We can help ourselves by unlearning some of the beliefs we've collected over the years, starting with these.

- Jason's just different; that's all there is to it.
- He's a misfit.
- There's something wrong with Jason.
- Our job is to make him fit in.
- Jason will never fit in.
- He belongs in a special setting, not the regular classroom.

Those beliefs aren't helping us, and they're not helping Jason. Instead, try looking at the kid in front of you and meeting them where they are.

PONDER THIS

It might benefit us to unlearn our curious preoccupation with diagnoses.

Sometimes, kids who behave, look, act, or think differently have an identified medical condition or learning disability. There may even be an acronym associated with the kid's name. Do you need a diagnosis to help a kid? I don't think so. In fact, sometimes having a diagnosis shoves the kid right back into a box. A different box than the Box, but a box, nonetheless.

Have you ever heard a colleague say this before? "Oh, it turns out he's dyslexic. No wonder! That explains everything." As if that colleague can now go to the dyslexia handbook, and that'll resolve all the struggles the student is having, because every kid with dyslexia is the same and needs the same thing, right? All the diagnosis does is provide a static definition of what dyslexia is, and your colleague will conform to their predisposed notion of what that means.

Gather your team and list the pros and cons of a child having a diagnosis, especially one with famous acronyms. Then, list the pros and cons of you, as professionals, knowing that diagnosis. What does this do to your sense of collective efficacy? What do you notice? What do you wonder?

First and foremost, let's unpack what we mean by not "fitting in." What we're really exploring is the child's sense of belonging. Because school is a social setting, and as humans are social beings, *belonging*—a sense of connectedness with others within an environment—is a big deal. In schools, experiencing belonging tends to lead to a myriad of positive outcomes. Kids flourish when they feel like they belong. When they feel like they matter. When they feel accepted, respected, and valued.

Not sure that kids who don't fit in actually need to become part of a community? Think about alternative or counter-culture movements. Hippies, punks, grunge, you name it. They've said, "Forget the masses; we won't conform! We're doing our own thing." Then, they find other like-minded people and share hairdos, facial piercings, fashion, music, hobbies . . . as well as beliefs, values, and identity.

When we feel misunderstood, overlooked, oppressed, ignored, or alienated somehow, we seek out others who share that experience. We connect and bond with others who feel as we do. Indeed, we're drawn to connection. To belonging. To community. To kinship. To feeling included. It's part of the human condition. People have always survived, and thrived, in clans.

This isn't just feel-good, hokey, lovey-dovey, campfire talk.

The term *belonging uncertainty*—in which an individual questions or doubts the quality of one's social bonds in a particular setting—was first coined in a paper published by the *Journal of Personality and Social Psychology* (Walton & Cohen, 2007). The research unmasks the powerful impact of belonging in motivation and achievement. When kids in the study felt like they didn't belong, or weren't sure if they belonged, their drive and participation in class, activities, and their own learning waned.

Kids flourish when they feel like they belong.

Now, what if kids feel like they *do* belong? As I mentioned before, this is where kids flourish. Belonging plays a significant role in promoting academic engagement and social functioning (McCabe, Kaskoun, Bennett, Meadows-Oliver, & Schroeder, 2024). As a result, according to a longitudinal study conducted by the U.S. Department of Education's Institute of Education Sciences, students who self-reported feelings of belonging experienced significantly higher rates of academic achievement than their peers, and those gains persisted over time (Sakellariou, 2025). Further, in a meta-analysis of ninety studies, researchers conclude that school connectedness and belonging has a significant protective relationship against substance abuse, mental health, and risky behaviors (Rose et al., 2024).

More belonging, less bad stuff. More belonging, more good stuff.

So, for all the Jasons out there, what might cause a lack of belonging? Let's explore the two big maybes I presented previously in this section: (1) physical differences and (2) brain differences.

Physical Differences

What's the first thing we notice when we meet somebody? Yes, all our senses are working in concert to upload information to our brains, and the most powerful of the five is . . . sight. At least, that's how humans tend to prioritize our senses. In fact, a OnePoll survey reveals that 77 percent of respondents value their eyesight more than their other senses (NVision, n.d.), and in a shocking statement of solidarity, participants in a survey would choose 4.6 years of life in perfect health over ten years of life with complete sight loss (Enoch, McDonald, Jones, Jones, & Crabb, 2019). Folks would rather die than go blind.

With that level of importance placed on vision, it's no wonder we prioritize our sense of sight when we encounter new people. From early childhood, kids visually scan their playmates and newcomers and look for differences and similarities. In that order. Biologically, humans are wired to first notice differences to help identify threats and danger, so encountering a person who appears to be different may cause the amygdala (the part of the brain that controls the flight, fight, or freeze response) to cue an immediate rejection based on fear (Levin, 2024). This automatic response (the amygdala is on autopilot) accounts for many kids' wariness of differences in height, body shape, hair color or style, skin color, other unique physical characteristics, and even clothing style and personal mannerisms.

Once the alert system calms down, kids look for similarities in an attempt to build *in-groups*—groups of peers who look, act, dress, and appear like them. Foundational research establishes that kids' self-esteem and confidence stem in large part from their sense of belonging in a group of like peers. Maybe that's why they tend to gravitate toward other kids who show similar characteristics (Tajfel & Turner, 1979).

Unfortunately for our kids growing up in an education system that prioritizes the Box, a lack of belonging and social identity within the "dominant" groups can cause significant damage. Groups develop reputations, causing kids to fear *stereotype threat*, the fear of confirming a negative stereotype, which adversely affects motor performance and learning, according to a massive meta-analysis covering thirty years of studies (Heidrich, Cardozo, & Chiviacowsky, 2025). Further, feeling excluded can shuttle kids down the social hierarchy ladder, resulting in ostracism, bullying, mental health challenges, academic struggles, behavioral incidents, and withdrawal from social and educational settings (Killen et al., 2024; Lanteri & Coley, 2024; Yu, Du, Li, Sun, & Pi, 2023).

Brain Differences

Australian sociologist Judy Singer first coined the term *neurodiversity* in her honors thesis, and the word saw its first mainstream use in *The Atlantic* (Blume, 1998). Taken technically, the prefix *neuro-* means something related to the nervous system, which includes the brain, and when added to *diversity*, which means a range of differences, creates this definition: a range of differences in nervous system (brain) functioning.

Knowing that the national conversation around neurodiversity—or *neurodivergence*, as we now know it—typically includes autism spectrum disorder (ASD); attention deficit/hyperactivity disorder (ADHD); learning disabilities like dyslexia, dysgraphia, and dyscalculia; and other neurological or developmental conditions (think of Tourette syndrome, obsessive-compulsive disorder, sensory processing conditions, and a host of other conditions), you might notice two things. One, your acronym alarm is ringing, and two, this category is much broader than just a collection of diagnoses. What do all those conditions have in common? They're indicators that the human is "different."

Let's build on the draft I started two paragraphs ago to establish a common definition of neurodiversity. If you'll allow me a little leeway, I'll use the term with its most overarching interpretation, as found in a Harvard Medical School article: *Neurodiversity* is "the idea that people experience and interact with the world around them in many different ways" (Baumer & Frueh, 2021).

Neurodiversity is "the idea that people experience and interact with the world around them in many different ways" (Baumer & Frueh, 2021).

Yes, neurodivergence describes differences in brain functioning from what most of us (the giant cluster toward the center of the bell curve—you know, the folks who fit rather comfortably in the Box) would expect in ordinary human interactions.

As a result, many individuals who are considered neurodivergent face considerable social and emotional challenges. We know what happens because we see it play out every day in our schools, classrooms, hallways, and gyms. Kids are ignored by peers, picked last for teams, and snubbed for group projects. Their input is discounted or overlooked, greetings are received with giggles or whispers, and behaviors and appearances are mocked or taunted.

Subsequently, and not surprisingly, many neurodivergent kids then experience significant mental health issues (Accardo, Pontes, & Pontes, 2024; Passarello et al., 2022). For instance, in studies of children with autism, nearly 70 percent report a mental well-being challenge such as feelings of isolation, loneliness, anxiety, or depression (Ivanović, 2021) and upward of 40 percent have practiced self-harm, expressed suicidal thoughts, or both (Ivanović, 2021; Mayes, Gorman, Hillwig-Garcia, & Syed, 2013). The long-term effects are becoming clear: A study at the University of Sussex finds that children with neurodivergent traits are more than twice as likely to experience chronic, disabling fatigue by age eighteen, compared to their peers (Quadt et al., 2024).

What would qualify a behavior, comment, action, or thought as "different," you ask? Where's the line? Neurodivergent, along with neurotypical, behaviors compose a spectrum, as shown in figure 2.1.

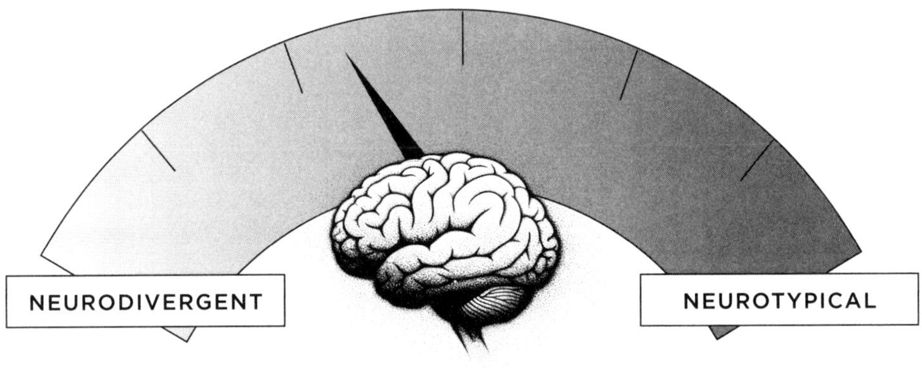

Figure 2.1: *Spectrum of neurodivergence.*

Have you ever paused to think about the nature of a spectrum? If you were to do so, you might realize we're all somewhere on every spectrum. If a spectrum truly is the broad range of qualities with one extreme on either end, then any spectrum would range from 0 percent to 100 percent. That might make us question the use of the deficit-focused terms like *disorder* and *disability* in the conditions named previously. With this concept in mind, I appreciate this emphatic and open-minded portion of Nicole Baumer and Julia Frueh's (2021) discussion of neurodivergent: "There is no one 'right' way of thinking, learning, and behaving, and differences are not viewed as deficits."

Judy Singer's early work, as a preliminary step to become more aware and inclusive of all people (kids in schools, employees at work, neighbors in the community, and so on), perfectly encapsulates the idea that our marvelous, intricate brains all operate with their unique strengths, structures, models, and tendencies (Blume, 1998). Not coincidentally, this was within a decade of the inclusion of autism in the Individuals with Disabilities Education Act (IDEA) in 1990 and the introduction of cinema's most famous neurodivergent character, Forrest Gump, in 1994.

Differences, indeed, cry out to be celebrated!

PONDER THIS

Here's an idea to generate a discussion with your staff or a team of teachers.

Have you ever been in a situation in which you felt out of place, like you didn't belong? Have you ever felt like the only one who was different somehow? What words and phrases describe that feeling? How long did it last? How did you cope or manage?

Now, imagine you were unable to cope or manage on your own, and exiting the situation wasn't an option. You were, for lack of a better term, stuck there. How might that feel? What might you do to combat this feeling? Who might you seek out for companionship? How long before you might give up hope and resign yourself to checking out?

Here's another set of questions to consider together, either as a follow-up to the preceding questions or as a separate discussion.

What are some words that describe your self-identity within your group? How aligned is your perception with your peer group's identity of you? For instance, do you ever feel like "the smart one," "the one who's always running late," "the organized one," or "the creative one"? Would your teammates describe you the same way?

How do these perceptions alter the way you work together and interact with one another? Do you sometimes feel you have to say or do things just to uphold a stated (or implied) perception? How does that make you feel? If you could break out of that box, how would you speak or behave differently?

Let's shift gears to look at your setting. Do you have a kid who "doesn't fit in"? How might we use this process, collectively and interdependently, to bring inclusion, as opposed to ostracism, to this kid's experience in school and within the peer group?

Are there other reasons—besides physical differences and brain differences—that kids don't fit in? Heavens, yes. A whole book full and then some! I'll address a handful of other reasons kids don't fit in the Box in subsequent chapters. For now, consider this chapter a catchall. It comes first because it's the most common concern I've heard from parents, teachers, education staff, coaches, and other concerned grown-ups: "This kid just doesn't fit in."

As you've been considering the Jason in your life or classroom, your first question was likely this: Why doesn't this kid fit in?

Your next question is, How can I reach and teach this kid?

WHAT DO KIDS WHO DON'T FIT IN REALLY NEED?

If the kid doesn't fit in, that's OK. Let's find a way to help the kid connect with others and become a part of the group. Belonging, social approval, and acceptance in the community are crucial human conditions. Our social ecosystem demands it. That doesn't mean Jason needs to conform; in fact, we want the opposite—we want the other kids to see what's incredible, valuable, and important about Jason!

We want what's different about Jason to be the standout characteristic that draws us to him. It's his special sauce. His ace in the hole. His power suit. And let's help him see leaning in to learning as a viable alternative to giving in, even if fitting in isn't in the cards.

This is a good time to return to the dog-eared, bookmarked pages in chapter 1 that include the four protocols and templates you'll want to use to frame your work. And, because clarity of the goal is a non-negotiable prerequisite for all the work that follows, I might also suggest that you revisit the list of questions I posed at the beginning of chapter 1 to hone your collaborative vision of success. Here's the result of that initial reflection for Jason.

GOAL STATEMENT

We want to help Jason connect with others, celebrate his uniqueness, and feel a strong sense of belonging within the social environment of his peer group and community of learners so that he can return to learning with passion, curiosity, and confidence.

With that clear goal in mind, let's see what your options are.

HOW DO WE DO THIS?

Before you dig in, just in case you're wondering, "If a kid looks different from the other kids or is neurodivergent and not really connecting well with peers, is there really anything I can do about it, as their teacher?" The answer is yes. Omnipresent researcher John Hattie's team's meta-analysis "What Schools Need to Know About Fostering School Belonging" uncovers the two most impactful factors in increasing belonging: (1) teacher support and (2) positive personal characteristics (Allen, Kern, Vella-Brodrick, Hattie, & Waters, 2018).

Stanford University professor Geoffrey L. Cohen (2022), in his book *Belonging: The Science of Creating Connection and Bridging Divides*, agrees that fostering belonging requires a multifaceted approach consisting of extrinsic factors like teacher interventions, environmental changes, and peer conditions and intrinsic changes such as belief sets, self-talk, and the development of interpersonal skills.

For kids who experience belonging uncertainty, a realistic approach would be to build structures to increase belonging.

That's where teacher support—or, depending on your position, the support, structures, encouragement, and interventions provided by the education professional in closest proximity to the kid—comes in.

Let's look at some specific options for my Jason and all the other Jasons out there. Here are several strategies to consider.

Strategy: Create Connections

One way to increase belonging is to forge a very clear, very explicit connection with another person, in particular one with some perceived social status. Gregory Walton and Geoffrey Cohen's (2007) study of the impact of belonging interventions includes this gem: When college students were led to believe, through an experimental ruse, that they happened to share a birthday with a mathematics major, the participants became more motivated in mathematics and worked harder and longer on a tough mathematics problem. We can nurture this sense of belonging by highlighting what our kids have in common with one another, despite the differences that might otherwise get top billing.

See "Tool 1: Characteristics Web" in the appendix (page 151) for guidance on implementing this strategy.

Strategy: Identify Interests

Often, students who are feeling left out find school irrelevant and struggle to connect with the content and curriculum. By utilizing topics, language, scenarios, and problems that have current, real-life applications for our kids, we can reverse this perception. By using interest surveys, we can find out what kids are interested in and use that information in our everyday lessons. Using kids' names in examples, writing story problems using current events and neighborhood locations, inviting kids to choose topics and titles for books to read, and posing riddles, incongruities, puzzles, or other questions—based on their interests—can hook disengaged students into the lesson and the learning.

See "Tool 2: Individual Interest Inventory" in the appendix (page 153) for guidance on implementing this strategy.

Strategy: Name Those Feelings

Often, students who struggle to fit in with their peers think there's something wrong with them or feel that they're abnormal. In reality, it's common to feel this way. In fact, most other kids probably do, too. What's more challenging is finding the words to describe the emotions to help our Jasons process how they're feeling, what they're thinking, and how to handle it. One key strategy is to unveil a list of emotions and help students discuss them in a productive manner. Engaging in activities like body scanning, using an emotion wheel, or identifying emoji can help teachers do this without detracting from instructional time in the classroom.

See "Tool 3: Name That Emotion" in the appendix (page 157) for guidance on implementing this strategy.

Strategy: Teach Social Skills

A lot of times, kids struggle in social settings because they haven't explicitly learned the social skills required of those settings. As adults, we often assume our kids have those skills; believing "they should know that by now" isn't helpful if they don't. We can help by teaching those skills and strategies. In *The EQ Intervention: Shaping a Self-Aware Generation Through Social and Emotional Learning*, Adam L. Saenz (2020) discusses the following four crucial elements of human connection.

Listening to Others

As Saenz (2020) writes, "Hearing is what our ears do, but listening is what happens in our minds and hearts with the words we hear" (p. 128). We can teach our kids to listen by using a talking stick, agreeing to wait to raise hands until after the speaker has finished, paraphrasing or repeating what the speaker has said, and playing games like popcorn storytelling, in which kids take turns adding on to an ever-growing story.

Connecting With Others

We can help our kids practice empathy by noting the *paraverbal* (tone of voice) and *nonverbal* (body language and facial expressions) messages others convey. Using emoji, pantomime games, role playing, and "in their shoes" activities, in which kids imagine themselves in someone else's situation, can help students understand the process and value of empathy and connection.

Communicating Effectively

Once we've listened to and connected with another person, how do we share our perspective? Of the four prevalent communication styles (passive, aggressive, passive-aggressive, and assertive), assertive tends to be most respectful, honest, and considerate. We can support our kids' development of an assertive communication style by providing examples, valuing openness and curiosity, helping to rephrase comments, and, for kids of all ages, offering sentence stems and suggested wording to communicate in a way that conveys our message and our meaning.

Resolving Conflict

Sometimes, things go sideways in a conversation, and feelings get hurt. We can teach our kids to address these situations by following a conflict resolution road map, which includes six steps (Saenz, 2020).

1. Calm down.
2. Clarify what happened.
3. Identify thoughts and feelings.
4. Apologize and forgive.
5. Negotiate next steps.
6. Involve a third party, if needed.

It can help to practice these steps in fun situations, such as role-plays, acting out scenes from books or TV shows, and using language prompts.

PONDER THIS

Gather your teammates, an instructional coach or administrator, or a trusted colleague, and pose the question, "How can we effectively teach social skills?"

Use the summary of Saenz's (2020) research to guide your exploration. Ask follow-up questions like the following to generate momentum and ideas to try out.

- What opportunities do we have to incorporate these four elements into our classroom routines?
- When could we weave these four elements into academic discussions?
- How might we remain vigilant and intentional about utilizing these ideas regularly?
- When could we practice these steps or strategies with our kids?
- What resources can we find that can help us teach social skills explicitly?
- Which teachers, colleagues, or local professionals can share their expertise with us?

Strategy: Promote Participation in Extracurricular Activities

Many schools have introduced models of extracurricular programming that blend student interests and staff passions. Do you love playing the guitar? Launch a beginner strings club after school. Got a passion for gardening? Lead a lunchtime greenhouse gang. Often, kids who spend time engaged with others outside of the classroom find themselves building a network of belonging—connecting with kindred spirits through a shared interest and a common experience. These are bonds that can extend well beyond the program itself. Even more, there's a huge benefit for kids being connected to *something* in the school environment beyond the classroom. When kids are involved consistently in athletics, music, clubs, activities, or other extracurricular activities, they're more likely to build strong relationships and learn vital skills, and their graduation rates increase dramatically (Crispin, 2017; Thouin et al., 2022).

PONDER THIS

A high school principal I was mentoring encountered a dozen kids skateboarding in the school quad one day after school. Rather than shoo them off and punish them for violating the school's *no loitering* rules, he rounded them up and challenged them to launch a skating club, establish safety protocols and boundaries, create an attendance policy, and solicit a staff sponsor. Not only did the kids follow through but they also initiated a fundraiser to construct a mini skateboarding facility as part of a city park remodel.

The last step was probably the most powerful. The kids dubbed their club "The Wheeled Deal" and designed attire (hoodies and beanies) that included the school logo. What began as a fun thing friends wanted to do together evolved into a school-sponsored club that tethered the kids to their school. That connection was just enough to keep them attending school, engaging in class, committing to their education . . . and graduating on time.

What activities, clubs, or extracurriculars does your school offer? Do they match your kids' interests and passions? For instance, if you have a slew of kids who enjoy table-top games, is there a time and place for them to gather, play, and create their own? Do you have an adult who is willing to oversee them? Or have you encountered kids who tote spray paint in their backpacks? Perhaps a staff member has some interest in launching a beginner muralist group.

What community resources beyond the school (recreation centers, churches, libraries, youth clubs, and so on) are available for your kids to engage and connect with others? How might you promote and celebrate these opportunities together? What are some ways you could intentionally build shared talents, interests, values, and beliefs into these experiences to enhance the kids' sense of connection and belonging?

Strategy: Encourage Positive Self-Image and Celebrate Differences

Belonging uncertainty, again, is the perception that you may not belong. Let's help our kids believe in themselves—even their independence. What kind of things can we do to help kids feel better about themselves and build their social identity in our classrooms and school settings? Utilizing a positive mantra (like "I can do hard things!") and conducting a "hero" interview, in which a kid introduces himself to a group using third-person language, can be great starts. Setting reasonable goals in the Goldilocks zone (just-right balance of effort required and success likelihood), sharing your high expectations for the child, and praising effort and attitude instead of just results foster what Stanford professor Carol Dweck (2006) famously introduced as a growth mindset. These can all help your kid look in the mirror and say, "Yeah, that's a pretty keen kid right there."

Plus, what makes each of us unique is also what makes our communities so great, strong, and interesting. If your kids have special interests, embrace them. With your kids' permission, create bulletin boards that showcase their skills and talents—students can "guess who" is an expert (in bugs, in cars, in crochet, and so on)—lists of hobbies, or the results of student interest surveys. Lauding their knowledge and accomplishments helps kids see their differences as positives rather than as liabilities. My daughter, Indy Anna, is a youth therapist, and more than once she's had her clients tell her, "Autism is my superpower!"

See "Tool 4: Hero Interview" in the appendix (page 160) for guidance on implementing this strategy.

BACK TO JASON

After meeting with Jason and his mom during my initial home visit, I sat down with my second-grade team to brainstorm strategies to help Jason connect with his peers. My goal for Jason was clear, plus I knew that if we didn't get Jason connected, we could lose him. If we left him on his current path, he'd eventually become so disconnected from his peer group, his school, his learning, and his support system that his future would be in jeopardy.

I used the information I gathered during the home visit to link Jason with his classmates. He became the class expert on stars, telescopes, microscopes, and researching things like wings from bugs, flowers, types of clouds, and so on. (Later, when teaching older kids, I switched the term to *star witness*, with great success!)

Jason lit up, and his peers celebrated him because we elevated his status within the classroom. By intentionally including him and his particular expertise, we were able to show his classmates that he was a smart, cool kid under his standoffish demeanor.

Taking a page out of the Walton and Cohen (2007) playbook, I also rigged a contest in which a student would win a free haircut. Jason and his mom couldn't afford a haircut, remember? And Jason made several comments about wanting his head buzzed, just like his teacher's. One day he told me, "Maybe if I were handsome, I could have friends, too."

So, I tried some derring-do. With his mom's permission, I brought my clippers to school one day and granted the winner of the contest—Jason, of course—with a buzzcut during recess. Kids made a circle around us in the school's courtyard and cheered as Jason's locks fell to the ground. When it was all said and done, we took a photo together, posted a copy on a bulletin board in the classroom, and labeled it, "Twins."

Jason beamed because we built a strong connection between him and someone with social capital (his teacher). His self-esteem got a boost, and he reveled in his new nickname, "Twin."

Watching the changes as Jason interacted with other kids in the classroom and the playground was profound. Seeing him at a table with his classmates in the cafeteria warmed my heart. And knowing that he was connected, engaged, and participating in his learning gave me a renewed sense of hope for his future.

At the end of the school year, during our field day, Jason's mom volunteered to run a moon viewing station alongside her son. They brought Jason's telescope, because, as he told me, "You can still see the craters during the day if the sun is out." They helped kids sketch what they saw through the lens.

Jason's mom also brought me a plate of homemade chocolate chip cookies with a note reading, "Thank you for being Jason's teacher this year. He's a different kid now than he was six months ago, and I owe that to you. I wish you'd been my teacher when I was a kid."

CONCLUSION

Some kids are different. Heck, all kids are different, if we're honest. And thank goodness that's the case! Can you imagine how dull and tiresome life would be if we were identical clones of one another? Often, however, some kids—represented in this chapter by Jason—are different in such a way that they don't fit in with their peers. They struggle to connect, and they don't feel like they belong. There's discord between the uniqueness we want to celebrate and the relationships we want to build. Fortunately, through implementing specific strategies, we can help Jason meet the goal we identified earlier: to connect with others, celebrate his uniqueness, and feel a strong sense of belonging within the social environment of his peer group and community of learners *so that* he can return to learning with passion, curiosity, and confidence.

3

SKYLA

THE KID WHO LACKS CONSISTENT SUPPORT

THERE ARE TWO words we've all said as educators, at one point or another, that really do us no good whatsoever: "If only . . ."

You can fill in the blanks following those two words with anything you like, and it doesn't matter. If only the parents supported this kid better. If only we could get this kid out of that environment. If only things would change at home. If only we were a boarding school and got to control what happens outside of class, too. If only, if only, if only.

We see the issues that inconsistent, unstable, or unsupportive environments create for kids: chronic absenteeism, mounting behavioral infractions, academic struggles, lack of engagement, inability to forge strong connections . . . They're outside the Box, and we want better for them. Desperately.

We see them struggling, and we'd like to wave a magic wand and—*voila*—fix everything. If only things were different.

Alas, wishing and hoping won't move the needle for our kids. The changes will come if—and *only if*—we're willing to take some significantly powerful actions ourselves, control the controllables, and ensure our kids get the support they need—from wherever they can get it.

MEET SKYLA

It was a crisp autumn evening, and I rejoiced in the vibrant hues of the various trees lining the meandering outdoor walk from my office to the school gymnasium. The sun crept ever closer to the horizon as nearby drivers began to flick on their headlights for the commute home.

I, however, was on my way to cheer on our eighth-grade volleyball team in a big match against a crosstown rival. OK, it wasn't that big of a match. Our team really wasn't very good, and the prospects of us winning were extraordinarily slim. However, our girls were always cheerful, eager to compete, driven to learn and improve, and ready for battle.

Sure enough, our girls were on the receiving end of an old-fashioned whooping. We'd lost the first game by about ten points, and we were down by about that much in the second. The ball just didn't seem to want to bounce our way. Nevertheless, I cheered them on, sitting peacefully in the bleachers with my popcorn.

Suddenly, a commotion on the gym floor caught my attention. A parent had come onto the court. She was screaming at one of our players, Skyla. Waving her finger and cussing, the parent grabbed Skyla by the arm and pointed to the gym door.

I was afraid a second whooping was about to go down, and I had to intervene. It was like a slow-motion daydream, yet it happened at lightning speed. Before I had time to put down my popcorn and race to the court, Skyla and the parent had left the building. By the time I waded through the volleyball team and a handful of other fans and got to the door, they were gone. Poof.

We settled everyone down, and I spoke briefly with our head coach, a science teacher named Andrea, before they resumed play.

"What was that?" I asked.

"That was Skyla's mother," Coach Andrea said, breathing heavily. "I guess she wasn't a fan of how the match was going."

From my office phone, I called the number for Skyla's mom and left her a message. "This is Mr. Hall from school. I'm concerned about what happened at volleyball this evening, and I was hoping you'd help me understand what's going on. Please call me back."

I didn't receive a call back, even after a couple more messages, and Skyla didn't come to school for three days.

On the fourth day after the volleyball incident, I hurried back to campus after a districtwide principals' meeting to oversee dismissal, and I crossed paths with Skyla as she was exiting the building. I ambled up next to her to chat.

"Hey, Skyla," I said. "What tickled your brain today? And how did you scratch that itch?"

Astute as any eighth grader I'd ever met, she looked at me sideways and said, "Is that really the question you want to ask me, Mr. Hall?"

"Guilty," I said. "What happened the other night at volleyball? Want to talk about it?"

"Nope," she said.

"Well, OK. Who's picking you up today?"

"My mom."

My eyes lit up. "Really? That's fantastic! I want to meet your mom. I'll walk with you."

"Mr. Hall, you don't want to meet my mom," Skyla said.

Undeterred, I walked with Skyla across the street to her designated pickup spot. A moment later, a minivan drove up and stopped in front of us. Sure enough, Skyla's mom was driving.

Skyla opened the door, and I stuck out my hand. "Hi, you must be Skyla's mom. I'm Mr. Hall, the principal."

Skyla's mom sized me up with a look that would have bent nails. "I know who you are," she said. "And I don't like you."

That caught me off guard, but I rebounded with what I thought was a witty retort. "How could you not like me if you've never met me? It takes most people at least an hour to realize they don't like me."

It didn't work. I got zero response. And my hand was getting lonely, so I retracted it and waved Skyla into the car, saying, "Well, I'm happy to meet you, and I wanted you to know what an amazing and intelligent daughter you have."

Now staring straight ahead, Skyla's mom said, "I know," as she slid the minivan back into drive. I'm pretty sure Skyla mouthed the words, "I told you," as she closed the door, and they drove away.

At that week's interdisciplinary team meeting for the eighth-grade teachers—a structure that proved to be indispensable as part of our professional learning community framework—we discussed a handful of kids we were concerned about. I'd added Skyla to the agenda, and I'd invited Coach Andrea to join us for that portion of our conversation.

Through a very robust discussion following some pointed questions and sharing, four big ideas emerged about Skyla.

1. She was intelligent, curious, and outgoing most of the time.
2. She tended to hold grudges and had a chip on her shoulder that alienated her from peers on occasion.
3. Her grades were decent, but she missed a lot of school, and there were holes in her learning.
4. Historically, the school (which included the elementary school she had attended) received little or no support from family members at her home.

I remember vividly the exchange that happened next. One of the teachers said, "If only we could just get her mom on board, Skyla would have a fighting chance. She's got brains and potential, and she could really become something special."

Coach Andrea's voice was next, and what she said stuck with me forever. "I wonder if we could look at this a little differently. What if Skyla's mom is doing the best she can with what she's got? What if our perception of her parenting style is the obstacle? Maybe we don't need to get her on board; maybe we need to create an authentic partnership with her to raise her intelligent, curious, outgoing daughter together."

As a team, we nodded and rolled up our sleeves. Our task, as we saw it, was threefold, and we separated our problems of practice into a timeline.

1. **Immediate:** How can we support Skyla to get to school more consistently and regularly?
2. **Short term:** How do we build an authentic partnership with Skyla's mom?
3. **Long term:** What supportive assets does Skyla need to have to grow and develop her potential, and how might the school and home collaborate to provide them for her?

WHAT'S REALLY GOING ON?

Thank goodness for Coach Andrea, right? She offered a tremendous slate-cleansing perspective and phrased it in a very palatable, curious way. She said "what if . . ." instead of "if only . . ."

Often, we become so immersed in our own game that we forget to empathize with the other players. We believe that what we're doing at school is good work (it usually is), that education is the most important thing for a young person to develop (it's certainly in the top three), and that it's the parents' responsibility to support our efforts (that's one of their jobs, for sure).

Inadvertently, when there's a gap between our beliefs about how things *should* be happening and what we observe, we can slip into a deficit-based mindset. The *if onlys* cast a pall of blame over our perception of our kids' parents. We begin to think of them as combatants. It's as if we need to overpower their teachings with our teachings. They say, "If someone hits you, hit 'em back." We say, "Wait, no, there's a nonviolent solution, and you'll get in trouble if you do what your parents say." (As an aside, I've been guilty of saying that aloud while simultaneously thinking, *Yeah, hit 'em back . . . harder!*)

Make no mistake, this all stems from us caring so much about our kids and their futures. However, how we express those beliefs—and our frustrations with the gap—can convey a judgment about family values, priorities, parenting styles, and the ultimate goal of raising kids. That's a tough spot to be in. How do we navigate this tension?

If we were to return to the goal I shared in the introduction, we'd obtain some clarity about what we're trying to do here.

We want our kids to be successful in life.

That's a significantly broader, all-encompassing goal than what we, as school people, tend to focus on: We want our kids to be successful in school. We need to let our gaze extend beyond the artificial and harmful walls of the Box and realize that *our* goal as educators and *families'* goals are one and the same.

We want our kids to be successful in life.

Differences in cultures, values, beliefs, and morals lead to differences in approaches, styles, actions, and attitudes. The sooner we open our eyes and hearts and approach the reality that, to paraphrase Coach Andrea, our kids' families are doing the best they can with what they've got, the sooner we can build true partnerships in this journey.

Instead of allowing our perspectives and biases to point our attention in the wrong direction, let's try looking at the kid in front of us and meeting them where they are.

If we were to view Skyla (or any of the Skylas out there) through an objective, inquisitive lens, we might see a kid who's missing a lot of class, whose parents are often at odds with the school, and who might not have the tools and resources to traverse this tangled path from childhood to adulthood fruitfully. Let's examine the research on attendance, family engagement, and asset development to see what's really going on beneath the surface.

Inconsistent, Poor Attendance

It stands to reason that missing school will affect academic performance. It also impacts the resources a school can offer its students, based on school funding formulas that take average daily attendance into consideration. But is attendance really that big a concern?

In a word, yes. Lots of kids miss a lot of school. Researchers at the University of Southern California find that nearly 20 percent of students hit the threshold to be determined chronically absent annually (that means missing 10 percent or more of the school year), a rate that increases for certain populations, such as multilingual learners, children in single-parent households, high-poverty communities, and Black, Native, and Pacific Islander families (Makori, O'Neal, Uka, McGee, & Jones, 2025).

And what happens if a kid isn't regularly in class? Nothing good. In one longitudinal study following kids from kindergarten through fifth grade, researchers noted that higher absenteeism led to lower academic, executive function, and socio-emotional outcomes (Ansari & Gottfried, 2021). The cumulative effects of chronic absenteeism seem to peak in middle school (Santibañez & Guarino, 2020) and can disrupt the learning of entire classes and buildings, not just the absent kid (May, Bailes, & Riser, 2025). Beyond the school years, high absence rates lead to lower health-related quality of life outcomes (van den Toren et al., 2019) and eventually produce greater economic hardships and decrease the likelihood of voting (Ansari, Hofkens, & Pianta, 2020).

Holy smokes. None of that is on our wish list for Skyla.

If a kid like Skyla misses a lot of school, that's *a* problem.

We often misinterpret chronic absenteeism (missing 10 percent or more of a school year), truancy (unexcused absences from school), and poor attendance (which can include skipping class; arriving late; leaving early; escaping to the bathroom, hallways, or school clinic for extended periods; or any other behavior that results in missing a significant amount of class time) as *the* problem.

Missing school is simultaneously the cause of the preceding effects and the *effect* of an even deeper root cause. So, what's the root cause prompting all of this?

Contrary to a commonly held belief, kids don't miss school simply because the parents won't send them or because they're just delinquent. In fact, there are a lot of reasons kids miss school. Consider the top reasons for the 2024–2025 school year (Barshay, 2025; Malkus, 2025).

- Feeling sick
- Not getting enough sleep
- Considering school boring
- Experiencing mental health challenges
- Caring for younger siblings
- Becoming stranded or having transportation issues
- Avoiding bullying or harassment
- Going to work instead
- Serving a suspension from school for disciplinary purposes
- Struggling academically

Interestingly, we can predict some of the spikes and trends in absenteeism. The *weekend effect*—in which more absences occur on Fridays than the other four days combined (Clifton-Sprigg & James, 2025)—is one very real example. Another is that, according to a study conducted in Baltimore, a student's attendance in the first month of school is a reliable predictor of whether their absences will adversely affect them throughout the school year (Olson, 2014). And some of the most glaring trends in absenteeism occur in conjunction with significant transitions between schooling levels (Coffin & Mason, 2025).

Attendance in school is a prerequisite to scholarly success, and it's a tangled knot that we need to unravel to fully understand.

Lack of Family Engagement

The family's role in a child's education and development can affect the kid's trajectory and success; this we know. That influence extends far beyond—and originates far before—any conversation about school attendance.

Before we discuss the lack of engagement, let's flip the script and examine what outcomes we can expect when families *do* engage with the school. In a nutshell—and this likely won't surprise you—it's a cornucopia of desirables.

- Better academic performance (Utami, 2022)
- More consistent attendance (Kearney, Benoit, Gonzálvez, & Keppens, 2022)
- Stronger community orientation (Erkenbrack, 2026)
- Elevated social-emotional competencies (Martinez-Yarza, Solabarrieta-Eizaguirre, & Santibáñez-Gruber, 2024)

- Decreased behavioral incidents (Calderon-Villarreal, Garcia-Hernandez, Olvera-Gonzalez, & Elizondo-Garcia, 2025)
- Increased ability to overcome obstacles (Sandoval-Reyes, Idrovo-Carlier, & Duque-Oliva, 2021)
- Greater likelihood of graduating from high school (Kantova, 2024)

With all these positive outcomes awaiting, you might be wondering why more families aren't engaged in their kids' education. Well, this is where it gets tricky. According to an Institute of Education Sciences survey involving over 19,000 families, more than 90 percent reported receiving communication from school, and families attended an average of six school meetings or activities in the past year (U.S. Department of Education, 2025). These two metrics are what we typically use to determine family engagement rates, but do they tell us the whole story?

The method, type, and intensity of family engagement can sway a child's educational trajectory. You may have read about *helicopter parents*—those who become overinvolved (Warren, 2024)—or *tiger moms*—those with rigid discipline and high expectations (Kang, 2024)—and emerged with a belief that there may be too much of a good thing. Consider the prevalence of *conditional regard*, in which kids' value is tied directly to performance, achievements, class ranking, and awards and often has debilitating effects (Haines & Schutte, 2023). Now compare that with *perceived cognitive competence*, which is one's belief in one's own potential to achieve success and often leads to . . . wait for it . . . success (Collie & Martin, 2024; Topor, Keane, Shelton, & Calkins, 2010). Both stem directly from the parents' interactions, expectations, and behaviors that shape a kid's identity, confidence, and attitude about self—which may correlate directly to feelings about school, education, and effort (Li et al., 2024).

Family engagement is complex and multidimensional. When we begin to look at some of the ways families demonstrate support for their kids (such as teaching skills, helping with homework, creating routines, shaping beliefs, reinforcing values, and promoting academic socialization), we realize how difficult a concept this is to measure. It's not as straightforward as *engaged* or *not engaged*.

While legislation requires American schools to partner with parents to access certain funds, there are no laws on the books compelling parents to engage reciprocally (U.S. Department of Education, 2025). So, for Skyla and a lot of the other Skylas out there who are struggling, their families may not be engaged to the extent the school would prefer—and almost definitely not in the manner that leads to the desirable outcomes listed previously. This disengagement stems from any of a number of sources: negative past experiences with schools; a fear or distrust of education (or any perceived governmental system); more pressing family, work, or financial needs; cultural beliefs; communication breakdowns due to language barriers; or the differences in values, emphasis, or attitudes about schooling (Ambroso, Dunn, & Fox, 2021). All of these, to some extent, play a role in the school-home partnership.

In short, some families put a premium on scholastic achievement, and others don't. This doesn't mean they're disengaged from their kids' development and future, only that they're disengaged from the school as an institution. Maybe they're just disenfranchised by the Box.

Dearth of Assets

Let's return, briefly, to the world of "If only . . ." In the perfect world, how would you complete that conditional idiom? What are the skills, supports, characteristics, tools, traits, influences, and resources that we wish all our kids possessed?

Wait a minute—put your pen down. You don't need to brainstorm; that examination has already been conducted. The Search Institute, a research organization that strives to support youth in becoming and being their best selves, identifies forty building blocks of healthy development for kids in each of four age ranges: (1) early childhood (three to five years old), (2) children (five to eight years old), (3) middle childhood (eight to twelve years old), and (4) adolescents (twelve to eighteen years old).

Within each age bracket, these forty developmental assets are divided into internal and external factors. The internal factors (commitment to learning, positive values, social competencies, and positive identity) are those that radiate from within the young person, and the external factors (support, empowerment, boundaries and expectations, and constructive use of time) originate from people, places, and activities throughout the home, school, and community (Search Institute, 2024).

As you might expect, the more assets kids possess, the more positive, healthy, and productive their lives tend to be. More assets equate to kids being less likely to engage in high-risk behaviors, such as violence, sexual activity, and drug use, and more likely to engage in thriving behaviors, such as helping others, doing well in school, and taking on leadership roles (Borowski, 2019; Scales & Leffert, 2004; Search Institute, 2024). And when we focus on doing positive, productive, fun things, as opposed to emphasizing the avoidance of harmful behaviors, the results—stronger relationships, deeper social-emotional competencies, increased academic motivation, and honed executive functioning, for example—are even more beneficial (Scales, Redmond, & Benson, 2023).

All told, it takes a lot to raise a kid to be well rounded, confident, and capable. Not to mention one who demonstrates compassion, courage, curiosity, empathy, fairness, generosity, honesty, integrity, kindness, perseverance, respect, and responsibility (you'll recognize those virtues from our original list of *characteristics we'd want our neighbors to possess* from the introduction). Indeed, as the popular saying states, it takes a village to raise a child.

Indeed, it takes a village to raise a child.

As you've been reading this section, you've probably been feeling rather optimistic. And you've been waiting for the other shoe to drop. Well, here it is. If kids don't possess a significant number of the assets, the prevalence of health issues, behavioral concerns, education struggles, financial instability, and even problematic driving habits increases (Kiadarbandsari & Fa'alau, 2025; Nurius, Prince, & Rocha, 2015; Sheehan et al., 2022).

And, according to the Search Institute's (2024) "State of Developmental Assets" report, over half (56 percent) of the 27,000 young people surveyed report experiencing most asset indicators only somewhat or infrequently, putting them in a vulnerable spot for at-risk behaviors. Presence of supportive assets drops for most youth between the ages of twelve and fifteen, a time of rapid development, change, and growth, and, especially in low-income communities, indicates a need for intentional emphasis on these resources (Min, Yoon, Minnes, & Singer, 2025).

The long and short of it is plain: We need more kids to have access to more assets.

As you've been considering the Skyla in your life or classroom, your first question was likely, Why does this kid lack consistent support?

Your next question is, How can I reach and teach this kid?

WHAT DO KIDS WHO LACK CONSISTENT SUPPORT REALLY NEED?

If a kid lacks consistent support, that's OK. Why? Because it takes a village to raise a child, and we're part of that village!

Raising and nurturing the development of a young person isn't an *either-or* proposition (that is, *either* we partner with the family to help them raise the kid *or* we focus on educating the kid). Harboring an *us-versus-them* mentality will get us nowhere. Converting our focus to a *both-and* mindset and embracing our collective pursuit of what's best for each individual kid will, however, give us a wide place for our steps so we can walk together along the journey to success.

We know Skyla needs to be in school and connected to her education. We also know she needs to be surrounded and uplifted by loving family members at home, in school, and throughout the community so she can develop the characteristics and traits that will carry her forward.

She needs her village, strong and sturdy, in her corner.

This is a good time to return to the dog-eared, bookmarked pages in chapter 1 that include the four protocols and templates you'll want to use to frame your work. And, because clarity of the goal is a non-negotiable prerequisite for all the work that follows, I might also suggest that you revisit the list of questions I posed at the beginning of chapter 1 to hone your collaborative vision of success. Here's the result of that initial reflection for Skyla.

GOAL STATEMENT

We want to partner as a village to rally around Skyla, to connect powerfully with her at home, in school, and throughout the community so that she can recommit to her learning, her relationships, her development, and her future.

HOW DO WE DO THIS?

You might be thinking, *Holy smokes, creating a village of support for a kid is a daunting proposition, and I'm only one person.* Yes, and . . . you're one powerful, committed, caring, influential person. You might just be the difference maker in your Skyla's life. And you're joined by colleagues who are similarly powerful, committed, caring, and influential.

Before we start examining strategies, let's make sure we're philosophically situated in a productive spot. Here are some questions for you to reflect on.

- What are your thoughts and feelings about your kid's parents? Are you channeling your inner Coach Andrea, remaining mindful that they're doing the best they can with what they've got? Have you opened your heart to believe they love their kid and they're looking for answers, just like you are?
- How committed are you to ensuring your kid's success beyond the schoolhouse? Are you simply looking for the home to support you in the education process, or are you seeking a true partnership to develop a kid's full, lifelong potential?
- What are your intentions related to communication? In a viable, equitable partnership, information flows two ways. Are you more

interested in sharing details or obtaining feedback? How open are you to receiving input from home and acting on it?

- Why is establishing this partnership important to you? What do you really hope to gain from this? Where did this goal originate? How might you keep this virtuous approach front of mind as you work with your kid and their parents?

With your positive, optimistic, energetic mindset firmly established, you're ready. Let's look at some specific options for Skyla and all the other Skylas out there. Here are several strategies to consider, organized in a memorable A-B-C-D-E format.

Strategy: Appraise Attendance Data

If the young person's school attendance is suffering, one question rises to the surface: Why? What's going on behind the scenes? What factors are influencing whether a kid goes to school, stays at school, arrives late, leaves early, or ducks out here and there?

To determine how to effectively address the attendance issue, it's best to collect and analyze as much data (as opposed to hunches) as possible. Unraveling and understanding the attendance picture includes a thorough look at the hard data, student factors, school factors, and home factors. With all this information in hand, the school-home partnership (and yes, this includes the kid in question) can set a collaborative and relevant goal and build a concrete plan for achieving it together.

See "Tool 5: Student Attendance Reflection Questionnaire" in the appendix (page 161) for guidance on implementing this strategy.

Strategy: Build a Clear, Common Goal

As educators, we want our kids to be successful. As parents, relatives, and guardians, our kids' grown-ups want their kids to be successful. Our kids want to be successful, too. Are our definitions of success the same? Are we shooting at the same target?

Research on effective goal setting, and even more pertinent goal achieving, informs us of five key characteristics that we'll want to consider. Here they are, along with a question to prompt your team's conversation for each.

1. **It's clear:** Together, with the team, picture success in your minds. Communicate it openly with one another and describe it in great detail (Saks, 2024). What is the goal we're aiming for?

2. **It's self-concordant:** Selecting a personally relevant, meaningful goal creates an upward emotional spiral that increases motivation and persistence (van Jaarsveld, Wong, Baars, Specht, & Paas, 2024). How is this goal important for the kid, the family, and the school?
3. **It's simultaneously process- and product-focused:** The outcome itself is the beacon calling us forward; the path and how we tread it from here to there are equally important (Pietsch, Riddell, Semmler, Ntoumanis, & Gucciardi, 2024). How will we focus on the *what* and the *how* of this journey?
4. **It's broken into chunks:** Establishing benchmarks along the way to gauge our progress will let us know if we're on track (Lawson et al., 2024). When—and how—will we take stock of our journey to note growth and calibrate as needed?
5. **It's written in the form of a question:** Posing a question to ourselves engages our interrogative self-talk, which fires the brain's problem-solving functions, meaning we're more apt to seek a solution to a problem than follow an order (Dharani, Witbooi, & April, 2024). How can we phrase this as a question we can seek to answer?

To illustrate these five characteristics in action, here's the short-term goal our collaborative team set with Skyla and her mother, along with an explanation of each.

How can we support Skyla to get to school more consistently and regularly?

1. **Clear:** As a team, we all pictured 100 percent attendance for Skyla—on time, every class period, every day. There's no confusion about what we were trying to accomplish.
2. **Self-concordant:** All parties (school, home, and Skyla) agreed that increased school attendance would have a snowball effect on Skyla's achievement and attitude. Skyla even said, "I think I get ruffled at school because I miss a lot of stuff—not just the schoolwork but also things with my friends and other kids. This should help."
3. **Simultaneously process- and product-focused:** The goal itself shone a spotlight on the outcome (Skyla is in school, on time, and more often) and what we all could do to support her. Eventually our plan would include those specific actions—and the habits we'd be helping Skyla develop to meet the goal.

4. **Broken into chunks:** The language we used, "more consistently and regularly," provided a comparison between current attendance rates and the goal. When we began this process, Skyla's attendance sat at about 80 percent, and she picked up an average of three tardies (for various classes) per week. We set benchmark targets of 85 percent attendance and two tardies per week within the first month, and when she met that, we celebrated and gradually raised the bar.
5. **Written in the form of a question:** This was a critical piece that we modified for Skyla so she could set a reminder on her phone for every evening: "What do I need to do tonight so I'm ready to get to school tomorrow morning?"

See "Tool 6: My Goals That Matter Goal-Setting Template" in the appendix (page 163) for guidance on implementing this strategy.

Strategy: Communicate, Communicate, Communicate

If you've ever heard the aphorism "97 percent of conflict is rooted in communication" and thought, *Yeah, that sounds about right*, then you likely understand the big idea: Clear, honest, early, frequent, articulate communication is critical for building trusting, collaborative, and productive relationships.

And if you've ever heard the expression "Keep your friends close and your kids' parents closer," then you've probably attended one of my professional learning workshops. How do we do this?

Communicate, communicate, communicate.

Remember, communication is a two-way street, and how a message is received is more important than how it is sent, no matter how it is intended. So, if a student is absent from school, for instance, how do you and your school communicate with families? Robo-calls, text messages, and emails? Those one-way tools, while convenient and often quite factual, tend to lack the personal touch that invites a relationship.

To combat this and to nurture partnerships with the home, schools (and individual teachers, for that matter) can build proactive, consistent communication plans. These plans tend to consist of six overlapping elements.

1. **Goal:** What is the purpose of the communication? What are you attempting to accomplish?

2. **Method:** How will you communicate? What various modes of communication will you employ?
3. **Frequency:** When will you communicate this message? How far in advance, how often, and how many repetitions will follow?
4. **Call to action:** What are you suggesting should occur because of this communication? Will you request a response, feedback, input, ideas, a visit, or something else?
5. **Invitation:** How will you elicit a response? What specific strategies will you utilize to ensure communication is a two-way street?
6. **Response to the response:** How will you demonstrate your openness and appreciation for the ongoing communication? How will you show you're using the information you gather and are interested in a communication partnership?

See "Tool 7: Communication Audit" in the appendix (page 165) for guidance on implementing this strategy.

Strategy: Diversify the Partnership

In many schools, the prevailing wisdom is *we need more parent involvement.* This phrasing and others like it (parent engagement, parent participation, and so on) imply that school and the child's education is the most important thing, and parents need to support us so we can do our jobs more effectively. While this isn't erroneous thinking, it leads to collecting superficial metrics like attendance at events such as multicultural night, parent-teacher conferences, parent-teacher organization meetings, and others—all hosted at the school building.

Because of work schedules, childcare needs, transportation issues, and a variety of historical contexts that may cause parents to be unwilling to step foot on a school campus, these events are often populated by the same group of grown-ups. Every sign-in sheet has the same names on it.

To build authentic partnerships and enhance school personnel's and parents' engagement in the education and development of each child, we've got to diversify the array of options. Implementing a strategic communication approach (see the previous strategy for some ideas); sharing information from local businesses and community members; cohosting events in familiar, neutral locations like the fire station or public library; planning informal get-togethers like a picnic at the neighborhood park; and scheduling events before school, during the lunch hour, and in the evenings can expand parents' availability to connect, engage, and become earnest partners in this important venture.

See "Tool 8: Authentic School-Home Partnership Tips" in the appendix (page 167) for guidance on implementing this strategy.

PONDER THIS

Gather your teammates, an instructional coach or administrator, or a trusted colleague, and pose the question, "What do we really want?"

In any given moment, our answer to this question will guide our next steps. As the expression goes, "form follows function," meaning once we have a clearly identified goal, we can build plans and implement strategies to accomplish that goal.

In other words, once we know what we want "family involvement" to accomplish, we can decide how to best go about it.

Sometimes, we have an event coming up and we need volunteers to help behind the scenes or during the event itself, so we reach out with that request. In other cases, we want to offer parenting classes, sessions on financial literacy, or information about the importance of sleep routines, so we broadcast the details. Often, we want to get families in the door, so we host a fun event (usually with food and kids' performances) and send out invitations.

What if we want families to feel like we're on their side? What if we want families to feel comfortable around us? What if we want to share the good vibes of the school people and build trust? What if we just want to create connections and stronger relationships?

Sometimes the best family involvement strategy is a positive phone call. A handwritten note. A quick conversation in the drop-off car line to ask how things are going. An email with a picture of their kid smiling and engaged in learning. These simple, quick, inexpensive approaches can do a world of good in creating the partnerships and involvement our communities and our kids so desperately need.

Strategy: Emphasize the Whole Child

We've got school, and we've got home. What else is there in a kid's life? Lots.

Earlier, you read about the Search Institute's (2024) research on the assets that help kids grow and develop into healthy, caring, and responsible young adults. School can contribute to that list, and home can contribute to that list. Since it takes a village to raise a child, let's recruit other members of the village to promote each kid's healthy development through cultivating these assets.

As you assess the building blocks your Skyla possesses and demonstrates, you might be asking yourself questions like these about her *external* assets.

- Does she experience support from caring neighbors and other adults in the community?
- Does she feel safe in and around her neighborhood?
- Does she witness adults modeling positive, responsible behaviors?
- Does she participate in programs, activities, or sports in the community?

Further, you'll explore questions like the following that address her *internal* assets.

- Does she engage in learning outside of school? Does she read for pleasure?
- Does she help other people? Does she tell the truth?
- Is she affected by other people's feelings? Can she resolve conflict?
- Does she feel proud of herself?

For each of the forty developmental assets you'll consider, the big question is this: To what extent or frequency does the kid experience this asset? You can access the full list of assets by visiting https://info.searchinstitute.org/developmental-assets-framework-download, where you must fill out a brief form to get the download.

With parents and the school team (and the kid as appropriate), review the forty items on the appropriate age-level asset list. Use a 1–5–10 scale to determine to what extent, frequence, or degree the kid experiences each asset: 1 meaning no, rarely, or with limited or negative impact; 5 meaning sometimes, to some extent, or with middling results; and 10 meaning yes, almost always, or with great positive impact.

Then, as a team, identify strategies, sources, and structures for augmenting or adding assets to support the healthy development of the kid. When analyzing the 1–5–10 scale, look for opportunities to incorporate or shore up those scoring 1, reinforce those scoring 10, and investigate ways to strengthen the 5 in a more consistent, widespread, or focused manner.

When our youngest daughter, Peja, was in sixth grade, my wife, Mindy, and I attended her parent-teacher conference. After the initial small talk, we sat at a table with her homeroom teacher. In front of her sat a stack of papers, and she clicked on a couple tabs on her laptop, saying, "Let's talk about your daughter, shall we?"

"Yes," said Mindy. "How is Peja doing?"

For the next fifteen minutes or so, we heard all about Peja's test scores, her points earned and grades in her classes, and we pored through the pile of work samples the teacher had brought. Together, we compared them with the grade-level standards and previous work, we analyzed them in light of the curriculum, and we projected her future academic performance.

To sum it up, the teacher said, "So, as you can see, she's in really good standing."

Considering all this information, I could see Mindy's wheels turning, and honestly, I wasn't too surprised when she said, "Yes, thank you, but how is Peja doing?"

Confused, the teacher asked, "What do you mean? I just told you how she's doing."

"You told us about her academic performance, which we appreciate," Mindy said. "From your perspective as a professional, how is she doing? How does she interact with the other kids? How does she handle frustration? What goals is she working toward? How would you describe her demeanor? What personality characteristics do you observe? We want to know about Peja the young person, not just Peja the student."

Though it was a tad awkward for a moment, the teacher recovered nicely, and we became engrossed in a conversation about our daughter—the kid—and what makes her unique and fantastic. The teacher had become so preoccupied and consumed with her singular focus on academic performance that she'd forgotten about the whole child.

It was at that moment that I vowed to prioritize the human element in education, knowing that every young person in our orbit is a delightful mix of hopes and fears, skills and struggles, halos and horns, and successes and flops, and those characteristics encompass every aspect of their multifaceted existence.

BACK TO SKYLA

After the rough encounter with Skyla's mom in the minivan and our subsequent interdisciplinary team meeting in which Coach Andrea dropped some serious wisdom, our team brainstormed some strategies to address the three-pronged goal.

1. **Immediate:** How can we support Skyla to get to school more consistently and regularly?
2. **Short term:** How do we build an authentic partnership with Skyla's mom?
3. **Long term:** What supportive assets does Skyla need to grow and develop her potential, and how might the school and home collaborate to provide them for her?

Not surprisingly, a lot of the approaches we pursued were interwoven. As Coach Andrea so shrewdly noted, it was as if we were constructing a web of support for Skyla. Here are three strategies we chose and the rationale or purpose for each.

1. We identified a point person to engage in frequent, multimodal communication with Skyla's mom. Since I was a source of irritation for Skyla's mom (because of my position as principal, my personality, or something else, I'm still not sure), it wasn't me. It also wasn't Coach Andrea, because she didn't know Skyla as a student. Skyla's English teacher, Kathryn, volunteered. At first, her calls and messages on our schoolwide communications app were simply reports of positivity and praise. After a couple of weeks, Kathryn asked if they could sit down to talk about Skyla and how we could partner to help her become even more successful. The two of them, along with Skyla, met at McDonald's during her mom's lunch break to begin that conversation.
2. We focused on first things first: attendance. As a result of that conversation, we learned a couple things about Skyla's attendance. First, she'd had some rough experiences in elementary school that soured her on school. She threw tantrums, and her mom would eventually give in and allow Skyla to stay home. Second, her mom confided in us that she really wanted Skyla to go to school and get her education. The fighting and screaming over getting to the bus became too much, and she opted to let Skyla stay home to prioritize the good vibes between her and her daughter. It had become a habit. Skyla didn't think her mom thought school was that important, so skipping was pretty easy to do. It was a source of real frustration for her mom, and she asked Kathryn for help.
3. We assessed her assets. A few months after establishing a strong partnership and continuing to communicate Skyla's progress back and forth, Kathryn invited Skyla and her mom to sit down with our team to go through the asset assessment and an individual interest inventory (see "Tool 2: Individual Interest Inventory" in the appendix, page 153). Her

mom was still reticent to come to school for this meeting, so we set it up for a gathering room at the local public library. This productive session revealed quite a bit about Skyla that we didn't know: She had a strong sense of right and wrong (thus the grudge holding we'd noted earlier), she wanted to serve others to make the world a better place, and she tended to gravitate more to adults than her peers. This gave our team (which included Skyla and her mom) plenty to work with.

As the school year ended, Skyla's attendance and attitude showed remarkable improvement. She participated in several community-service projects that our school coordinated, including a neighborhood cleanup effort for which she created and distributed a flyer (and a social media post) to local homes and businesses, recruiting volunteers.

When it came time to facilitate the transition of our eighth graders to the high school, we offered to bring our team to Skyla's mom during a work break. To our surprise, she said, "Actually, I'd like to meet with y'all at the high school. I want to see that place and get a feel for it so I know what Skyla's talking about when she comes home every day."

At the transition meeting, we covered as much ground as we could, handing Skyla off to the high school staff with love, thoughtfulness, and a bucket of information. They immediately put some plans in place to ease the transition and ensure Skyla's success, to continue the partnership with her mom, and to enhance Skyla's assets.

As we set to leave, Skyla's mom walked directly up to me. I had flashbacks of our earlier interactions, so I must have tensed up. Holding out her arms for an embrace, she laughed. "Mr. Hall, I don't bite."

Then, quietly, she told me, "Your staff has been phenomenal. This is the first time I've heard more good things than bad things about my daughter from the school. I was about ready to pull her out of school or something, but y'all really changed my mind. Thank you."

Several years after Skyla graduated from high school, I crossed paths with her at the local airport. She was working as a gate agent for one of the airlines, and she recognized my name from a flight manifest. I was just minding my own business, waiting to board, when I heard my name called to the podium over the loudspeaker.

She asked, "Mr. Hall, do you remember me?"

"Absolutely, Skyla. It's great to see you."

"Well, I'm happy to inform you that you've been upgraded to first class for this flight," she said.

I'm pretty sure—OK, I'm 100 percent positive—that my name wasn't at the top of the upgrade list, but I wasn't about to make a scene.

"Thank you, Skyla."

"You're welcome," she said. "I figure it's the least I could do, since you made sure I got a first-class education."

As I boarded the plane, I made a mental note to ask Skyla about her mom . . . next time.

CONCLUSION

Some kids arrive at school with a hundred people in their corner and a parade of resources, scaffolds, safety nets, ladders, and tools at their disposal. Others, like Skyla, have bits and pieces of supplies. Their support networks are incomplete. There are gaps in their stanchions. As it stands, they don't have the means to grow, develop, thrive, and meet their full potential. That's where we come in. By building strategic, authentic partnerships with families; setting clear goals; and working relentlessly to provide thorough structural support, we can partner as a village to rally around Skyla and help her meet the goal we identified earlier: to connect powerfully with her at home, in school, and throughout the community *so that* she can recommit to her learning, her relationships, her development, and her future.

4

ANTHONY

THE KID WHO DOESN'T CARE

I'm bored.

Why do we need to learn this?

Is this going to be on the test?

This is dumb.

Who gives a ______?

When am I ever going to need this?

PHRASES LIKE THESE echo off the whiteboard walls, tiled ceilings, and linoleum floors of classrooms everywhere as young people try to make meaning of school. As a result, we—the professional educators in the room—lament the absence of initiative, discipline, and commitment shown by the newest generation.

Our kids, it appears, are less and less interested in their education. They're disengaged at school. They're not motivated by anything. They're disconnected from their peers, their teachers, even their future. They don't participate in—sometimes even resist—courses, lessons, and activities. Their attitudes range from indifferent to sour and sometimes worse.

Despite our noble efforts and our best intentions, we can't seem to crack the code. We haven't yet unlocked our kids' potential and drive. And as we pour our blood, sweat, tears, and coffee-fueled selves into our work, the kids stare back at us, blankly or defiantly, and say the one thing that burns us the most.

I. Don't. Care.

MEET ANTHONY

I heard the tears in her voice all the way from my office. Dolores was Anthony's grandmother, and she was at her wits' end. By the time I joined her at the welcome desk, she'd already been through two tissues and was working on a third.

"Oh, Mr. Hall," she pleaded. "Is there anything you can do? Anthony refuses to come to school and has locked himself in his room again."

As I walked with Dolores back to my office, I reflected on what I knew about Anthony. He was in sixth grade and found himself near the top of just about every list we kept in the office. Because of his low grades and poor test scores, he was on the academic watch list. Because of his history of missing school, he was on the attendance watch list. Because of his tendency to get in fights, argue with teachers, and create a ruckus, he was on the behavior watch list. And because of his athletic ability, friendly disposition, and generous smile, he was on that other list we all keep but don't talk about: the "why is he squandering his potential?" list.

"Tell me what happened this morning," I said to Dolores.

Anthony's grandmother shared the tale. Here's the short version: Anthony refused to get up and get going today. School's stupid, no one cares if he's there or not, classmates tease him for being dumb, all he does is get in trouble, so what's the point? He wouldn't even come out of his room to eat breakfast. The bribing, the ordering, and the sweet-talking had run its course, and Anthony wasn't having it. All he wants to do is play football. Real football, video football, fantasy football, that's all he cares about.

I had an idea. "Let's go," I said, standing up.

Dolores looked at me sideways. "Where are we going?"

"Your apartment. Let's go get Anthony." Dolores smiled and held the door for me.

During the ten-minute walk, I asked a ton of questions about Anthony, his past, his goals, what his life at home was like, and what—besides football—was a motivator for him. By the time we got to the apartment, I felt like an Anthony expert.

Dolores knocked on Anthony's door. A groan emanated from within.

"Hey, Anthony. What could you possibly be doing that's better than coming to school with me today?" I said.

"Is that Mr. Hall? Gramma, why'd you get Mr. Hall?"

"I don't talk to closed doors," I said. "Open up, will you?"

The door opened, and Anthony, still groggy-eyed, shook my outstretched hand. "No disrespect, but I don't want to go to school. It's a waste of my time," he said.

"You're coming to school with me right now; that's non-negotiable," I said. "The question is, how can we make it worthwhile for you? Maybe you and I could talk about it while we play catch after lunch. Grab your favorite football and brush your teeth, let's go."

Anthony's eyes lit up. "Really? OK, hang on."

Dolores thanked me as she readied to go to work, then Anthony and I headed out. I carried the football so it wouldn't be a distraction. As we walked, we came up with a rough draft of a plan to help Anthony feel better about coming to school, staying focused, and keeping out of trouble. The long and short of it was this: Anthony would check in with me first thing every day and drop off his football. He'd go to class, behave himself, and do his best at his schoolwork. If he needed help, he'd ask for it. If kids teased him, he'd ignore them. At lunchtime, he and I would play catch and talk about how the day is going and what he needs to do to finish it strong. He seemed excited about it.

Now, I never played football, not even in grade school, but I could throw and catch a football just fine. Anthony, as I learned that first afternoon and confirmed over the next two weeks, was an exceptionally skilled receiver, and he beamed with joy during those lunchtime sessions. Even when he'd gotten in trouble or failed a test in the morning, we played catch and talked, and his afternoons were always better.

The first step seemed positive. He was coming to school, which is the lowest rung on the ladder and the prerequisite for every other element of school success, so we considered that a win. Also, he was engaging with me, his assistant principal. Another win. This setup wasn't sustainable for the long run, however, and not just because my shoulder wouldn't survive too much more pseudo-quarterbacking. It was still built on external motivators, and we needed Anthony to find his own internal inspiration.

So, we needed to learn more, make a more enduring plan, and put it into place. This is where the real work began.

WHAT'S REALLY GOING ON?

Anthony is just one of many kids who, in one way, shape, or form, demonstrate to us that they simply don't care about school. How they communicate this indifference tends to rankle us, doesn't it? As a professional educator, consider what goes through your mind when you witness a kid turn in a blank paper, stare out the window when it's time to get to work, dawdle in the hallway when you've clearly set a deadline, mark *B* on every item in a multiple-choice test, throw their book in the trash, leave their tablet at home, shrug, roll their eyes, laugh and joke when it's silent work time, or snarl and say, "You can't make me do this."

You've seen all these behaviors before, and you've heard all the snarky comments. And if you're like me and the tens of thousands of educators out there facing it every day, you probably sink into thoughts like these.

- "He doesn't care about his future."
- "She's given up."
- "They're going to end up helpless, hopeless, and homeless at this rate."
- "He hates me."
- "She's destined to be a failure."
- "If they don't care, why should I?"

However, what we see on the surface is rarely the reality. Those descriptions and thoughts are deduced solely based on the inputs we receive.

As a result, we view and interpret their absence, their struggles, their lack of effort, their opposition, their disruptions, and every other outside-the-Box behavior as wayward disobedience. Some kind of naughty.

If we take it at face value, then we respond in kind: If the kid's not going to put any effort into learning, I'm not going to put any effort into teaching. Done.

Looking beneath the surface, however, at the message itself—rather than the unfortunate delivery method—reveals the truth: The kids who appear disengaged, who seem indifferent, and who give the impression they don't care actually care a lot about life, their future, their dreams, their relationships . . . they just don't care about school and the way it's currently imposed on them. Caring about school and caring about one's own future are two different things.

While it may initially upset us, as educators, to see our kids refuse to "do school" and grumble about it, it's actually a blessing. Hearing those phrases and observing those behaviors signal to us that it's not over yet. The kid's still here. We still have time.

While Anthony may appear disengaged and might tell us straight up, "I don't care," if we listen carefully to discern the underlying message, it's even more powerful: "This ain't working for me."

With our newfound open minds and open hearts, let's try looking at the kid in front of us and meeting them where they are.

Why don't some kids care? Why are they disengaged from school? Why ain't this working for them?

Before we start scrutinizing the reasons for disengagement, let's define *engagement* together. A lot of us believe—erroneously—that the term, and the behavior it describes, is dichotomous. You're either engaged or disengaged. You're either in or you're out.

While Anthony may appear disengaged and might tell us straight up, "I don't care," if we listen carefully to discern the underlying message, it's even more powerful: "This ain't working for me."

The truth is that engagement is much more complex than a simple pair of binary options. It exists on a scale, described in fabulous detail for educators by Phillip Schlechty (2002) in *Working on the Work* (see figure 4.1, page 80). When presented with a task, assignment, or other schoolwork, students will respond in one of the following five ways:

- Authentic engagement: The task, activity, or work the student is assigned or encouraged to undertake is associated with a result or outcome that has clear meaning and relatively immediate value to the student.
- Ritual engagement: The immediate end of the assigned work has little or no inherent meaning or direct value to the student, but the student associates it with extrinsic outcomes and results that are of value.
- Passive compliance: The student is willing to expend whatever effort is needed to avoid negative consequences, although he or she sees little meaning in the tasks assigned or the consequences of doing those tasks.
- Retreatism: The student is disengaged from the tasks, expends no energy in attempting to comply with the demands of the tasks, but does not act in ways that disrupt others and does not try to substitute other activities for the assigned task.
- Rebellion: The student summarily refuses to do the task assigned, acts in ways that disrupt others, or attempts to substitute tasks and activities to which he or she is committed in lieu of those assigned or supported by the school and by the teacher. (Schlechty, 2002, pp. 1–2)

Source for levels: Schlechty, 2002.

Figure 4.1: *Levels of engagement.*

As you can see, there's more nuance than *they're either engaged or defiant*. Under the surface, the factors influencing a kid's level of engagement on this scale may vary from day to day, content area to content area, even minute to minute, depending on what's on the kid's mind, the task in question, who's sitting nearby, the temperature in the room, what the cafeteria served for breakfast—literally anything.

We need to know what that *anything* is in any given moment if we're going to try to affect it in a positive way. Let's unpack the research to explore the top five most significant *anythings* that influence our kids' engagement in school and in the classroom. Back to the original questions of this section: Why don't some kids care? Why are they disengaged from school? Why ain't this working for them?

They're Bored

In a survey conducted by Yale University, nearly 70 percent of high school students in the United States reported feeling bored at school (Moeller, Brackett, Ivcevic, & White, 2020). This may or may not shock you, since "I'm bored" has long been a part of teenagers' vernacular, especially when it comes to school. In even less shocking news, a Gallup poll (dubbed "The School Cliff") of over half a million students showed a marked and consistent decline in student engagement from elementary to middle to high school (Bushaw & Lopez, 2012), a disheartening reality that the Brookings Institution's report "The Disengagement Gap" confirms (Winthrop, Shoukry, & Nitkin, 2025). And an even sharper dagger is this: Only 12 percent of teenagers look forward to coming to school every day (Manno, 2025).

During a workshop on student engagement, a teacher participant took umbrage at the notion that school being less engaging is the problem. The culprit, she believed, was our kids' short attention spans and inability to tend to their responsibilities as students. She asked me, "What do you expect us to do—perform all day like a reel of social media posts?"

While it's true we're morphing into a population that craves bite-sized data inputs from social media, feeds, and apps, there's an equal reality: Our kids pay attention to things that matter to them. So, when you read the line, "They're bored," how did you first interpret it? That school should be more stimulating by teaching fifteen-second tidbits with expert editing and a soundtrack? Or that school should be more stimulating by eliciting mental activity through curiosity, high-interest topics, relevant queries, and important challenges?

Capturing a kid's attention for fifteen seconds does little to fire up the brain. Providing opportunities to wonder, to seek, to learn, and to master articles of significance will go a long way toward alleviating boredom and replacing it with inspiration, dedication, and resolve.

Another teacher at that workshop stepped in to share a strategy that might address the concern. "If you're comparing a garden-variety classroom lesson with a social media post," she said, "try this: Ask your kids to open whatever social media app they choose and start scrolling until something compels them to stop. Ask them: Why did you stop? What about that post caused you to turn on the volume and listen? Why did you click on it instead of scrolling by?"

Their answers will most likely reveal what I shared in the previous paragraph: Our kids are curious about something, interested in learning something, or captivated by something that matters to them. It's incumbent on us to figure out what that is.

Curiosity is all the rage when little humans begin to notice, think, and speak. When little kids ask why something is the way it is, we think it's cute. Over time, our responses to that simple, curious question change. Why? Because, little by little, we've substituted what kids are curious about with what *we* think they ought to focus on and know. When a little kid asks why the sky is blue, we take time to explain it (as best as we can). When older kids ask the same question, we think they're trying to challenge our intelligence or position of authority. When high schoolers ask, we think they're trying to launch a full-on, mutinous coup. We often respond with things like, "Great question, but that's not what we're doing in class today. Nice try. Put your attention back on the learning targets and your worksheet." When we do this, we're often redirecting our kids away from what piques their interest, what's on their minds, what they're wondering . . . and straight onto activities that may or may not have any relevance to their current (or future imagined) lives. A learning target, no matter how well written, rarely serves as a suitable substitute for good old-fashioned question marks in the thought bubbles above our kids' heads.

They're Not Challenged Enough

Is it possible that some of our kids become bored—and disengage from school—because the classwork assigned to them doesn't cause their engines to fire and smoke to rise from their brains? Absolutely. Spending too much time doing busywork, only covering topics at surface level, or repeating learning that's already been mastered can cause kids' attention to wander, their motivation to diminish, and their commitment to wane. By contrast, rigorous work, as defined by lifelong educator Robyn R. Jackson (2011), requires students to "create their own meaning, integrate skills into processes, and use what they have learned to solve real-world problems, even when the 'correct' answer is unclear and they are faced with perplexing unknowns" (p. 15). That's the kind of work that increases participation, motivation, and enthusiasm. And in case you're wondering, no, it's not just the high-achieving kids that need the challenge, so the solution isn't to reassign the bored kids to honors and AP courses. The expectation that learning is positioned nicely in the Zone of Proximal Development, the sweet spot between what a student can do alone and what requires assistance (Vygotsky, 1978), supports all students.

They're Disconnected

It's no surprise to hear a student ask, "Why do we need to learn this?" or "How will I ever use this in the real world?" Often, we have answers to those questions ready, written on sticky notes in our lesson plans. However, what if the question they ask is, "I want to do *such-and-such* when I grow up. Why can't I learn about that?" This query unearths a new reality: For a lot of kids who are outside the Box, there's a disconnect.

The disconnect doesn't stem from a lack of caring about the curriculum, though it eventually lands there. This particular disconnect originates from the kid's goals, dreams, interests, and ambitions and the perceived lack of opportunities and availability to indulge in learning, work, and activities that are relevant to that future. The result? Kids experience *school alienation*, which is exactly what it sounds like: a set of negative cognitive and affective attitudes toward school (Hascher & Hadjar,

2018). This manifests as the estrangement from the institution itself, a drop in academic performance, withdrawal from relationships, and a decay in motivation (Buzzai, Sorrenti, Tripiciano, Orecchio, & Filippello, 2021; Labokas, 2024). Let's address the elephant in the schoolhouse: Many kids have given up. Why? They don't see schooling, as it's currently being executed, as a viable part of their future.

They're Stifled

Many kids complain that school is something that is done *to* them, rather than it being a collaborative enterprise that helps to build them. Because of several factors (for example, a standardized curriculum, the sheer number of students in a defined space, the need for order, the aforementioned myth of control, and the idea of discipline), school is a place where the adults are in charge. Kids are the consumers, and, as the Box so consistently teaches and reinforces, the consumers often lack autonomy, choice, and voice—elements that are proven to increase attendance, engagement, student performance, and learning outcomes (Conner, Mitra, Holquist, & Boat, 2025). There are few places in society as regimented and controlled as school, where kids are told where to go, when to go there, how to get there, what to do when they're there, how long they'll be there, and when they can leave. It's no surprise that many young people, eager to develop their own personalities and virtues, cultivate their strengths and passions, and demonstrate their free will and independence, resist in one form or another against this structure. Often that dissention is quiet and subtle, as defined by the middle stages (compliance and retreatism) of Schlechty's (2002) engagement continuum, before hitting outright rebellion.

They're Antsy

Imagine wanting—or needing—to do something and being told that you can't do it. Now, imagine that happening for six hours a day, one hundred eighty days a year, for at least thirteen years. I think we might all get antsy if that were the case. Our bodies were designed to move. To go outside. To explore. To do stuff. To pick things up. To walk and climb. School, the way it's currently set up, has very few opportunities for kids to experience learning with the level of movement we biologically, and developmentally, need. John Medina (2008), author of *Brain Rules*, sums it up perfectly: "If you wanted to create an education environment that was directly opposed to what the brain was good at doing, you would probably design something like a classroom" (p. 5). Many kids have learned to acquiesce to the demands of the Box, and they can sit for hours under artificial lights, processing theoretical information and completing a litany of tasks, and they often do so successfully.

The kids we're interested in, for the purposes of this book, generally cannot. They need to get up, to move, to access all their senses, and to explore things of interest to them.

Chances are pretty good that a light bulb illuminated above *your* head while you read through these five descriptors of disengaged students. Maybe several. Perhaps an entire chandelier. And as you've been considering the Anthony in your life or classroom, you may now have a viable response to your first question, Why doesn't this kid seem to care?

Your next question is, How can I reach and teach this kid?

WHAT DO KIDS WHO DON'T CARE REALLY NEED?

If kids act like they don't care, that's OK. What's not OK is dismissing them and focusing solely on the kids inside the Box who exhibit the characteristics of a "good student": behaves well, follows directions, works hard, pleasure to have in class.

We often misinterpret our kids' disengagement as a challenge to us: How can we make our lessons, our units, and our school experience more engaging?

While there may be shards of truth to the notion of this challenge (if they're disengaged, we need to engage them, right?), the primary charge isn't to unilaterally alter our delivery model to become more engaging—it's to find out what hooks will serve to engage our disengaged kids. We must identify and capitalize on what our kids care about. What matters to them? What are they curious about? What links them to their goals?

We don't need to engage Anthony. We need to craft an environment in which Anthony engages himself.

This is a good time to return to the dog-eared, bookmarked pages in chapter 1 that include the four protocols and templates you'll want to use to frame your work. And, because clarity of the goal is a non-negotiable prerequisite for all the work that follows, I also suggest you revisit the list of questions I posed at the beginning of chapter 1 to hone your collaborative vision of success. Here's the result of that initial reflection for Anthony.

GOAL STATEMENT

We want to help Anthony engage in school and his education so that he can rediscover his passion for learning, develop the skills he needs, and keep every conceivable door to his future open.

HOW DO WE DO THIS?

How do we engage the disengaged? Remember, it's not about unilaterally changing who we are. The answer isn't in the unsustainable practice of face painting, dressing up in character, and sprinkling pixie dust in the classroom while a walk-up anthem plays loudly in the background. It's not about theatrics, flash, and dazzle. It's about capturing our kids' brains. It's about supporting our kids as they lasso their hopes, dreams, and interests and then guiding them to flick their learning brains to *on*, roll up their sleeves, and immerse themselves in their learning journey.

The more you sing and dance, and the more you add sizzle and Tony Award–worthy theatrics to your lessons, the more likely you'll exhaust yourself, burn out, become frustrated, and throw up your own hands while exclaiming to the heavens, "I guess it's true. You can lead a horse to water, but you can't make him drink."

So, don't do that! There's a better way. Remember when folks first started championing the expression, *Work smarter, not harder*? Well, this is where it comes into play. Your goal isn't just to make a horse drink; it's to help him discover how thirsty he is.

Your goal isn't just to make a horse drink; it's to help him discover how thirsty he is.

Let's look at some specific options for my Anthony and all the other Anthonys out there whose behaviors look like a game of "I don't care" show-and-tell but are really a cry of "Help me make this work for me." Here are several strategies to consider, couched in handy *if . . . then* . . . language for each of the five primary causes of disengagement.

Strategy: If They're Bored, Then Stimulate Them

Let's face it, school is often boring. And maybe that's OK sometimes; however, before you jump on the "let the kids learn how to handle boredom" bandwagon, know this: Our kids' brains will focus on something, and if what's happening around them in school and the classroom isn't interesting or relevant and doesn't hook their brains, our kids will focus elsewhere.

And does school need to be boring? If *boredom* is, as John D. Eastwood, Alexandra Frischen, Mark J. Fenske, and Daniel Smilek (2012) define it, "the aversive experience of wanting, but being unable, to engage in satisfying activity," what satisfying activity would satiate this urge? Couldn't school provide opportunities for all our kids to engage in mentally stimulating activities that lead to satisfying feelings?

One such strategy is the application of *cognitive interest cues*, prompts that spark kids' intellectual curiosity and prime their brains for learning—one of the fourteen research-supported strategies found in *The New Classroom Instruction That Works* (Goodwin & Rouleau, 2022). Cognitive interest cues aren't free-for-all questions or gimmicks that simply attract kids' attention. Instead, they serve to hitch kids' mental focus to the existing learning outcomes; indeed, they are questions and methods to help kids reveal the significance of and drive their motivation to immerse themselves in the guaranteed and viable curriculum you're already committed to teaching.

For example, to launch a lesson on finding the volume of a shape, the teacher might ask the class, "How many bags of concrete would we need to buy to build a staircase from the amphitheater's stage to the ground?" Or a teacher could introduce a lesson on grammar by asking, "What's the difference between how you might begin an email to the school board, a text to your best friend, or a love song?"

See "Tool 9: Cognitive Interest Cues" (page 170) in the appendix for guidance on implementing this strategy.

Strategy: If They're Not Challenged Enough, Then Challenge Them

We tend to think our kids behave like water: Left to their own devices, they'll seek the path of least resistance. However, the opposite is true; their brains thrive off challenge. Learning new material, mastering skills, engaging in rigorous tasks, solving problems . . . these are what brains are designed to do. Mental challenges create new neural pathways, sharpen cognition, and enhance overall brain function (Attarha et al., 2025). How do we do this in our classrooms? Here are five ideas.

- **Curate the learning tasks:** Kids don't need to complete increasing amounts of work to be challenged; they simply need to engross themselves in challenging work. Instead of having them read an entire book and have cursory conversations about it, perhaps let them choose a passage to read deeply and then engage in a Socratic seminar. Rather than having them complete problems 1–31, odd, and skipping the story problems, have them choose any four of the problems until they feel confident in their skills, and then team up with classmates to solve and thoroughly explain story problems 33 and 35. It's about quality, not quantity. When you do this effectively, you should see the steam emitting from your students' brains.
- **Chunk learning with timely feedback:** To stay within the Zone of Proximal Development (Vygotsky, 1978), break the learning into manageable pieces. After each chunk is completed, guide your kids to engage in a feedback discussion about learning goals, success criteria, and unanswered questions with classmates and you or as a self-reflective

exercise. As they self-assess, celebrate their progress, reset their goals, and identify their next steps, your kids will generate momentum and unlock new levels of achievement.

- **Provide cognitive challenges:** One of the most tried-and-true methods of ensuring cognitive challenge is to access the higher-order thinking skills in Bloom's taxonomy. Why reinvent the wheel? Use a healthy balance of activities, prompts, and projects that hit each of the six levels: (1) remember, (2) understand, (3) apply, (4) analyze, (5) evaluate, and (6) create (Anderson & Krathwohl, 2001). What else can you do? Incorporate brain games (Wordle, anyone?), hypotheticals (What if . . .?), and the liberal use of the question, *Why?* The more we challenge our kids' brains, the sharper they become and the more adept they are at learning new and complex material.
- **Assess on real-world applications:** The soccer team is assessed on the match, not on practices. Archaeologists are assessed on their discoveries, not on their tools. In class, rather than using multiple assignments, tests, and quizzes to keep kids on their toes and to force them to work and comply along the way, we could look for relevant applications of knowledge, content, and skills to use as assessments of learning. Authentic assessments (for example, performance assessments, solutions to real-world problems, simulations, or collaborative projects), when utilized effectively, not only would help determine each kid's learning trajectory with relation to the ultimate target but would also dramatically streamline our assessment strategy and boost in-class motivation (Arnold & Croxford, 2025).
- **Gamify it:** Studies have shown that kids who play games—this includes video games, puzzles, memory games, and other similar challenging brain games—show upticks in memory, attention, and problem-solving abilities (Chaarani et al., 2022). Too much of the same kind of game, however, nullifies the benefit, and excessive video-game play has detrimental effects on cognitive function (Kappi, El-Etreby, Badawy, Ebrahem, & Hamed, 2024). However, in the Goldilocks zone (the just-right amount) of mixed-type games, kids remain engaged and focused on the content, helping them grow stronger brains. The more opportunities you can take to gamify the learning, the better your kids will learn and the more interested they'll be.

See "Tool 10: Bloom's Revised Taxonomy Tasks" (page 173) in the appendix for guidance on implementing this strategy.

Strategy: If They're Disconnected, Then Connect Them

For many kids, school is a positive place full of joyous experiences, friendships, and meaningful activities. The Box invites those who have common interests, skills, personalities, and other traits into dozens of opportunities to build connections: with other kids, with adults, with programs, and with the curriculum. For others, especially those who have dreams and ambitions that the institution ignores—or, at the very least, doesn't focus on—school can feel like a deserted island. For kids who find themselves on that island, motivation to engage can be hard to summon.

How can we help kids form a connection between their life goals and their formal education? Instead of remaining tethered to the Box because "that's the way we've always done it," let's free ourselves and our kids to connect to topics and learning that are interesting and relevant to them, fostering motivation by using a novel technique called *motivational interviewing*.

What is motivational interviewing? Well, have you ever knelt next to a kid who has shown you, in no uncertain terms, that school and the curriculum, due dates, projects, tests, and grades just aren't interesting enough to invest in . . . and you've tried to have a conversation that inspires them or helps you understand what's going on beneath the hood of this disinterested vehicle? Those discussions often go nowhere—until you realize your goal isn't to load motivation *into* this vehicle; it's to extract what motivation already exists.

Motivational interviewing is a communication approach designed to support an individual's commitment to making a change. Originally used in a clinical setting as part of substance abuse and addiction therapy, motivational interviewing is a flexible and dynamic methodology that empowers someone—in this case, a disconnected kid—to explore and enact their own motivation to engage (Miller & Rollnick, 2013). By asking a series of open-ended questions, posing forward-thinking prompts, utilizing reflective listening, and evoking goal statements and commitments to specific plans, educators can coax the kid to feel they have a reason to try (Orchard, 2025).

See "Tool 11: Motivational Interviewing Guidelines" (page 175) in the appendix for guidance on implementing this strategy.

Strategy: If They're Stifled, Then Help Them Become More Autonomous

If we have kids who feel school is something that's being done to them, how can we help them feel like they've got some ownership in the process? Two words: *voice* and *choice*. Let's explore them one at a time.

Student Voice

If we, as professional educators representing the institution of school, are open to it, there are many ways we can incorporate student voice into our decision making, policies, and practices. From the classroom level (having our kids create norms together for how the classroom will operate or asking for suggestions about how to make the classroom better) to the school level (inviting student leaders to represent their peers at school board meetings or seeking input to identify what needs to be improved in the school), the more ownership our kids have in the process, the more stake they have in the outcomes. Researchers isolated a key three-pronged strategy for using student voice productively: Provide opportunities to solicit input, encourage participation, and take actions responsively to the feedback (Conner, Holquist, Mitra, & Boat, 2025).

See "Tool 12: Student Voice Scales" (page 177) in the appendix for guidance on implementing this strategy.

PONDER THIS

Tammy Campbell, former superintendent in Washington state, advocated fiercely for the inclusion of student voice across her districts. She hosted monthly Lunch With the Superintendent events, included student representatives in key decision-making meetings, and collected surveys from students every six months. In addition, she insisted that her district leaders imagine a kid sitting right behind them at all times. This helped keep the main thing the main thing.

Her adamant prioritization of student voice compelled me to do the same. When I took over a struggling middle school as principal, one of our first action steps was to identify the foundational ideals that would guide our upcoming transformation. In addition to surveying families and working together as a staff, we engaged all six hundred seventh- and eighth-grade kids in a robust protocol to arrive at six core values: (1) commitment, (2) grace, (3) grit, (4) hope, (5) love, and (6) unity. These became the basis of our school-improvement plan, our decision-making processes, our conflict resolution strategies, and our character development approaches. And, because each of our kids had their fingerprints on the creation of the list, we (as a staff and leadership team) didn't have to *sell* them on it; we simply reminded them to *live* their commitment to this ambitious vision of the ultimate school setting. You might say we didn't make them drink; we helped them discover how thirsty they were.

Now, gather your teammates, an instructional coach or administrator, or a trusted colleague and pose the question, "What opportunities do we have to invite, share, and celebrate our students' voices in our day-to-day and long-term operations?"

Student Choice

Providing our kids with the opportunity to make decisions related to their education can be a powerful motivator (Lane, Buckman, Iovino, & Lane, 2023). How can we do this without losing our professional control? The first step is to remain mindful of the learning outcomes. If those outcomes are truly guiding our work, then "all roads lead to Rome," as the expression goes—different paths, different choices can lead to the same goal. Here are a handful of relatively simple ways to offer your kids choices in classroom settings.

- **Connect choice to goals:** Clarify and agree on the goals as a class first. All roads only lead to Rome if everyone agrees that Rome is the intended destination.
- **Offer limited, related choices at first:** Expand the field of alternatives as kids become adept at making savvy decisions.
- **Discuss pros and cons:** Consider multiple choices and help your kids become aware of their decision-making processes and the impact of those selections.
- **Model it:** Show kids—explicitly—how to make effective, informed, rational decisions.
- **Debate with a mock jury:** Structure a discussion with kids arguing each side and a select group of kids serving as the jury. The jury's "verdict" determines what happens next.
- **Vote:** Finalize the vote—majority rules.

What can our students choose? Here are some relatively straightforward elements of the school experience that we can grant our kids autonomy over.

- **Seating:** Where would you like to sit so you can be most productive? High tables, on the floor, at desks, in a group, or by yourself?
- **Partners:** Would you like to choose a partner or work independently?
- **Order:** Which would you prefer to work on first?
- **Timing:** Would you prefer to complete this task at the beginning of class or at the end?
- **Assessment:** Written or oral? Whole-class or one-on-one? Recorded and submitted or presented live? Multiple choice or open-ended?
- **Materials:** Which book would you like to read and analyze?
- **Content:** Choose any six of the ten problems and explain your thinking and your work for those six.

In the bigger scheme of things, how can we share the reins of the learning journey with our kids? If our goal is truly to help every young person be successful, let's put our money where our mouth is. Here is a sampling of some relatively powerful ways to help our kids own and manage their own trajectory in the school system.

- **Course schedule:** Matching our kids to the right teacher, taking particular courses at the right time of day, and managing breaks can be powerful elements in increasing motivation. As curators of the master calendar, we can influence the construction of schedules that meet individual kids' needs.
- **Electives:** When our kids have choice in what courses they take and what they're learning about, the ripples from that curiosity and commitment often impact the kids' performance and engagement in other (required) courses.
- **Graduation plan:** Here's where the Box can be excruciatingly constraining. We've become so beholden to a certain number of courses in each of the core subjects, a certain number of credits, and certain boxes to check that we sometimes miss the point. Flexibility in all the preceding points may allow us to captivate—and keep—our aforementioned disengaged kids in school, on trajectory, and in a position to be successful on graduation day and beyond.

For Anthony and all the kids out there who are disengaged, present as if they don't care, and are teetering on the edge of rebellion or dropping out, the more say they have in their day, the more they'll commit to their educational experience.

See "Tool 13: Choice Boards" in the appendix (page 181) for guidance on implementing this strategy.

Strategy: If They're Antsy, Then Help Them Move More

Human beings have a biological need to move. The more we move, the longer we stay alive. The more we move, the more we thrive (Stults-Kolehmainen, 2023). Kids who have higher energy levels, need more sensory input, or tend to express themselves physically will, developmentally, need to move more at school. The longer they sit—especially at a desk in a classroom—the more restless they're going to become (Medina, 2008). And we know where that road leads (hint: it's not Rome—it's more likely the principal's office). Simple adaptations in instructional delivery, classroom layout, and daily experience can address this need for movement in a positive, proactive manner.

For example, collaborative structures such as turn-and-talk can expand to walk-and-talk, stand-up conversations, and even track chats (in which kids talk while walking laps together on the athletic track). Incorporating performances, role-plays, charades, and other up-and-out-of-your-seat activities also builds engagement while helping our kids' bodies move. Using a variety of hands-on approaches (such as dissecting bear scat, sorting different colored leaves, rearranging words on index cards to hone syntax skills, or creating a model) instead of just talking about it can also satisfy that urge. And nothing beats going outdoors (into the courtyard, under the breezeway, or on the field) to engage in class discussions, take part in quick physical exercises, complete a project, or simply meditate and take a brain break.

See "Tool 14: Ten Ways to Help Your Kids Stay Active in School" in the appendix (page 182) for guidance on implementing this strategy.

I have three children, and I admit I'm part of the disengagement problem. Why? Because I often asked my kids, "How was school?" Their answers, as they progressed through the grades, inevitably became the same: "Fine." "Meh." "Whatever." I thought I'd reached a point of enlightenment when my wife suggested we ask a slight variation of that question, and it helped a bit: "What did you learn today?" We got middling responses, from "Some math" to "Nothing much."

What we've since learned, and what my wife and I encourage our kids to use with our grandchildren, is a strategy designed to elicit these five elements of engagement. Here's a starter list for you to try out.

1. Boredom
   - What's something you got excited about today? Why were you jazzed about it?
   - What tickled your brain today? How did you scratch that itch?
2. Challenge
   - What's one thing you struggled with today? Why was it hard for you?
   - What tough task did you tackle today? How did you go about it?
3. Connection
   - How did you seek out learning that you found relevant and meaningful? How did that play out?
   - What caused you to prick up your ears today? Why is that topic appealing to you?

4. Autonomy
    - What was one choice you made today that you're proud of? Why did you make that decision?
    - When did you speak up for yourself today? How did you approach the situation?
5. Movement
    - When did you move your body today? How did it feel to return to work after that?
    - What new thing did you explore today? How did you go about it?

BACK TO ANTHONY

As a team, we built a robust plan to try to hook Anthony—body and brain—back into school and his education. After a couple of weeks of playing catch with the football during lunch recess, I let Anthony know that I had a couple hundred other kids I was responsible for, so I'd have to save my shoulder for special occasions. However, because we have a whole staff full of amazing, loving adults working here, perhaps we could come up with some options to help make school less "stupid," as he called it, and to help him feel more successful.

He shrugged and said it wouldn't hurt, so we set up a couple of sessions with our school counselor, Lisa. She and he talked about his hopes, his dreams, his frustrations, and his future. He didn't know it, but she was taking notes on an individual interest inventory form (see tool 2, page 153).

One item of significance was Anthony's resolute desire to play football. He had the skills, the speed, and the hands to be an NFL receiver, he stated confidently. After a little digging online, Lisa found clips of the NFL teams' introductions of their starting lineups on TV.

"What do you notice about how they introduce themselves?" Lisa asked.

Anthony responded, "They're all huge, and a lot of them mumble. And they say their positions."

"What else?" Lisa pressed.

"They say what college they attended," Anthony said.

Lisa used that quick conversation to prompt an investigation into colleges. With no family members who had attended college, Anthony had never spoken with anyone about college. About entrance requirements. About scholarships. About what courses he'd have to take in high school to be able to go to college. About what grades he'd have to earn. And about what he'd need to do now, as a sixth grader, to put himself in a position to do all those things in the future . . . if he wanted to ever make it to the NFL.

Together, they drafted a personalized success plan (tool 16, page 189). Lisa shared it with Anthony's teacher team, administrators, and his grandmother, Dolores, to get feedback and refine it. Once some of the elements of the plan were agreed on, we conducted a SWOT analysis (chapter 1, page 26) and launched the plan in full force.

In the plan, Anthony was allowed two seven-minute breaks per day: one in the morning and one in the afternoon. During these self-selected times, Anthony could elect to walk to the office to check in with his counselor, Lisa, or take a pass to the gym or library. During the allocated time, Anthony would reflect on the situation that preceded it using prompts printed on the back of his student ID card (right next to the NFL logo, which served as a visual motivator for Anthony).

At first, admittedly, it was clunky. Anthony would use his breaks almost immediately in the mornings then find himself struggling to focus, engage, and remain positive until lunchtime. His teachers couldn't always identify reasonable and authentic consequences for Anthony's disruptive and argumentative behaviors, which had decreased but not disappeared. Whereas we once used recess as a carrot, and removal of it as a stick, we realized taking away opportunities for Anthony to move his body had a dramatic negative effect on future behaviors, so we began to teach him the self-discipline of addressing the issue at hand.

So, if Anthony argued with his teacher, the logical consequence was a one-on-one conversation with that teacher during a quiet time later in the class, in which they restated their commitment to their partnership, Anthony's education, and the harmony required in the classroom. Sometimes those conversations occurred after school with Anthony's grandmother, who kept a handy list of chores posted on the fridge for such occasions. "If you're going to make things ugly at school, you're going to make things pretty at home," she'd tell him. He'd roll his eyes, and then he'd do those chores before any free time.

As the weeks and months progressed, Anthony's plan evolved. Eventually, he didn't need a daily afternoon check-in, as he was able to get that connection need addressed in the mornings. As our staff participated in more collaborative team meetings and incorporated more of our professional learning on well-crafted core instruction, Anthony increasingly remained engaged in class.

As part of her ongoing investigation into Anthony, our counselor, Lisa, uncovered a secret skill Anthony possessed. His grandmother revealed to Lisa that she and Anthony often cooked dinner together at home. Anthony reluctantly admitted to this and eventually expressed his feelings of freedom, creativity, and satisfaction from cooking a delicious, healthy meal. Would he be interested in learning more about that? Preparing and eating the right foods might just help him put his body in a good position to become a professional athlete.

Our team met with the middle school team in the spring to help transition Anthony seamlessly into the new building the following year, including his personalized success plan. Together, we guided him to take an elective course in fundamental cooking and food safety and connected him with the school's kitchen manager. As he grew and matured, he began to thrive. His grades were tolerable, his attitude shifted considerably, and he showed signs of leadership across campus and on the sports field.

In high school, he was elected student body vice president (he came back to my school and told me it was as close to assistant principal as the associated student body offered), participated in the culinary arts program, starred on the football field, and eventually went to college on a full athletic scholarship. Though he didn't make it to the NFL, he found his direction: After two years of playing football at the university, he enrolled in culinary school and eventually got a job as a chef in a local restaurant.

For a kid who locked himself in his room, refused to come to school, and emphatically stated, "I don't care about school," Anthony ended up experiencing quite a bit of success in school and, more important, creating a marvelous life for himself and his family. Our team wouldn't have had it any other way.

CONCLUSION

For a lot of us, as educators, nothing pierces the skin more deftly than the sharp teeth of indifference. When our kids tell us "I don't care"—whether it's about the lesson, the topic, the learning objective, or anything else, for that matter—we bleed a little bit. We care so much about our kids, our craft, and our impact . . . and sometimes those cuts find their way to our souls. If we're willing to decrypt the message within the message, however, we might reveal the source of our kids' frustrations and lack of engagement. Then, with careful, intentional precision, we can create the conditions that counteract the perceived apathy and help Anthony meet the goal we identified earlier: to engage in school and his education *so that* he can rediscover his passion for learning, develop the skills he needs, and keep every conceivable door to his future open.

5

MAYRA

THE KID WHO'S WAY BEHIND

ACADEMIC STANDARDS ARE a critical piece of our schooling system. They form the skeletal structure of the knowledge and skills we expect all our students to master, systematically, throughout the preK–12 experience. We build curricula and assessments around the standards. We design instruction with them in mind. Graduation requirements, credits earned, course progressions, grades, athletics eligibility, honors tracks, and a host of other elements of schooling are determined by the degree to which students learn the standards along the way.

What happens, though, when our kids struggle to master the academic standards and find themselves behind? Way behind? Years behind?

Most teachers progress through the curriculum with a predetermined pacing guide. The content keeps flowing, the concepts become more complicated, and no matter how much the curriculum spirals and returns to itself, it's always at a more sophisticated, complex level that requires prerequisites and leaves our struggling learners abandoned, on the outside looking in.

Learn it now, and you can keep moving forward. If not, you'll be stuck in the thorny underbrush of failure. The Box wasn't built for the kids who fall behind.

There's outside the Box, and then there's this chapter's kid. This chapter's kid is *behind* the Box. *Below* the Box. Stranded. Deserted. Forsaken because of a dearth of skills, a lack of knowledge, and a shortage of proficiency.

MEET MAYRA

It had already been a long afternoon by the time our child study team meeting convened. Our collaborative task was to design academic support for every one of our struggling learners. Sure, it was an ordinary Thursday in October, and that meant we'd had a faculty meeting before school, the honeymoon period of the school year was over, kids' behaviors were starting to veer off the rails, teachers were running on fumes, and it was probably a full moon.

This was my induction into the assistant principal role, and I didn't know it then, but that ordinary Thursday child study team meeting would change everything.

We had a full docket of kids to talk about that day, and as we progressed through the list, an uneasy feeling blanketed the room. There were about ten or eleven of us, and the sheer magnitude of the work before us became overwhelming.

When the team's chairperson read the next name, Mayra, an audible sigh sounded around the table.

"Can we skip her?" someone asked. "She's so far behind, we're better off allocating our resources to other kids."

I was sitting next to our principal, a grizzled veteran and a fierce advocate for kids. Frank C. Garrity, or "Chief" as I called him, was the kind of leader who would be just as likely to pick a fight in the parking lot as get teary-eyed talking about a kid's future, and I felt him bristle at this comment.

"Good question," he said slowly. "Tell you what, team. Everyone grab a note card and a pencil."

We did as we were told.

"Now, scan the agenda in front of you, and scan your mental lists of all our kids," he said. "When you're ready, write the name of a kid who doesn't have any potential on your note card."

We paused, pencils poised.

"And just in case you're wondering," Frank said. "If you write down a name, I'll consider that your resignation."

His meaning was clear. All means all; 100 percent means 100 percent. If we're going to say we're here for each and every one of our kids, we're going to mean it. And we're going to follow through.

The pencils hit the table. Fast.

"Good," Frank said. "Now, let's talk about what Mayra needs."

No one resigned that day, and—thank goodness—no one got into a fight in the parking lot. We may have gotten a bit teary-eyed about Mayra, however, as we discussed her plight.

Mayra was a fifth grader, though she was performing academically at a first-grade level. She had only rudimentary literacy skills, could compute only basic mathematics, and seemed lost in most other subjects throughout the day.

Her family had arrived in the United States when she was seven years old and told us Mayra had completed kindergarten in their native country the year before. Despite her low scores on a screening assessment, she was placed in a first-grade classroom. Her parents had experienced limited schooling themselves, and they spoke a different language at home. As an English learner, Mayra often seemed confused by directions, jumbled her vocabulary, and sought fellow classmates to translate for her.

Despite all that, everyone loved her. She was a delight! She smiled a lot, stayed out of trouble, went out of her way to help her teachers, and survived in the classrooms through a combination of mimicry, emotional intelligence, and charm.

Because she was a sweet, quiet, compliant girl, she did not rise to the top of her schools' watch lists. Yes, schools . . . plural. For one reason or another, the family kept moving, and as a result, Mayra switched schools several times. When she scored at the bottom of the lowest category on the state-mandated third-grade reading and mathematics tests, her previous school had retained her.

She landed at our school at the beginning of fifth grade, burdened with a full four years' worth of academic gaps, and during this ordinary Thursday child study team meeting, our team was stumped. In reviewing her records, we noted that she was in a leveled reading class, worked weekly with the English language development specialist, and had daily pullout interventions in reading and mathematics, yet her struggles continued.

Was it language? Was it a learning disability? Was it a lack of background knowledge? Was it something else? And what could we possibly do to help Mayra traverse the chasm that had been carved over the past few years?

We didn't have the answers that day, but we sure as heck knew there wasn't a stone we wouldn't overturn to find some.

WHAT'S REALLY GOING ON?

The topic of this chapter is not at all surprising, and it may well cast a wide net for the myriad of kids out there who confound us. After all, being way behind academically is something most of the kids who don't fit in the Box tend to have in common.

We often see a kid like Mayra, who's well behind the standards, and ask, "Why is she so far behind?" We then skip to judgments that are unhelpful and, frankly, ungenerous.

- She's lazy and unmotivated. (It's her own fault.)
- She's a second-language learner. (She'll always struggle outside her native language.)
- It's probably a learning disability. (She needs special classes.)
- She could just have a low IQ. (There's no realistic expectation for growth.)
- She'll never be on grade level, and we just have to accept that. (Poor thing, let's move on.)

With those debilitating thoughts in our heads, how do we often proceed? We want Mayra to be successful, of course. We have big hearts. We also know she's outside the Box looking in, so we place Mayra in remedial classes, remove electives and choice from her schedule, exclude her from activities, lower our expectations (that's a self-serving euphemism for *dumbing it down*), bypass her in favor of the "bubble" kids (those whose quick gains represent low-hanging fruit and provide a statistical bump to misidentify a school or student as being successful), and, likely to her detriment, retain her.

If we continue to see Mayra as the problem, then our primary solution is to sit back and hope Mayra changes on her own . . . and hope ain't a strategy. Our mindsets determine our reality, and this is an invitation to shift our mindsets in order to shift our reality.

In short, we have to own our impact. We must acknowledge the role that teaching quality has played in this equation. Most likely, poor instruction contributed to Mayra's struggles. If we can admit that, then we can consider the accompanying reality: Great teaching can help Mayra overcome her struggles. We must embrace the causal relationship between teaching and learning if we're to develop the efficacy to positively impact Mayra's learning outcomes. We must believe we're the X factor.

We must embrace the causal relationship between teaching and learning if we're to develop the efficacy to positively impact Mayra's learning outcomes.

Yes, in our schools and classrooms, we find the Box, and Mayra's not in it. We must resist the urge to continuously compare Mayra's station in relation to the Box, pitting her against grade-level standards, her peers, and the curriculum's relentless pacing guide. She'll always come up short. Instead, our charge is to view Mayra for who, what, how, and where she is, and help her to stride forward.

So, what's going on? At first blush, the answer to that question is straightforward. Mayra's behind academically. Below grade level. Credit deficient. Failing. She's not cutting it. She doesn't know and can't do what her classmates know and can do. In a world of reading groups named after eagles and bluebirds, she sits with the quails.

Digging deeper, what Mayra's experiencing is much more complex. There are a million possible explanations for why kids struggle academically, and it behooves us to examine the origins of Mayra's challenges. Though we can't address every cause, we can certainly explore options for mitigating their harmful effects and take steps to usher our Mayras along the learning journeys.

There tend to be three primary categories from which our kids' academic struggles stem.

- **Home and family factors:** Socioeconomic status, family history with schooling, beliefs about education, distrust of the system, more pressing needs (family, work, or financial), competing cultural beliefs, and other influences of home
- **Personal and health factors:** Individual motivation and attitude, school connectedness, social and peer pressure, physical health, mental health, brain functioning, and other influences of the individual
- **Educational factors:** Curriculum, instruction, interventions, assessment, and other influences of the school

Rather than unpack all three of these factors here, we're going to split them up. You can read more about home and family factors in chapter 3, "Skyla: The Kid Who Lacks Consistent Support," and personal and health factors are the primary focus of chapter 6, "Penelope: The Kid Who's Struggling Emotionally." Honestly, because our kids' situations are so complex and interwoven, you'll find bits and pieces of all three causes in every chapter of the book. I urge you to read thoroughly as you consider the young people under your charge.

For now, we're going to unpack the third set: educational factors. As professional educators, it makes sense for us to dissect and explore things that we can control more directly. Yes, things happen outside school that influence how our kids experience school as students. And yes, who the kid is makes a difference. No one is going to argue either of those. However, I'm going to emphasize the cause-and-effect relationship between teaching and learning and suggest that modifying the education factors that helped dig Mayra's hole will also help extract her from it.

Here are the five most influential educational factors at play.

Clunky Implementation of Curriculum

What do our kids need to learn in school? That's an essential question that experts from Plato to John Dewey have sought to answer for centuries, and one that current experts like Linda Darling-Hammond and Bryan Goodwin continue to wrestle with. To best prepare our kids for the "real world" beyond the school walls, we've come up with a scope and sequence, a road map and pacing guides, timelines, and lists of standards we want our kids to master in each course and grade level to meet the requirements to graduate. According to Richard DuFour and Robert Marzano (2011) in *Leaders of Learning*, a guaranteed and viable curriculum is the variable most strongly related to student achievement at the school level. What does that mean? Well, the fact that it is guaranteed assures us that specific content is taught in specific courses and at specific grade levels, regardless of the teacher to whom a student is assigned. The fact that it is viable indicates that there is enough instructional time available to actually teach the content that's identified as important.

Here's the rub: When we become too reliant on the pacing guides, we march along and take the proficient kids with us . . . leaving the strugglers to become stragglers. When we require lockstep adherence to the curriculum and prioritize covering content, we misplace the essential purpose of ensuring that our students learn. When the textbooks and teacher's manual dictate what is said and done in class, we inadvertently gloss over our individual kids' needs.

Ineffective Core Instruction

Having a guaranteed and viable curriculum is a fabulous start. Not surprisingly, providing a road map, blueprint, or checklist—even a fabulous one—isn't sufficient. How that curriculum is applied through teaching makes all the difference in the world. Research has been incontrovertibly clear that instruction is the primary determinant of student success in school (Bernhard, McDermott, Hasenhüttl, Burn, & Sammons, 2024; López-Martín, Gutiérrez-de-Rozas, González-Benito, & Expósito-Casas, 2023). And if we're to fly that flag, shouldn't we also fly its unfortunate companion banner, that instruction is the primary determinant of student failure in school (Havis, 2023)?

Covering material does not necessarily equate to teaching it, and teaching it doesn't mean the kids have learned it. What our kids need in school is high-quality instruction across the board that results in high levels of learning for every child. The insightful meta-analysis *The New Classroom Instruction That Works* reveals fourteen research- and evidence-based instructional strategies that reliably result in increased student learning outcomes (Goodwin & Rouleau, 2022). The book is a remarkably thorough crosswalk between what brain science tells us about how students learn and what decades of research tells us about the most effective teaching strategies. Great teaching is a game changer for every kid . . . especially those who have found themselves behind.

Have you ever watched a master chef at work in the kitchen? Or a first-chair cellist in the concert hall? They may start with a recipe or sheet music, and there's a clearly identified outcome they're aiming for, but there's also their individual *je ne sais quoi*, that special something they bring to the challenge that adds immeasurable value.

By contrast, an ordinary chef could take an incredible recipe and cook a mediocre meal. An ordinary cellist could take a delightful score and produce a mediocre tune. And yes, an ordinary teacher could take a magnificent guaranteed and viable curriculum and produce mediocre learning.

In the classroom, do you know what your *je ne sais quoi* is? Maybe it has something to do with how you bring energy and enthusiasm into every lesson. Maybe it's your uncanny ability to build connections with students that compel them to engage. Maybe it's your attentiveness to the lesson as it's progressing to know when to call time-out and address misconceptions before they get too deeply ingrained. Whatever it is, pay attention to it, link it to your guaranteed and viable curriculum, and weave it through your high-impact instructional strategies.

Dearth of Targeted Interventions

When the first indications of student struggles rear their heads, we react. If a kid isn't mastering a standard or demonstrating a skill, we reteach it. If the struggles are persistent or significant enough, we enlist the support of specialists, aides, and others within a structured model of interventions. Whether it's a response to intervention (RTI) or multitiered system of supports (MTSS) approach, the goal is the same: to provide the kids who need more, more.

Unfortunately, many intervention models fall into the same traps that exist outside the interventions. Reteaching using the same ineffective instructional practices, pulling students out of key content for remedial boosts (Pegram, Watkins, Hoerger,

& Hughes, 2022), overlooking kids that really need help in favor of "bubble" students, and using retention as an intervention (Davis, 2021) result in the struggling students struggling even more. The gap often widens rather than closing.

Our kids need interventions that are based on their needs, are delivered with high-quality instructional techniques, and are prepared in partnership with the kid's greater goal or goals in mind. Interventions, like their core instructional counterparts, must be chosen and delivered strategically. They cannot be performed through plug-and-play automaticity: *Open book, turn to page* x, *do as instructed* might work for kids in the Box, but it won't help our struggling students catch up, and it won't help them thrive. Remember, it's not just about mastering a standard; it's about preparing a kid for successful, productive adulthood and citizenry.

Unreliable Assessments

Most discussions about assessment in American schools begin and end with the almighty standardized test. As part of a thorough, comprehensive, and strategic assessment strategy, standardized tests offer significant value at the policy, system, or even classroom level . . . but rarely for individual students.

However, most standardized tests operate as islands. They're often one-and-done snapshots, and their results frequently have high-stakes ramifications for individual kids. From classroom placement to interventions, from grade-level progression to eligibility for electives, and ultimately to graduation requirements and college admissions, standardized test scores can accelerate a kid's trajectory . . . or halt it in its tracks. To a certain extent, standardized tests gatekeep the Box. And because very few standardized tests accurately, reliably, and validly assess what is intended to assess (Maroun & Tienken, 2024), we often make erroneous judgments and placements of kids with damaging consequences.

I feel obligated to include a note about the school settings where everything leads to the standardized test. I've worked with districts that count down the days until the big state test, dedicate a significant amount of time to test-prep activities and materials, and convey an unhealthy amount of stress and importance on individual kids to "do their best on the test." Well-intended, loving, dedicated educators carry this pressure on their shoulders, and it plays out in a very unhealthy manner.

I've often felt that if the assessment is designed to determine whether, and to what extent, a student has mastered a concept or skill, then we really shouldn't have to prep them for how to take the assessment; they should simply demonstrate their level of mastery in an authentic manner. If the test does its job well, the results will convey helpful information. If not, fix it or scrap it.

In those test-driven settings, when the test is over, what do the staff do? They celebrate, then ratchet down the rigor for the remaining six weeks of school. Many teachers and administrators have shared with me that new learning is all but done after the test. They leave it to next year's teacher to pick it back up again in the fall. It's not because we, as educators, are lazy and unmotivated; rather, it's a result of a natural letdown following a long-term buildup and climactic event. It is, indeed, "the way we do things" within the parameters of the Box.

Other Influences of the School

Since this is an exploration of school factors that impact student learning outcomes, academic success, and appropriate development, I must acknowledge the differences made by the school setting itself. On a broader scale, these three elements also factor into many of our kids' academic struggles.

- **Leadership:** As a former school principal myself, I certainly like to believe that my presence and efforts impacted the schools, staff, communities, and students I led. In a decades-long study, researchers found that, quite succinctly, "Principals *really* matter" (Wallace Foundation, 2021). Of course, principals aren't the only leaders in a school; verily, the influence of the leadership structure of a school determines the direction, priorities, efficacy, quality of services, and a host of other environmental factors (Mincu, 2022). Strong leadership results in high levels of achievement and success; poor leadership does the opposite.
- **Access to adequate resources:** Despite knowing the impact of poverty on educational outcomes, the United States has a long history of allowing zip codes to determine the quality of kids' education. The outcomes of funding disparities are exposed clearly and devastatingly—schools in lower-income neighborhoods receive less funding and perform lower, and it's the opposite for higher-income communities (Learning Policy Institute, 2025).
- **School climate:** The environment in which students spend a big chunk of their prime wakeful hours every day makes a big difference. How

positive and optimistic are staff members? How explicit and consistent are the values and norms? How are relationships prioritized to foster belonging across campus? The experience of the kids and adults at the school, as curated by all stakeholders, fluctuates greatly and impacts a host of academic and social outcomes (Harris & Jones, 2023).

PONDER THIS

Remember the Mayra story—*"Write the name of a kid who doesn't have any potential on your note card"*—at the beginning of this chapter? In direct contrast to Frank C. Garrity's note card test, take out a note card and write down the name of a kid you've known who was way behind in school, didn't perform well academically, and still became a successful, productive, happy adult. It's OK this time; write down a name.

Now, with your staff or a team of teachers, discuss these questions.

- What determines a person's worth? Is it their grades? Their test scores? Which reading group they were in?
- What determines how successful a person is as a grown-up? Is it their job? Their income? What college they attended?
- As a teacher, administrator, or other education professional, what do you value in your students? What are your school's or district's values? How do you demonstrate what you value, what you treasure, what you prioritize, and what you love each and every day?
- How do you handle it when a kid demonstrates potential that isn't aligned with your values?

Let's shift gears to look at your students. Do you have a kid who is way behind? Typically, a kid who struggles in school faces a pretty steep, daunting uphill battle, one in which they aren't considered victorious until they master identified standards. And the longer a kid is in school, the farther behind in the steep uphill climb they fall.

Your task, individually, collectively, and interdependently with your colleagues, is to identify the talents of your struggling kid. Your challenge is to bring joy back into the school experience for this kid. Your quest is to elevate your Mayra's academic skills.

As you've been considering the Mayra in your life or classroom, your first question was likely, "Why is this kid way behind?"

Your next question is, "How can I reach and teach this kid?"

WHAT DO KIDS WHO ARE WAY BEHIND REALLY NEED?

If the kid is way behind, that's OK. Rather than dwell on that fact and duck into the If Only Saloon—where they pour pints of "If only we'd delivered better teaching earlier" and "If only we started the interventions sooner"—let's remember the wise words of career educator and speaker Richard DuFour, who often referred to an old proverb when asking his audience, "When's the best time to plant a tree?" The response, of course, was "twenty years ago." Richard would follow up with "When's the second-best time, if you didn't plant it twenty years ago?" That's correct: It's right now (DuFour, 2012).

When we consider school success, we tend to think in terms of the K–12 progression, the first eighteen years, or, for some young adults, college and graduate school. If we shift our mindsets to embrace *life* success as the ultimate goal, there's no hard and fast timeline. Life is a long, thickety path that requires a diverse, nimble, complex array of knowledge, skills, and attitudes.

We needn't try to shove our struggling learners back into the Box and force them to meet milestones that may or may not be developmentally appropriate for them. What we ought to do, instead, is help our kids rediscover the magic in learning, unearth the joy of curiosity, reveal the passion in solving mysteries, delight in the enthusiasm of pursuing goals, and revel in finding school one of the many places that help propel them forward.

This is a good time to return to the dog-eared, bookmarked pages in chapter 1 that include the four protocols and templates you'll want to use to frame your work. And, because clarity of the goal is a non-negotiable prerequisite for all the work that follows, I might also suggest that you revisit the list of questions I posed at the beginning of chapter 1 to hone your collaborative vision of success. Here's the result of that initial reflection for Mayra.

GOAL STATEMENT

We want to help Mayra accelerate her academic progress so that she can remain connected to school, amplify her love of learning and growth, and develop the knowledge and skills required for her continued success, no matter how it's defined.

HOW DO WE DO THIS?

Notice that the preceding goal statement is not, "We want her to master fifth-grade standards by June" or "We want her to be reading on grade-level by the end of seventh grade." Those are common, yet unhelpful, targets. In the grand scheme of things, whether Mayra is on grade level at any point in her academic career is immaterial. We want her to love learning, remain connected, and pursue her passions.

You may also notice that the strategies that follow are centered on the classroom, team, and school levels. Because you, reading this text, are a boots-on-the-ground, in-the-field, sleeves-rolled-up practitioner, you aren't looking for approaches that alter the system (such as requiring preschool for all children ages three and up), need unanimous support (such as universal prenatal care that includes mandatory preacademic parenting sessions), or fundamentally change the schooling machine (such as adopting a scientifically proven, guaranteed and viable curriculum). Those would be great, of course, yet they're outside your locus of control. Those policy decisions are above your pay grade. For now, you're going to stay in your lane and do amazing things for incredible kids.

So . . . what's in your lane? What can you impact? What influence can you have? More than anything else, you can influence the teaching. Classroom instruction. Delivery of lessons that meet our struggling learners' needs, in both the core classroom and the intervention settings.

With that clear goal in mind, let's tackle some strategies to support the kids who are way behind age- and grade-level expectations, one Mayra at a time.

Strategy: Deliver High-Quality Core Instruction

We've all had a colleague mutter, "I taught it; they just didn't learn it," right? Because there's a fundamental difference between *teaching* something and someone *learning* it, we mustn't conflate the two. In fact, in our planning, teaching, and analysis of lessons, we should prioritize the learning part of the equation. As it turns out, human brains tend to learn information in a predictable pattern. So, if we build experiences in our activities, lessons, and units that follow the pattern, our kids will be primed to learn more quickly, efficiently, and effectively. We have to teach the way our kids' brains learn. In *A Reflective Teacher's Guide to Planning for Learning*, Bryan Goodwin and Pete Hall (2023) provide an overview of the six phases of learning and offer dozens of reflective prompts to generate thoughtful discussion and deliberate planning for teachers and teams. As you build strong core instructional practices in your classroom, team, department, or campus, following these six phases will help transform the focus from *teaching* to *learning*.

We have to teach the way our kids' brains learn.

Phase 1: Become Interested

For so long, we've faced struggling learners and succumbed to coaxing, pleading, or cajoling them into the learning process. What's more effective, and less exhausting for us, is to whip up a little anticipation. How can we pique our kids' interest and tap into their innate curiosity? When kids are genuinely interested in a topic, find it personally relevant, and want to learn it, they're much more likely to perk up their ears and engage with the process.

Phase 2: Commit to Learning

We humans (adults *and* kids) tend to get distracted easily, and our brains often seek out the path of least resistance: What's the lowest amount of effort I can get away with? So, if we really want kids to learn something, we've got to help them commit to it. They have to care about learning it. They must switch their learning brains on and make explicit the connection between their effort and the outcome. When our kids set personal learning goals and view their hard work as the path leading to success, they will stick with it.

Phase 3: Focus on New Learning

Once our kids are interested in and committed to learning, it's time to buckle down and put their short-term working memory into action. We can help by providing information in multiple modes (for example, visual, verbal, and auditory) and offering opportunities for them to unpack complicated concepts and reformat them in concrete ways. Seeing examples, creating models, practicing vocabulary, and describing it in their own words are effective ways to enact this phase.

Phase 4: Make Sense of Learning

We've all heard of hands-on learning. What's even more effective is minds-on learning. What do we want our kids to be thinking about while they're learning? How do we equip them with these skills? When we build experiences for our kids to think about the concepts and material, their brains process their learning in a way that leads to retention. And when we chunk the learning into bite-sized pieces and offer opportunities to reflect after each chunk, the learning becomes even more solidified.

Phase 5: Practice and Reflect

Practicing something—in a quest to master it—provides us with information. When our kids practice the skills, procedures, and their new learning, it offers them feedback. As educators, we can highlight and emphasize that feedback, which guides our kids to learn from their attempts and allows them to repeat their successes, correct their mistakes, and revise their practice to make the learning *permanent.* The reflective process that began with minds-on effort continues to drive our kids' learning. And of course it does: Learning isn't the result of simply doing things. It's a cognitive change that happens in our brains because of these experiences, exposure, and input.

Phase 6: Extend and Apply

How do we know if our kids learned the material we wanted them to learn? To answer this, we need to look way beyond the pop quiz, the end-of-unit assessment, the final exam, and the standardized test. We'll know our kids learned the material if they can use it. If they can recall it. If they can employ it in a novel situation. To prepare our kids for that, we can create opportunities for them to solve a problem, conduct an investigation, or complete a task that require the successful application of the skill, the implementation of new knowledge, or a thorough understanding of the process they learned. Marking the correct bubble on a multiple-choice test does not mean they've learned it; applying it to a real-life situation is a better way to show mastery.

See "Tool 15: Planning for Learning Road Map" in the appendix (page 184) for guidance on implementing this strategy.

Strategy: Implement a Personalized Success Plan

We have Individualized Education Plans (IEPs) for students with documented learning disabilities, but what about our struggling learners who don't qualify for that level of assistance? Wouldn't you agree that every child deserves an educational program that is tailored to their interests, their strengths, their needs, and their goals? In the spirit of differentiated instruction—an approach brought to the mainstream by Carol Ann Tomlinson in her 1995 book, *How to Differentiate Instruction in Mixed-Ability Classrooms*—wouldn't it make sense to adapt and adjust the learning experiences of our varied and diverse school populations to help them reach the goal? You might be thinking, *Holy smokes, that means creating a separate guaranteed and viable curriculum, presenting a unique lesson, and performing one-on-one assessments for every kid. That's unmanageable!* And you'd be correct. What is manageable, however, is offering options and varied pathways for our kids to hit the goal of becoming productive, happy, uplifting grown-ups and neighbors in our communities.

Yes, we want our kids to learn and master the curriculum. Yes, we want our kids to demonstrate the characteristics I shared in the introduction. Perhaps having a personalized success plan, one written specifically for a struggling kid, could help us achieve both goals. A personalized success plan narrows the focus by highlighting a high-interest goal; prioritizing the relevant academic, behavioral, social-emotional, and organizational skills; and streamlining the approaches and supports to ensure the kid's success and positive momentum.

Remember, most kids perform well, succeed, and thrive in the Box, so they won't need this option. For those who are way behind, a personalized success plan that guides their educational journey might just be the most viable alternative to trying to cram them back in the Box.

See "Tool 16: Personalized Success Plan" in the appendix (page 189) for guidance on implementing this strategy.

Strategy: Provide Targeted Interventions

Often, our struggling kids are lifted from class (sometimes, even the core class in which the student is struggling) and inserted into an intervention group. Offering interventions to struggling kids is, indeed, a high-yield strategy . . . when it's done well. Interventions done well tend to include these characteristics.

- **Based on needs as identified by relevant assessments:** Every intervention has a clearly acknowledged goal and outcome, is directly connected to the guaranteed and viable curriculum, and is determined by data that shows the kid's clear needs.
- **Explicit, systematic instruction:** Lessons and sessions build on one another, allowing the learner to maximize progress.
- **Laser-like focus:** If the goal is to increase vocabulary related to microorganisms, that's what the intervention includes. Period. Every session remains firmly connected to the pinpointed target.
- **High dosage:** Generally, the greater the frequency and duration of the interventions, the higher the impact.
- **High interest, high relevance, and high motivation:** Similar to the first two phases of learning, kids in intervention sessions must become interested and commit to their learning, which requires the professional adult to create the conditions in which that happens.

Too often, interventions are provided in a haphazard, inconsistent manner. Kids are pulled from high-interest activities and classes, removed from recess or lunch periods, kept after school, and denied opportunities to connect with the school community. We do this with the best intentions, of course, because we believe the answer to kids being way behind the Box is to shove them more and more forcefully toward the Box. With a clear focus, tactical precision, and a streamlined plan, we can do better.

See "Tool 17: Targeted Intervention Planner" in the appendix (page 193) for guidance on implementing this strategy.

PONDER THIS

Gather your teammates, an instructional coach or administrator, or a trusted colleague, and pose the question, "Why are there only three strategies in this chapter?"

If low academic performance is such a gigantic concern, why aren't we given dozens and dozens of strategies to choose from and implement?

I'll share a bit of my thinking here. As educators, we tend to consume—almost voraciously—the latest research and the most innovative approaches. And then we try to put them into practice. All of them. All at once. When we do too much simultaneously, the impact of any specific strategy is diminished greatly. This is called *implementation overload*. What we need, instead, is a concerted, focused, strategic approach. In this section, as we've explored Mayra and her low, low academic performance thus far, our solutions are threefold.

1. Deliver high-quality core instruction.
2. Implement a personalized success plan (tool 16, page 189).
3. Provide targeted interventions.

It isn't rocket science, as they say, because it's not complicated. It is rocket science, in a way, because there's a formula. If we can provide Mayra—and all the struggling Mayras out there—with strong, reliable core instruction; create and implement a learning plan that's tailored to her needs; and offer her timely, focused interventions, she's much more likely to fast-track her advancement toward her goals, successes, and passions.

BACK TO MAYRA

Our child study team collaborated to draft a plan to support Mayra's academic acceleration on that ordinary Thursday in October, and our English language development specialist, Jennifer, was designated as the lead to coordinate Mayra's personalized success plan. Over the next couple of weeks, the plan evolved as more information about Mayra, her learning profile, her experiences, and her goals came to light.

A side-by-side comparison of Mayra's daily schedule with an on-grade-level fifth grader showed a remarkable difference. Several of Mayra's pullout interventions occurred during the same content block, so she was essentially missing her core instruction in reading while receiving reading support. Same for mathematics. Couple that with the loss of instructional time during transitions—it took five to seven minutes for the students to report to the small-group room and for the intervention groups to get started and five to seven more at the end—Mayra was receiving less instructional time than her peers.

"Interventions are intended to support, not supplant," stated Lisa, the school counselor, at the next fifth-grade team meeting. "And kids who need more actually need more, not less. We've got to do better."

The next questions, as we expected, were these: If we're going to accelerate Mayra's academic skills in something, which content area is the priority? And if we're going to provide those additional interventions during a different content area, which one is it going to be? What's Mayra going to have to sacrifice to meet her goals?

As a team, we chose literacy as the priority. As a staff, we had already identified reading, writing, and communicating as the top skills we were going to ensure all our kids had before they headed to middle school. Literacy skills, after all, are the basis of all interactions and the foundation of all learning in every other content area. With literacy skills, everything is possible. Without them, Mayra's future would look awfully bleak.

With literacy elevated to DEFCON 1 priority, what would fall by the wayside? That's something we took very seriously, and in collaboration with Mayra's teachers, counselor, interventionists, family, and Mayra herself during a direct interview, we made a decision. As of that moment, everything else would be placed on hold, and we'd focus on helping Mayra learn literacy skills in every context we could.

Mayra had indicated an interest in becoming a nurse one day, and because of her sweet demeanor and kind soul, we could see that as a viable option. Her personalized success plan, then, included two creative interventions that linked her passions with her needs. First, we assigned her to become a "big sister" to a first-grade classroom during their literacy block each day so she could build her foundational reading and writing skills while "teaching" younger kids. Also, we set up a thirty-minute block right after lunch and recess during which she would shadow our school nurse. (In case you've never worked in an elementary school clinic, the thirty minutes immediately following lunch and recess are notoriously the busiest.) Not surprisingly, she thrived, interacting with kids—and adults—while learning the terminology and flow of the nurse's station.

Next, we amended her intervention periods. She was no longer pulled for mathematics support, and the pullout reading group was moved to an unoccupied reading nook adjacent to Mayra's fifth-grade classroom. Transition time decreased and on-task time increased. The interventions themselves also became more streamlined. With her thirty minutes broken into chunks that addressed fundamental skills she was lacking, front-loaded upcoming content in her core classroom, and emphasized key English vocabulary, she began to progress rapidly.

Within six weeks, her "big sister" responsibilities had moved to a second-grade classroom, and by the end of the year, she was in a fourth-grade classroom for ninety minutes a day, mastering standards left and right. Her work in the clinic earned her special recognition from our school nurse, who invited Mayra and her parents to a special luncheon one day to celebrate her work ethic, empathy, and contribution to the culture of the school.

Did we get her to grade level by the end of the year? No, not quite. Did she pass the state's standardized test that spring? No, she didn't. Was she on par in mathematics, science, social studies, and the other content areas? Nope.

However, in our final child study team meeting of the year, when Principal Garrity asked each member of the team to take out a note card and write down the name of a kid who had grown the most, who had shown the most potential, and who we were most proud of, we thought of the fifth grader who had arrived four years below grade level, who had tripled a year's growth, whose confidence had grown exponentially, and who had put herself in a position to be successful . . . and every member of that team wrote the same name: Mayra.

CONCLUSION

Being below grade level and struggling to meet identified standards do not need to become a one-way ticket to remediation classes, surrendering, and dropping out of school. As we learned from Mayra's story, there's always more to the story than we see on the surface, and sometimes the most effective solutions are the most obvious. In this case, let's use our knowledge and our resources to provide stronger core instruction, build personalized success plans for our struggling learners, and ensure that interventions are targeted to their specific, individual needs. With clarity of our goals and plan, and with a broader view of success than the checked box next to "Meets Standard," we can help Mayra meet the goal we identified earlier:

to accelerate her academic progress *so that* she can remain connected to school, amplify her love of learning and growth, and develop the knowledge and skills required for her continued success, no matter how it's defined.

6

PENELOPE

THE KID WHO'S STRUGGLING EMOTIONALLY

WHEN A KID walks or bikes in, gets dropped off, disembarks from the bus, or drives up to the school, a remarkable transition occurs. That kid, and everything about that kid—hopes and dreams, fears and worries, attitude, health, emotions, experiences, thoughts, values, all of the podiums and baggage, all of it—disappears, melting away to leave behind a new being. They're not a kid anymore; in their place is a *student.*

Actually, that doesn't happen.

Kids—even as students in school settings—carry everything about them with them. What we used to refer to as the *invisible backpack* is now much more visible. As a society and as a profession, we've evolved to notice and respond to others' emotions and their situations. Kids are—and bring to school with them—the totality of their experiences.

Sometimes, those experiences yank the rug right out from under them. Then, staggering through an emotional fog, they arrive at school, home, or somewhere in the community, and are forced to navigate the setting, social dynamics, expectations, and their own conduct through the lens of this rickety reality.

As you might expect, the Box isn't inviting to kids who are experiencing anxiety, loneliness, hopelessness, uncertainty, and other intense emotions.

MEET PENELOPE

Lunchtime at the middle school. A principal's dream, right? Actually, the lunch periods—we had three—were something I really looked forward to. In fact,

I prioritized being on campus, in the cafeteria, on the field, in the gym, around the kids, for that entire two-hour block of time in the middle of every day. It was there, in the splendor and peace and chaos and awkwardness, that I got to experience the realness of thirteen- and fourteen-year-olds.

Amid a conversation with a table full of authentic, fantastic kids, my walkie-talkie buzzed. Of course it did. That, like the lunch periods, occurred like clockwork.

I responded, since everyone in my walkie-talkie network knows that it's *emergency only*, especially during lunchtime, so this must have been an emergency.

On the line, our attendance clerk said, "Mr. Hall, we have a new student registering, and ordinarily we'd follow our welcome protocol, but this young lady is asking for you specifically."

I excused myself from the table and headed to the office. When I arrived, imagine my surprise and joy to see Penelope and her father standing in the foyer! Penelope had been a student at the elementary school where I'd been principal for the previous five years, and I'd known her from second grade through sixth grade. And now, here she was, registering for middle school in late October. I looked at her dad with an eyebrow raised.

"Hi, Mr. Hall," he said. "You remember Penelope, right?"

"Of course I do. How are you, young lady?" I asked. I took a half-step toward a potential hug, but when Penelope gave me the textbook teenager head nod, I stopped and reciprocated with a not-so-textbook administrator head nod.

"You're probably wondering why we're here," her dad continued. "Penelope was zoned for a different middle school, as you know, and when she got there, it was, well, it was a mess. She's been a hot mess since sixth grade, honestly."

"Dad!" Penelope hissed, halting her dad in his tracks. This caused my other eyebrow to raise.

Her dad shrugged and gave me an exasperated half-smile. "We needed a change, and honestly, you and your staff at the last school were so good for her, so we wanted to bring her here to you."

Throughout elementary school, Penelope had been a very carefree, happy-go-lucky kid. She'd done well in school, had a solid peer group and plenty of friends, played the cello, was on our school soccer team, and seemed to thrive in the Box. I'd watched her progress through the education system—skate through it, really—without ever causing so much as a blip on our radar to indicate she might be struggling. It was easy to be good for her because she was a model student and a superb kid!

But now? Now, something about Penelope was different. Something was off.

I made an in-the-moment decision to separate dad and child to do a quick intake. Penelope went with our seventh-grade counselor, Linda, to talk and fill out some forms, and I invited her dad into my office to talk freely.

"I don't know exactly what's happened," her dad said, a cup of coffee in his hands. "It's like she went to sleep one night as a princess, then woke up the next morning as a monster."

"Tell me more," I said.

"She and I were so excited for middle school. When summer came, she stopped going out and doing things with her friends. It seemed like every day, she'd spend less time out of her room. We used to eat dinner together every night, and that time got shorter and shorter until now she just says, 'I'm not hungry,' and I eat alone."

"What kind of things did she stop doing with her friends?"

"Well," Penelope's dad said. "They used to do regular kid stuff, right? They'd go to the mall, head over to the park, ride their bikes wherever, soccer on the weekends, have sleepovers. And it was summertime, right? Sunshine, warm weather. All Penny wants to do now is sit in her room."

"When she's in her room, what's she doing?" I asked.

"Doomscrolling," he said. "Posting stuff on her social media. Honestly, she's thirteen; she really shouldn't be putting all that stuff out there. I mean, it's appropriate and all, but it's not appropriate, know what I mean?"

"I do, indeed," I said, and I reflected on the challenges my wife and I shared of raising our two daughters through their teenage years.

Her dad continued, "I try to be outside every day, before and after work. I invite her to sit on the porch with me while I mess around in the yard, pulling weeds, watching the sunset, whatever. Nope. Like a tractor beam, she's being tugged inside all the time."

"And how's her attitude? Her mood?"

"You saw that out there, right?" her dad winced. "She's on edge. Snappish. It's like she thinks I'm out to get her. Like the whole world is out to get her. But you want to know what's funny? On her social media posts, she's delightful. Smiling, chipper, like everything's roses. It's weird."

I spoke with her dad for another fifteen minutes or so, then suggested he take Penelope home while we get her class schedule set up so she could start the next morning with a full day, fresh slate, ready to go. He agreed, we met Penelope at the counseling center, and off they went.

I sat down with Linda to compare notes.

Sure enough, Penelope's account was similar in tone, though her perception of events was glaringly different.

Despite having only just met Linda, Penelope was surprisingly forthright. She'd started puberty about two years ago, so that didn't explain the recent mood swings. Her parents had split up, and her mom had exited the picture before she entered kindergarten, so living with just her dad wasn't new.

According to Penelope, her dad was the one who changed. He had grown more bossy and demanding, teased her for her fledgling influencer pursuits, and never listened to anything she said, wanted, or was interested in. She resented the change in schools because her dad was dragging her away from her friends and peer group. "What kind of monster does that?" she'd asked.

After exchanging tales, Linda looked at me and offered an executive summary: "Sounds like a middle school kid who is navigating her teenage years as a girl without a positive female role model—at least she didn't share about one with me—and facing intense social media scrutiny. She craves attention and validation, but doesn't know how to handle it appropriately, especially when it's negative. Emotionally, she's all over the place. And her expectation for growing up seems to be different than her father's expectations for her. That strains their relationship. She seems to be quite anxious and worried. We'll need to wrap her up with support pretty quickly."

Our responsibility was clear: We had to help Penelope find her footing. The next morning, the real work began.

WHAT'S REALLY GOING ON?

Penelope is one of the growing number of kids who are having a hard time. In every community, we have kids who are struggling mentally and emotionally with life, with love, with the world, with themselves, with their future, with school, with friends, with adults, and—thanks to the ubiquitous nature of smartphones and social media—with complete strangers.

The schoolhouse is not immune to this epidemic. As you'll read in the next section, kids tote their emotions along with them. Emotions are real, they're natural, and they're always with us. We cannot avoid them, pretend they're not real, or stop them from happening.

To open our minds to this reality and to create a safe environment for our kids to learn, we must adapt our approach. One of the first things we can unlearn is any mindset that aligns with the phrase, "Kids should leave their baggage at the door and come to school to be students."

Humans are emotional beings. If our schools and classrooms were devoid of feelings, they may as well be run and inhabited by machines. Kids aren't cogs, teachers aren't widgets, and learning doesn't happen through robotic, monochromatic, hollow, lockstep processes. It's magical, dynamic, exciting, and inspiring. Learning happens through relationships, and relationships are packed tightly with emotions. So, rather than becoming bothered by them, wishing they weren't so prevalent, or brushing them under the multicolored, story-time classroom rug, it would behoove us to embrace them.

One of the first things we can unlearn is any mindset that aligns with the phrase, "Kids should leave their baggage at the door and come to school to be students."

In fact, we can use emotions to our advantage in the schoolhouse. If positive emotions help us interact more openly, work more productively, and learn more effectively, then we ought to craft a setting and experiences that exude more positive emotions. We'll dig into that big idea in a little bit.

In the meantime, we have Penelope. Because of whatever's happening in her life, she's struggling. Her emotional reactions aren't something she can just turn off or change at the click of a button. So, when she—and your Penelope—shows us her big feelings through a litany of emotion-driven behaviors, we mustn't diminish her, ignore her, or persecute her for disrupting the Box.

Have you heard colleagues say things like this before?

- "She's just being dramatic."
- "He's doing this for no reason."
- "They're just trying to get attention."
- "She's overreacting."
- "He must have a mental illness."
- "Why are they making such a big deal about it? Get over it."

None of these statements are helpful, and we'd be better served to eliminate them from our vocabulary. It does us (and our kids) no good to criticize or assume there must be something wrong with a kid who's experiencing intense emotions. You have your emotions, I have mine, and Penelope has hers.

In that vein, let's try looking at the kid in front of you and meeting them where they are. When we come face to face with our emotions, a reality stares right back at us: We're experiencing what it means to be human. Emotions are neither good nor bad; indeed, they are our natural responses to stimuli. That includes happiness, sadness, anger, guilt, surprise, love, a thousand others, and . . . anxiety.

Anxiety and the Brain

So, what is anxiety, and why is it so prevalent in our young people? The American Psychological Association (APA, 2018) describes anxiety as an emotion, often producing a long-lasting response, characterized by the apprehension or anticipation of a future-oriented, diffuse threat.

Anxiety is worry to the *n*th degree. It's like standing on stage before the curtain rises, certain the audience is waiting for your mistake rather than your performance. It's the lingering dread of what no good, horrible, very bad thing could possibly happen. And, to a certain extent, it's the belief that the no good, horrible, very bad thing *will* happen.

If we were to have a moment of lucidity, our rational mind would probably tell us not to worry. Unfortunately, when we're experiencing intense emotions, our rational mind—controlled by the prefrontal cortex—is disconnected. Here's why.

Think of your brain as a computer. The prefrontal cortex acts as the main processor. It makes reasonable, rational, calculated decisions based on the information it collects, manages, and filters. When we're operating out of our prefrontal cortex, we're intentional, thoughtful, careful, reflective, and self-aware. We tend to focus on our goals, analyze data objectively, create manageable plans, monitor our progress, and adjust our actions accordingly. In short, we do our best work when we're operating out of our prefrontal cortex, when the main processor is online.

However, for information to get to the prefrontal cortex, input from our senses comes through the brainstem like data through an internet connection or USB port, and it has to pass through two doors, each guarded by a sentry. The first sentry, the amygdala, acts like a built-in security firewall, asking, "Are you safe?" If the amygdala senses a threat—even a perceived threat—the door remains closed. It's as if the computer has been hijacked by the antivirus software, shutting down all the programs and apps while it runs. It's the computer's equivalent of our brain's flight, fight, or freeze mode. (We'll address this, and the traumatic experiences that tend to trip it, later in this chapter.)

For now, if the answer is "Yes, I am—or feel—safe," the information proceeds through the first door and heads toward the second door.

When the information arrives at the second door, the new sentry—the limbic system, acting as the brain's emotional firewall—asks simply, "What emotions are you experiencing as you process these inputs?" Our response, determined by whether our emotions motivate *approach* behaviors or *avoidance* behaviors, governs the lock on that second door (Beckner, 2023).

Emotions like happiness, joy, and curiosity make you want to *approach*, or continue, an experience, and they contain the encrypted passcode to open the second door and allow access to the prefrontal cortex.

Other emotions like sadness, frustration, and anxiety prompt you to *avoid*, or stop, an experience. When these emotions are present, the firewall holds, the sentry remains steadfast, and the door stays shut. Only when the parasympathetic nervous system has flushed the stress chemicals and the emotion has subsided (to continue the computer metaphor, once the limbic system has repaired the corrupted files) will that second door open, granting a pathway to the prefrontal cortex.

One of the trickiest parts about embracing the emotional reality of our kids in the schoolhouse is, well, interacting with kids experiencing intense emotions creates an emotional response in us! The kids aren't the only humans in this equation.

So, what do we need to do so we can be at our best for our kids? Like flight attendants tell us on every airplane, "Put on your oxygen mask before helping others." That means managing our emotions, remaining self-regulated, and operating out of our prefrontal cortex. Fortunately, in my travels, I've had the opportunity to work with some phenomenal people who have shared proven, valuable, effective approaches to do just that. Here are some of my favorites.

Remain grounded in your purpose.

From Kristin Van Marter Souers, Keith Orchard, and Pete Hall (2025) comes the importance of knowing why you're doing what you're doing. They state, "The key is to stay grounded in who you are and how you want others to experience you" (Van Marter Souers et al., 2025, p. 13). Having clarity of purpose might not change the work you have to do, though it will alter the way you do it, thereby transforming the end user's experience. I equate this to the quote attributed to Mother Teresa:

"Wash the plate. Not because it is dirty, nor because you were told to wash it. But because you love the person who will use it next."

Pause and reflect.

Ignacio Lopez (2024), author of *The EQ Way: How Emotionally Intelligent School Leaders Navigate Turbulent Times*, suggests that calling a time-out to connect with your emotions and thoughts can be incredibly important and helpful. This might be as simple as stepping out for a minute, taking a deep breath, going for a quick walk, or even reaching for a fidget spinner. (Yes, adults can use self-regulation tools, too. I always had a little basketball hoop in my classroom or on the back of my office door that I'd shoot stress-balls through when I began to feel overwhelmed.) These moments allow you to build your self-awareness by asking questions like these.

- "What emotion am I feeling right now?"
- "Why am I feeling it?"
- "What is actually happening right now?"
- "How might I think more rationally about it?"

Take regular brain breaks.

Wendy Turner (2024), the 2017 Delaware Teacher of the Year and author of *Embracing Adult SEL: An Educator's Guide to Personal Social Emotional Learning Success*, advocates for taking consistent, proactive brain breaks. We tend to work and work, grind and grind, toil and toil, even through our lunch "hour," and our bodies wear down over time. So, our watches ding every hour to remind us to stand up. Meanwhile, our minds also become exhausted, and we're susceptible to emotional upsurges. What if we had an alarm ding to remind us to give our minds a break? Why wait for the stressors to overwhelm us? By taking a short break, focusing on something lighthearted and even fun, moving our bodies, and interacting with people, music, prayers, or pets that provide us with an emotional boost, we can "foster more calm and pleasant emotions" (Turner, 2024, p. 90).

The long and short of it is this: With a little preventive care and some self-awareness, we can put ourselves in a position to be at our best for our kids.

Kids and Trauma

Let's take the brain-as-a-computer metaphor even further. Sometimes, when information reaches the first door in our brain and the sentry—the amygdala—asks,

"Are you safe?", the answer is "No. No, I'm not." The amygdala signals all the door's locks to remain bolted. The portcullis drops. Meanwhile, the brain releases cortisol and adrenaline, stress hormones that increase energy, heart rate, and blood pressure, as it prepares for a flight, fight, or freeze reaction. Everything else, like the immune and digestive systems, remains shut down, until the danger—or the perception of danger—passes. What causes this biological response? Trauma.

According to the Substance Abuse and Mental Health Services Administration (n.d.):

> Individual trauma results from an event, series of events, or set of circumstances that is experienced by an individual as physically or emotionally harmful or life threatening and that has lasting adverse effects on the individual's functioning and mental, physical, social, emotional, or spiritual well-being.

That's a lot to process, so I'll break it down.

1. An individual experiences something—an event occurs.
2. The individual interprets the event as dangerous or harmful.
3. This interpretation cues the amygdala's "lock it down" response.
4. The flight, fight, or freeze reaction affects the individual for some (undesignated) period of time.

During this heightened state of alert, our kids' brains shift to survival mode and will guide them to escape the threat (or perceived threat) by any means necessary. Often, these means are disruptive and distracting to the Box and everyone in its orbit—just think for a second about some of the flight, fight, or freeze behaviors you've seen kids exhibit. Experiencing trauma is often quite debilitating. You might consider it like this: If anxiety is worry to the *n*th degree, trauma is anxiety to the *n*th degree.

PONDER THIS

Gather your teammates, an instructional coach or administrator, or a trusted colleague, and pose the question, "If you can see a kid is hurting, do you really need to know the details of what happened?"

In the decades following the groundbreaking adverse childhood experiences study (Felitti et al., 1998), educators and policymakers across the globe have keenly investigated the causes of trauma responses. With a list of the ten original adverse childhood experiences posed as an assessment checklist (you can read more about these at www.cdc.gov/violenceprevention/aces/about.html), we've seen kids who are struggling and asked, "What happened to you?"

With all due respect to the many professionals who calculate kids' adverse childhood experience scores, that information does us, on the ground, very little good. If you return to my breakdown of the definition of *trauma*, you'll read the following: The individual interprets the event as dangerous or harmful (Substance Abuse and Mental Health Services Administration, n.d.). It's the individual's *interpretation* of the event, not the event itself, that prompts the trauma response.

Say, for instance, you have two kids in your class whose parents recently got divorced (this is one of the original ten adverse childhood experiences). One of the kids might proceed with business as usual, while the other might fall into a deep funk. The divorce itself was not traumatic; the kids' history, interpretation, coping mechanisms (or lack thereof), and support networks (or lack thereof) create the stressful or traumatic response.

So, if you've ever heard a colleague say, "If only I knew," the reality is this: It doesn't matter if you *know* what happened. It doesn't even matter if you *agree* that the event was traumatic. The only thing that matters is that you meet kids where they are and support them the best you can.

Not surprisingly, kids who are experiencing (or have experienced) trauma may be sitting in our classrooms, but their brains are focused on safety and escape, not learning targets, group projects, assignments, and today's pop quiz. In that "No. No, I'm not safe" state, they are unable—not unwilling—to learn, connect, or attend to the things their prefrontal cortexes could handle.

You might be wondering, *How many kids are we talking about here?* In the 2023 Youth Risk Behavior Survey, researchers found that 80 percent of respondents reported experiencing at least one adverse childhood experience, and over 20 percent reported experiencing four or more (Swedo et al., 2024). Without a doubt, statistics like these prompted Kristin Souers and Pete Hall (2016) to write this devastating statement in *Fostering Resilient Learners*: "We know that childhood trauma has become an epidemic" (p. 23).

A Mental Health Crisis

How many of our kids need to struggle with anxiety or its enervating sibling—depression—for it to be considered a crisis? Five percent? Ten? According to the

Centers for Disease Control and Prevention (2025), in 2022–2023, 11 percent of kids ages 3 to 17 had a current diagnosed anxiety disorder, and 4 percent had current diagnosed depression. That's 15 percent (though there may be some overlap there), and that seems like a lot. That said, our mental health crisis isn't about diagnosed mental illness; rather, it's a byproduct of the sheer number of kids who feel out of sorts. Our schools and communities are full of kids who are experiencing tough situations, including adverse childhood experiences, prompting normal emotions to an extent that adversely affects them. Survey data offers a glimpse: 40 percent of teens reported having persistent feelings of sadness or hopelessness in the last two weeks, and 20 percent of teens reported seriously considering suicide in the past year (Centers for Disease Control and Prevention, 2025).

What is the cause of this crisis? In a word, stress. More specifically, how our young people respond to stressful stimuli is affecting their mental health. The Center on the Developing Child (Harvard University, n.d.) describes three types of stress responses.

- **Positive stress response:** This typically includes a brief increase in heart rate and mild stress hormone elevation that occurs when facing everyday challenges. An example is when a kid is asked to answer a question aloud in class and feels butterflies. With teacher support and classmate encouragement, the kid answers the question and feels a sense of pride.
- **Tolerable stress response:** This is a more severe, longer-lasting reaction that activates the body's alert systems to a greater degree. One example is when a kid's pet passes away, leading to feelings of grief and sadness. Over time, and with family support and perhaps a ceremony to commemorate the pet, the kid processes the loss in a healthy, safe manner.
- **Toxic stress response:** This occurs when a child experiences strong, frequent, prolonged adversity and trauma, leading to intense activation of the stress response system without adequate supports in place. Living in an environment of frequent domestic violence, for example, can cause this response. Without a responsive caregiver to provide safety (from the violence itself and from witnessing the violence), the stress response remains chronically activated.

This offers us a peek into what's going on behind the scenes, beneath the prefrontal cortex. At the core, many of our kids wield underdeveloped coping mechanisms. Theoretically, experiencing hard things would make us better at handling hard things. We cultivate healthy stress response systems by gradually experiencing more adversity and learning strategies for coping with the increased challenge. When we have tools to help us manage stress (like supportive relationships, self-regulation strategies, breathing techniques, and so on), we develop the resilience that allows us to tolerate more of it. Because of some of the most common and impactful stressors, our kids' healthy experience of the positive stress response has been short-sheeted, and those tools are insufficient to combat them. It's as if the limbic system's emotional firewall is caught in a doom loop and changes the password to the second door faster than we can type it in. What are the stressors responsible for this downturn? Here are some of the culprits.

- **Smartphones and addictive behavior:** In *The Anxious Generation*, Jonathan Haidt (2024) contends that the prevalence of smartphones "may be the key to explaining the sudden collapse of adolescent mental health" (p. 34). With the constant dinging of notifications alongside a "firehose of addictive content" (Haidt, 2024, pp. 3–4), our kids' reward systems are overwhelmed with hits of dopamine, the pleasure chemical. This causes them to seek out that experience (scanning for comments, mining for likes, scrolling the feed, checking for messages) again and again, each time needing more repetitions to get the same dopamine boost, creating addiction-like behavior (Poisson, Engel, & Saunders, 2021).
- **Social media:** Closely following the omnipresence of smartphones is the darling of the cyberworld—social media. Not only does constant posting, commenting, and liking expose preteens and teens to the daggers of comparison, bullying, and cyberbullying that harm mental health and increase suicidal thoughts and ideation, but it has also been shown to affect cognitive functioning and impact academic performance and memory (Nagata et al., 2025; Young et al., 2024).
- **Strained, insecure relationships:** When kids have strong, supportive relationships with others, including connections with parents and caregivers, teachers and coaches, and friendships and peer groups, they thrive (Badcock, Holt-Lunstad, Garcia, Bombaci, & Lim, 2022). When these relationships are lacking, however, our kids' mental health and physical health decline (Holt-Lunstad, 2024). Whether it's a result of the swollen reliance on electronic communication instead of face to face, the increased retreatism to cyberworlds, the superficial nature of interactions online, or the reduction of time spent in interpersonal connections, the lack of secure, supportive relationships affects

youth mental health (Imran & Jackson, 2022) and follows them into adulthood (Zhang et al., 2022).

- **Insufficient exercise, breaks, and unstructured playtime:** With the onslaught of information flooding their brains, it's no surprise that our kids just don't have the bandwidth to process it all in healthy ways. As it turns out, there are three approaches that help, though our kids aren't engaging in them enough. Exercising, especially when coupled with proper nutrition and adequate sleep, promotes mental health and well-being in youth (Hosker, Elkins, & Potter, 2019). Sometimes our kids just need a break, and a simple rest—where they can chillax, device free, for even brief periods—can strengthen brain functioning and support deeper learning (Buch, Claudino, Quentin, Bönstrup, & Cohen, 2021). Sometimes, those healthy breaks can include unstructured, exploratory, adventurous play—either alone or with peers—which can build resilience, enhance creativity, increase happiness, hone decision-making skills, and strengthen friendships and relationships (Dodd, Nesbit, & FitzGibbon, 2023). Unfortunately, according to the Physical Activity Alliance's (2024) report card, only about a quarter (21–28 percent) of children aged 6 to 17 meet the 60 minutes of daily physical activity guideline, earning the United States a grade of D–.
- **Low self-esteem:** Does self-esteem matter? You bet it does. Self-esteem, defined by the APA (2023) as "the degree to which the qualities and characteristics contained in one's self-concept are perceived to be positive," has been debated for decades by fans of Mr. Rogers and critics of fourteenth-place ribbons. Researchers at the University of California at Davis settled the dispute in a massive study, determining that the lack of self-esteem leads directly to stress and anxiety, while its presence provides calmness and confidence (Orth & Robins, 2022). Have you ever heard a kid say some version of "I suck at this; I'm worthless"? Where does that type of self-talk come from? Consider the tone and timbre of the information that pours into our kids' brains via geopolitical events, news feeds, social media posts and comments, political rhetoric, and even the conversations of nearby adults. Then, think of the prevalence of bullying, the pressure to fit in (the Box), the demands levied on kids, and the typical challenges of navigating childhood and young adulthood. It's a lot to manage.

The preceding list is full of potential stressors, and growing up with stress is not a new phenomenon. These are just different stressors than previous generations may have faced. However, if this list is indeed responsible for the epidemic of anxious, depressed, forlorn kids, it's not just because they're more stressful stressors than we've ever experienced. The common thread is our kids' abilities—or, too often, their inabilities—to safely and consistently develop effective coping mechanisms for them.

OK, that was a lot of information, and it may seem overwhelming. Most likely, as you've been considering the Penelope in your life or classroom, your first question was likely, Why is this kid struggling emotionally?

Your next question is, How can I reach and teach this kid?

WHAT DO KIDS WHO ARE STRUGGLING EMOTIONALLY REALLY NEED?

If the kid is struggling emotionally, that's OK. Emotions—even those like anxiety, sadness, frustration, worry, and melancholy—are a large part of what make up the human experience. When those feelings begin to overwhelm our kids, however, they need the scales of influence tipped so the positives in their lives outweigh the negatives.

You can help, because one of the primary scale-tippers is the presence of strong, consistent, supportive, loving relationships with positive adult role models. Such connections can impact a kid's *perceived cognitive competence*, which is the belief in one's own potential to achieve success (Topor et al., 2010). This is a key part of bolstering self-esteem and enhancing a kid's feeling of value.

The reality is that there will always be stressors, and kids will forever experience stress. How they handle that stress will be determined by the self-regulation skills and coping mechanisms they develop under the watchful, empathetic tutelage of adults like you. You can help them process the events in their lives that climb into their brains and chip away at their sense of self-worth. You can help them learn the skills that open the second door and grant access to the prefrontal cortex.

Penelope and kids like Penelope who are having a tough time with big emotions need the tools to march confidently through the mess.

This is a good time to return to the dog-eared, bookmarked pages in chapter 1 that include the four protocols and templates you'll want to use to frame your work. And, because clarity of the goal is a non-negotiable prerequisite for all the work that follows, I might also suggest that you revisit the list of questions I posed at the beginning of chapter 1 to hone your collaborative vision of success. Here's the result of that initial reflection for Penelope:

GOAL STATEMENT

We want to strengthen Penelope's relationships, boost her self-esteem, and support her self-regulation to help her develop effective coping mechanisms for life's stressors so that she can boldly and purposefully step into her learning.

HOW DO WE DO THIS?

When kids have nurturing, supportive relationships; coping mechanisms and self-regulation strategies; and access to their rational prefrontal cortex, they can progressively withstand more stress and thrive amid life's ongoing, ramped-up challenges.

How do we help our kids develop those skills? One effective approach is to follow a gradual release of responsibility model. With the guidance and security of trusted adults, our kids tackle increasingly more intense stressors and develop slightly stronger coping mechanisms, responsibility, and independence. It's like a series of workouts for the tolerable stress response system.

What's the result? Often, the words that frequently pop up here are grit, resilience, stick-to-itiveness, perseverance, courage, fortitude, persistence, doggedness . . . you know the terms. They're the characteristics of people who rise above their conditions and forge optimistic, successful worldviews and experience a host of successes throughout their lives (Jadhav et al., 2025).

Let's look at some specific options for my Penelope and all the other Penelopes out there. Here are several strategies to consider.

Strategy: Create an Empathetic Classroom

When kids are having a tough time managing big emotions, it can be just the ticket to be surrounded by—and enveloped by—other human beings who are attuning to their emotions, empathizing with their current state of mind, caring for them at a personal level, and supporting their healthy regulation. In the classroom setting, this means classmates, teachers, volunteers . . . and anyone else with a heartbeat.

Counselor and educator Maria Munro-Schuster (2025) shares the characteristics of an *empathetic classroom*. All members of the environment do the following.

- Notice and understand their own emotions.
- Seek to attune to others' emotions.
- Anticipate challenging interactions.
- Anchor themselves in experiences that assist with self-regulation.
- Consider emotions as valuable data.
- Emphasize relationships and connections with one another.

To create a classroom as a refuge, teachers can incorporate the skills of attunement, attachment, validation, play, power, emotions, and change in their settings (Munro-Schuster, 2025). Whether it's a full seven-hour day, a fifty-minute period, or a twenty-minute group, these approaches can address the mental health needs of our kids to allow them to boldly and successfully step into their learning.

See "Tool 18: Four Steps to Setting Up an Empathetic Classroom" in the appendix (page 196) for guidance on implementing this strategy.

Strategy: Build Self-Esteem Through Deliberate Praise

If the barrage of negative messaging is at least partially responsible for our kids' low self-esteem, it stands to reason that an even more overpowering salvo of positive messaging would raise it. Here we enter the confusing world of praise. Tread carefully here, because praise can be a double-edged sword. Sometimes, the positive, complementary words we use inadvertently harm the way our kids see themselves and their worth . . . and have the opposite effect of what we intended. A savvier approach would be to use language that assumes and emphasizes our kids' intrinsic motivation (Anderson, 2019). Here are some tips for becoming more deliberate with our praise.

- **Focus on effort, strategy, and process:** To encourage a growth mindset, persistence, and grit, you can highlight specific actions, choices, or strategies rather than innate ability. Here are some sample phrases.
    - "I noticed how carefully you planned each step before starting—that shows great strategy."
    - "You kept trying different ways until it worked. That perseverance really paid off."
- **Be specific and descriptive:** Descriptive praise informs students about exactly what they did well and boosts intrinsic motivation. Avoid vague praise like "good job!" Focus on observable behaviors or choices. Here are some sample phrases.
    - "You summarized the main ideas in your own words and checked for accuracy—excellent attention to detail."
    - "You asked clarifying questions when you weren't sure. That curiosity is how you learn best."
- **Attribute success to controllable factors:** Students learn they can control outcomes through effort and strategy, increasing self-confidence and grit. Praise effort, choices, and persistence, not "talent" or intelligence. Here are some sample phrases.

    - "Your careful proofreading shows you're developing strong habits."
    - "You improved your score because you practiced consistently—that's real progress."
- **Recognize progress and improvement:** To build self-esteem, encourage risk taking, and highlight that learning is a process, you can notice small gains, revisions, or attempts, not just perfect results. Here are some sample phrases.
    - "I can see how much better your paragraph structure is compared to last week."
    - "Even though it was challenging, you didn't give up, and that persistence is paying off."
- **Link praise to reflection and self-awareness:** To help students recognize their own learning strategies and develop self-awareness, you can encourage students to think about what they did and why it worked. Here are some sample phrases.
    - "You solved that problem using a method you developed yourself. What made it effective?"
    - "You checked your answers carefully; how did that strategy help you succeed?"
- **Support autonomy and intrinsic motivation:** Praise that respects students' control and choice strengthens intrinsic motivation. Connect praise to students' goals and encourage ownership over learning. Here are some sample phrases.
    - "You chose a creative approach that reflects your own thinking—great decision!"
    - "You decided to revise your draft before submitting, and it really improved your work."
- **Be authentic and timely:** Students detect insincerity; authentic praise is more motivating. Offer praise immediately after an action and make sure it is genuine. Here are some sample phrases.
    - "I'm impressed by how focused you were during that group discussion; it made a big difference."
    - "I noticed the effort you put into explaining your reasoning. That clarity helped everyone understand the concept."

- **Balance praise across students:** Avoid favoritism or over-praising top performers; this builds equity, self-esteem, and engagement. Recognize improvement, effort, and perseverance in all students. Here are some sample phrases.
    - "Your progress on this assignment shows that your consistent effort is paying off."
    - "Even though this was tricky, you stayed with it—well done!"

As a school principal, I paid a lot of attention to how the kids in my schools were doing. Sure, I pored over data for attendance, behavior, and coursework . . . and I closely monitored their attitudes, energy, and physical, mental, and emotional health, too. I felt very strongly that it was our responsibility, as the adult professionals working in the setting kids inhabit for seven hours a day, five days a week, to care for the whole human.

Having done a ton of work myself in the field of self-improvement and the art of self-reflection, I read Carol Dweck's seminal 2006 book, *Mindset: The New Psychology of Success*, with great enthusiasm. Immediately, the idea of a *growth* mindset leading to greater success than a *fixed* mindset resonated with me. If we believe we can continuously learn, grow, and improve, of course the sky's the limit! I emphasized this approach in my conversations with kids, with staff, and with families, and it proved quite effective . . . until it didn't.

There's a natural limit to how far you can take yourself with a can-do attitude. Your belief in yourself is critical, of course, but . . . it's not sufficient. For us to truly approach our potential, we must couple our mindsets with the guidance of mentors, teachers, parents, coaches, and other role models, collaborators, partners, and supports.

How did this shift my language approach to support the lifelong pursuits of the whole humans in my schools? I sought to balance the following, which creates the memorable acronym MUUST.

- **Motivational optimism:** "TGIM, my friends! You can do some amazing things this week!"
- **Uninhibited compliments:** "Did you get a new haircut? That looks fabulous!"
- **Unconditional regard:** "Your outburst during the exam sure made a spectacle, didn't it? I believe in your ability to fix this with your teacher." (This factor is opposed to *conditional regard*, where kids' value is tied directly to performance, achievement, and awards.)

- **Savvy praise:** See the tips for building self-esteem (page 132) for some examples and guidelines.
- **Targeted reflective prompts:** "If that's really your goal, who are you going to ask for help along the way?"

I remember reading an article in which the authors claimed children experience, on average, thirteen to fourteen negative interactions for each positive, to which I replied aloud, "Unconscionable." Stephen R. Flora's (2000) article, "Praise's Magic Reinforcement Ratio: Five to One Gets the Job Done," set a new standard that you probably know by heart: five positives for each negative. And for kids with low self-esteem, battling mental health issues, fighting anxiety? A ten-to-one ratio or more might be in order (shoot, a one hundred-to-one ratio sounds good to me).

As educators, we talk a lot. And make no mistake: When we're talking to kids, our words matter. A lot.

See "Tool 19: Daily Checklist for Effective Praise" in the appendix (page 198) for guidance on implementing this strategy.

Strategy: Practice Self-Regulation

Self-regulation is the ability to manage the brain's stress response system. In technical language, Ross A. Thompson (1991), University of California at Davis distinguished professor of psychology emeritus, defines self-regulation as the "intrinsic processes responsible for monitoring, evaluating, and modifying emotional reactions." This means when kids experience the emotions that accompany life's stressors, they're able to notice their feelings, reduce the intensity of the emotions, calm the body's physiological reaction to the stress, and shorten the duration of the dysregulation, allowing them to get back to work, engage with peers and adults, and return to learning.

Make no mistake: When we're talking to kids, our words matter. A lot.

There are roughly one billion self-regulation strategies available to our kids, and many of them are school- and classroom-appropriate. From meditation and journaling to deep breathing and cross-lateral stretching, from drinking water and eating an apple to coloring and working on a puzzle, the array of options is truly endless. The key for us, as educators, is to identify the handful of strategies we can logistically manage, then help our kids learn about, practice, and choose the two or three approaches that work for them. There's no single tool that works for everyone, but all your kids can find a tool that works for them. How do we best do that? Take them through the buffet line of self-regulation aids and test them all out; it won't take long to determine which ones are tools and which are toys.

See "Tool 20: 101 Self-Regulation Strategies" in the appendix (page 200) for guidance on implementing this strategy.

Strategy: Get Creative With Coping Mechanisms

When our kids are experiencing stress, they need to be granted access to the prefrontal cortex to make sense of the event, analyze it rationally, and file it in the correct compartment of their brains. Engaging in self-regulation strategies, as you just read, is an extremely effective way to start this process. Another is to build creative, innovative coping mechanisms to help get the operating system back online. What fits the bill?

- **Pattern interrupters:** By doing something unexpected, we can jolt our kids' neural network and force the prefrontal cortex back into command. Why? Just like the viral slap-a-cheese-slice-onto-a-crying-baby's-forehead trend, the shock of the startling event causes the brain to flick on, and the intense emotion is bypassed as the rational brain asks, "What in the world was that?" Instead of keeping a stock of cheese slices on hand, try a simple bird call or point to the classroom window and gasp.
- **Movement:** As the saying goes, "Motion changes emotion," so challenging kids to crab walk or bear walk either as a body break or while quizzing each other on multiplication facts can help shift the focus from big emotions to big motions.
- **Pink or brown noise:** Playing *pink noise* (like a flowing creek) or *brown noise* (like a roaring waterfall) in the background while students work independently or complete a project can help with relaxation, cover other environmental sounds, and soothe inner thoughts.
- **Draw it:** Drawing requires the coordination of the entire brain, so drawing the emotions one is feeling, the definition of vocabulary words, or a summary of a recent reading passage can help manage emotions. For an additional challenge, try finger paint or shaving cream.
- **Role-play:** When your kids' brains are regulated, using emotion flash cards, emoji, situations from books or historical events, or scenarios to

prompt a role-play can help kids attune, empathize, and communicate various emotions in productive ways.

- **Improv, miming, and stand-up comedy:** Take role-play to the next level by teaching kids to think on their feet and access the imaginative part of their brains. Challenge kids to act as numerators jealous of denominators, characters of two novels arguing about who was next in line for a taxi, or a historical figure trying to make friends during modern times. By incorporating laughter, we can help our kids process emotions with more optimism and lightheartedness.

Sometimes, the best defense is a good offense. Preparing your kids (and yourself) for those moments of high stress and anxiety *before* they occur can help develop healthy, safe coping mechanisms for *when* they occur. And as you develop your skills and experiences in this realm, you'll discover lots of ways they can be incorporated into academic lessons, using content from the curriculum, thereby saving you time by remaining focused on learning outcomes as well as supporting mental health awareness.

PONDER THIS

Gather your teammates, an instructional coach or administrator, or a trusted colleague, and pose the question, "How might we weave some of these creative coping mechanisms into our day-to-day operations?"

One of the chief complaints of educators who resist any sort of instruction or discussion about empathy, emotions, and feelings is about time. When are we supposed to do it? What are we supposed to take out of our curriculum to make room for this lesson or activity?

Those are valid questions. And since I used up all my political capital in the introduction, I can't address the excess content in the curriculum anymore, which leaves me with this: Expert teachers do both. Simultaneously.

The teachers whose names I wrote in the acknowledgments, as well as thousands more I've met on my travels, realize education isn't an either-or battle between curriculum or kids. By doing what's best for kids, we meet their needs, create a safe space for them to learn and develop, facilitate the learning of the curriculum, usher them ever closer to their goals and dreams, and watch them thrive when they leave.

So, as a team, contemplate this: How can we heighten our kids' emotional savvy and help them master the learning standards?

Strategy: Run a Multi-Age Advisory Program

Relationships, relationships, relationships. You know they're important to kids for a heap of reasons, yet they're challenging to establish, maintain, and strengthen over time, especially with academic and curricular needs demanding our time and energy. This strategy may appear, on the surface, to double down on the "relationships first, achievement second" tune. However, when we remember relationships are the means, not the end, it makes a heap of sense.

Offering a multi-age advisory program where students of different grade levels meet regularly with a trusted adult boosts cross-age connections (Burton, Raposa, Poon, Stams, & Rhodes, 2022), provides a stable relationship with that adult adviser for multiple years (Gambone, 2024), promotes social-emotional growth (Jenner et al., 2021), and supports smoother transitions from grade to grade and school to school (Hill, 2025).

Imagine fifth graders mentoring kindergartners during the first weeks of school. Picture a handful of first and second graders who progress through the school system together for a full decade. Envision the promotions and onboarding that occur between elementary and middle schools, and again between middle and high schools—and now visualize them with peers and classmates handling the heavy lifting and imparting their wisdom and experience along the way. In a multi-age advisory program, relationships throughout the school environment are strengthened, building a culture of connection (Hernández, Darling-Hammond, & Nielson, 2024).

See "Tool 21: Tips for a Multi-Age Advisory Program" in the appendix (page 204) for guidance on implementing this strategy.

Strategy: Detox From Devices

At the appropriate age and in moderation, smartphones, social media, and other technologies can be immensely powerful learning tools. The technologies and apps themselves are not inherently damaging; it's when they're used without limits in the hands of developmentally unready kids, causing cravings and addictive behaviors, that they become dangerous. While there's an argument to be made for embracing them as tools for learning, research shows that the benefits of keeping phones out of the classroom outweigh the potential bump of engagement you might envision. As caring, trusting, concerned adults, we must sometimes make uncomfortable decisions based on what's best for our kids.

What happens when kids eschew social media, log off, and leave their phones in a drawer, locker, or office during school hours? This ought to whet your appetite for a digital detox.

- In two weeks, kids in a Kentucky school district checked out half as many books from the school library as the entire previous school year (Grose, 2025).
- In a year, four Connecticut school districts reported higher student engagement rates and fewer discipline issues (Stanford, 2025), and a study in Norway demonstrated a significant positive mental health impact and lower bullying incidents (Abrahamsson, 2026).
- In two years, academic performance in a Florida district increased 2–3 percentile points (Figlio & Özek, 2025).

Clearly, banning cell phones at school is part of a much broader approach to supporting our kids' mental health. Putting smartphones in a special locker when kids arrive at school is certainly a powerful start.

See "Tool 22: Tips for a Digital Detox" in the appendix (page 206) for guidance on implementing this strategy.

Strategy: Let Them Play and Explore

Recess was one of the first casualties of the Accountability Era of the early 2000s. Who would have thought that allowing children free time to play outside would become such a lightning rod? As it turns out, playing and learning aren't diametrically opposed after all. In fact, research supports the notion that kids who play more, learn more (Miller et al., 2022). And for kids who struggle emotionally, getting outside and breathing fresh air, being active and participating in games and sports, creatively digging and building with tools, collaborating and negotiating with peers, and resolving boredom in authentic ways can work wonders for equipping them with the resilience and wherewithal to manage stressors more effectively (Jiang & Hussain, 2023). So, take the kids outside, let them play and explore and act like kids, and protect chunks of time throughout the day for this natural behavior . . . from birth, through high school, and beyond.

PONDER THIS

Gather your teammates, an instructional coach or administrator, or a trusted colleague, and pose the question, "How important is play to our kids' development?"

If we trust the research and understand the natural need to move, explore, and fidget with things, how are we going to put our money where our mouths are? How are we going to demonstrate this priority?

BACK TO PENELOPE

When Penelope came to school the next morning, her advisory teacher, Elise, was there to greet her. Because we had launched a multi-age advisory program the year before, Penelope could bank on having a long-term (well, our school had seventh and eighth graders, so two years at least!) connection with Elise, the first of several positive female role models we positioned for her. She also had eighth-grade mentors in that advisory period to show her the ropes, easing the transition for the new kid.

We had also instituted a cell phone lockup policy during the school day. While Penelope and her peers had access to their school-issued laptops (which had a firewall to prevent social media sites from popping up), their phones and the accompanying distractions of notifications, communication with peers, social media posts, likes, comments, and constant need for the dopamine hits were tucked away in the office until the school day ended.

Implementing and managing the cell phone policy was clunky at first (kids learned to bring stowaway phones, parents had a lot of questions, and we had to be extra aggressive for the first couple of weeks about tracking down kids with phones and then partnering with their parents to get them to fall in line), but as we ironed out the details and established a system, the kids (and adults) acquiesced rather quickly. To our surprise, once the phones were locked up, our kids just rolled up their sleeves and got to learning. Out of sight, out of mind.

What did this mean for Penelope? At first, she was a bit standoffish with her new schoolmates. Then, since there was no social media pressure to perform or add filters to who she was, she began to interact, smile, and spend time with other kids. Before long, she acted very much like the carefree, happy-go-lucky kid I'd known from her elementary school days.

Because Penelope had played the cello in elementary school, Elise brokered an introduction between her and our orchestra teacher, Drew, and she was instantly hooked. Academically, because she was on Elise's interdisciplinary team, her adviser was able to keep close tabs on her performance, attitude, and effort in her core classes.

Was it all sunshine and rainbows? No, that wasn't realistic or expected. Penelope still struggled with her emotional self-regulation at times, and it took her a while to determine which tools and approaches were most effective for her to restore homeostasis (that sense of calm that serves as an emotional baseline). After some specific explorations with her advisory class, she settled on three: (1) a tessellations coloring pad she could keep in her backpack, (2) a stress ball that she decorated with a marker, and, for more extreme moments, (3) a "feed the fish" pass she could use once per day to drop flakes into the aquarium in Elise's classroom (and spend a moment with her trusted adult, coregulating).

One evening, a couple weeks after Penelope had arrived, I encountered her dad at the grocery store. We shook hands, and he said, "She's a different kid, man. Actually, she's not. She's the kid she was before. I don't know what magic y'all are using over there, but I say keep it up!"

I smiled. "Thank you, I'm glad to hear you're seeing the changes. We are, too. And I assure you, there's no magic—just a bunch of people who love Penelope and are dedicated to helping her make positive decisions for herself. How's the influencer thing going?"

Her dad smiled. "She's still at it, but it's not something we argue about anymore. In fact, we have a deal. First dinner—together—then she can go be a content creator or influencer or social media personality or whatever her goal is. And I follow her online, so I can keep track of what she's posting and how she's presenting herself. So far, so good."

As the school year ended, I made a point to pop into the end-of-year one-on-one meeting between Penelope, her adviser, Elise, and her grade-level counselor, Linda. As was our standard operating procedure for these discussions, the adults asked open-ended, reflective questions, and Penelope talked at length about herself, her school year, and her goals for the future. Toward the end of the chat, Elise said, "OK, Penny, here's the deal. We've been so impressed with how you've conducted yourself this year, used your self-regulation strategies so openly and honestly, that we'd like you to be a part of the mentor training team that prepares next year's eighth graders to welcome the new crop of seventh graders. What do you think?"

Penelope smiled. "I think I could handle that," she said. "I've been working on my influencing skills, anyway, so I may as well put them to good use."

The adults laughed, and I gave Penelope one of my now-famous, not-so-textbook administrator head nods as I got up to leave. Leaping up, Penelope said, "Hold on, Mr. Hall," and rushed to give me a hug.

CONCLUSION

Emotions. What else can I say? Simply uttering the word in a room full of educators evokes all sorts of emotions! And the reality we face in our schools, at home, and throughout our communities is that we have a lot of kids experiencing big emotions—often bigger than they can handle. Some kids, like the Penelope I introduced in this chapter, have support networks that allow for developing healthy coping mechanisms for the stressors that lead to worry, anxiety, and even trauma. Others don't and need us to help. Fortunately, there are a ton of strategies at our disposal that fit the bill, and it's our common challenge to match our approaches to the kids' needs. When we do so, we can help strengthen Penelope's relationships, boost her self-esteem, and support her self-regulation to help her meet the goal we identified earlier: to develop effective coping mechanisms for life's stressors *so that* she can boldly and purposefully step into her learning.

EPILOGUE

SCHOOL SHOULD BE a magical place, full of joy, love, curiosity, learning, relationships, growth, passion, laughter, and celebration. Now, if you know me, you know I really try to avoid using the word *should*. Nobody likes getting *should on*, right? That said, school really *should* be magical, shouldn't it? I mean, it really should.

That's our collective responsibility. We need to bring that magic with us and spread it around like pixie dust. When kids feel marvelous, when they feel like they belong, and when they're excited about what they're doing and learning, amazing things happen. That's magical, and I've seen it. In schools and classrooms and the nooks and crannies in which educators meet with kids, I've seen this magic elicit kids who possess and demonstrate the very characteristics we want in our graduates and our neighbors (the following is the list I shared in the introduction).

We need to bring that magic with us and spread it around like pixie dust.

- Compassion
- Courage
- Curiosity
- Empathy
- Fairness
- Generosity
- Honesty
- Integrity
- Kindness
- Perseverance
- Respect
- Responsibility

WE DO THIS TOGETHER

There's a lot of *stuff* getting in the way of that noble, magical goal, however, including the "That's the way we've always done it" mindset. The predicament we face in modern education is almost paradoxical: Our problems are *inside* the Box, yet the solutions are *outside* the Box, which necessitates some *outside*-the-Box thinking from the people *inside* the Box.

Over the course of the past six chapters, this is what I hope you've been able to do.

- You've learned a mental model for processing, reflecting, and enhancing your impact.
- You've read and felt the stories of very real kids and their struggles.
- You've unlearned some of the unconscious thoughts that might be getting in your way.
- You've clarified the goal for each of the kids and their challenges.
- You've dug into the research about what's happening beneath the surface and what our kids need to be successful.
- You've surveyed a collection of strategies designed to meet those goals.

At the end of each chapter, you read the story of how a team of wonderful, well-intentioned educators worked collaboratively to meet the needs of that chapter's hero. The element of shared responsibility, of cooperation, of team accountability isn't one to glaze over. In fact, it's essential.

Following the well-traveled proverb "If you want to go fast, go alone; if you want to go far, go together," my professional preference has always been to build a strong team. As a teacher, I often served as a bridge between colleagues, grade levels, and even the teaching staff and administration. As an assistant principal and then principal, I learned and espoused the tenets of the professional learning communities process, and I emphasized the power, the authority, the influence, and the impact of our grade-level, department, and interdisciplinary teams in each of my schools. We thrive or struggle together; it's that simple. Now it's time to commit to making a change. My suggestion: Gather your team, whoever that includes. Send out invitations, hand-deliver them, link arms, and engage in this noble, magical work collectively.

MCKENNA AND TERRANCE

When I was a middle school principal, I struggled to find the correct words to accurately and honestly answer the neighborhood-barbecue question, "How are things at work?" Then, I thought of the analogy of water's journey from the fresh, clear, babbling brook emerging from the spring (elementary school) to the raging, salty waves of the ocean (high school). And how do we describe the water in between, where freshwater meets saltwater in a special blur?

Brackish.

Is there a better word to describe the middle school setting and those special middle school years, when kids are, indeed, a special blur of innocence and expectations, of excitement and frustration, of body odor and body spray, of wonder and skepticism?

How are things at work? Brackish. And I love it!

All that to set up this story.

The high school where we sent our kids was positioned in a historically low-performing, low-income neighborhood. At the time, their graduation rate stood at 55 percent, and that was using generous metrics. No matter whose perspective you used to view this, it was not OK. The entire community was struggling, and we weren't making much headway.

As part of a multipronged effort to raise the collective bar, the high school launched a "First in Family" initiative to inspire kids to become the first ones in their family to graduate from high school. As a capstone event, the high school hosted a special dinner gala for the kids who met this criterion in the spring of their senior year. It promised to be an extraordinary affair, with a plated dinner, linen tablecloths, and guest speakers. And, as a special nod, each graduating kid was allowed to invite one educator—someone who had played a vital role in supporting the kid's educational attainment—to join in the festivities.

Imagine my pride when McKenna, a former student of mine, sent me an invitation to the First in Family event to join her and her parents. *Finally*, I thought. *Someone acknowledges how great a principal I've been!*

Years before, McKenna had endured all the torrent and tumult one might expect from a brackish middle school experience. From social dilemmas to academic struggles, self-doubt and identity crises, the stressors seemed to gravitate toward her. I had counseled her on many occasions, providing support and encouragement and making sure she was connected to all her wonderful, well-intentioned teachers, counselors, and staff.

And here she was, graduating. The first in her family. I was incredibly proud. I got all dressed up and met McKenna and her family at the event, and we basked in her glory together. And at some point during the evening, I got up to fill up my glass at the punch bowl.

Imagine my surprise as I crossed paths with Terrance.

Terrance had been a thorn in my side. Like McKenna, he and I had spent a lot of time together during his middle school years. The principal's office is where a lot of kids end up when they act out in class, and I'm pretty sure *tomfoolery* was his middle name. Terrance and I would talk at length about his choices, his goals in life, and the path he probably needed to be on to reach those goals. Still, his troublesome habits ran the show, and repeatedly he'd land in my office.

Yet, four years later, here he was, graduating. The first in his family. Dismissing my surprise, I outstretched my arms when I saw him, saying, "Terrance, man, you did it. Congratulations! Bring it in!"

I'm not kidding when I tell you Terrance crossed his arms in an X in front of him, looked at me quizzically, and said, "Who are you?"

Instinctively, I laughed. "Terrance, it's me. Mr. Hall, your middle school principal. I'm so proud of you!"

There was not even a glimmer of recollection as he said, "Yeah, not ringing a bell."

The sting of those words shot through my veins. How could he not remember me? We spent so much time together, and our conversations had been so powerful. I mean, my advice was outstanding, I'm sure.

And then, as my parasympathetic nervous system flushed the stress chemicals and the emotion subsided, I had an epiphany: It's not about me. Whether or not Terrance remembered me, my outstanding advice, or anything else about me was immaterial. He was graduating. First in his family. This was about Terrance.

I gathered myself, put out a hand to shake his, and said, "Terrance, congratulations, young man. We're all very proud of you." He shook my hand with a slight nod, then returned to his table.

As I refilled my glass at the punch bowl, I reflected on the accomplishments of McKenna and Terrance. McKenna had invited me to the event, and Terrance had evidently invited someone else. I looked around the room. It was clamoring with graduates, each of whom had invited a different educator to honor, and it struck me again: We do this together.

Celebrating McKenna and Terrance also means honoring all the educators, parents, relatives, and community members who supported them along the way. No single educator can ever expect to be the sole contributor to a kid's success. For McKenna, it wasn't me. And for Terrance, it wasn't not me. For both of them, it was us.

We do this together.

Now, let's go do this. Together.

APPENDIX

IF YOU'RE LIKE most readers—or, more important, practitioners trying to do right by kids—you already popped into this appendix looking for a specific tool. If that's the case, terrific! Welcome. And if you just finished the meaty middle of the book and turned to the appendix for the first time, terrific! Welcome.

You may be wondering, *So, Pete, how do we use these tools?* Great question, and my response will refer you back to what I wrote in the introduction: We do our best work together. Collaboratively. In partnership.

Whether your titled position is classroom teacher, principal, social worker, office manager, counselor, bus driver, assistant principal, advocate, superintendent, cafeteria staff, classroom aide, coach, therapist, or something else, you have a valuable role: You're a part of the team that's wrapping its arms around a kid.

And as you wrap those loving, shielding, encouraging arms around that kid, you'll want to keep your collective goal front and center. Remember to use the templates and protocols I introduced in chapter 1 to guide your work and focus your efforts, then choose and employ the tools and strategies that are most likely to yield the results you're targeting.

As you move forward, I urge you to do so with confidence. The tools that follow aren't built on hunches; they're constructed and compiled through years of research-driven field tests, application, and refinement by education professionals across the globe. I've used many of them myself, both in my buildings and in the many districts, schools, and classrooms I've supported as a coach and mentor.

Figure A.1 includes a full list of the tools in this book and the page numbers where they may be found.

Figure A.1: *Comprehensive list of tools and where to find them.*

TOOL 1: CHARACTERISTICS WEB

Purpose

This tool highlights the similarities (and uniqueness) of every young person in a given setting and provides opportunities for educators to discuss what each kid has in common with others (as well as what makes each person special).

Directions

On a bulletin board, create a chart (or other creative graphic organizer) that provides enough space for each kid in the class to be represented. Then, beginning with the most obvious (or outer) characteristics, collect data on physical features, names, backgrounds, and so on. When all members of the setting are posted, engage in a data-driven discussion together, asking questions like these.

- "What do you notice about our class?"
- "What's something you have in common with someone else?"
- "What's something that's unique to you or a classmate?"

This process can be repeated with hidden (or inner) characteristics like favorite foods, skills or talents, goals, fears, or anything else that can surface commonalities and differences.

As a fun twist, after collecting multiple characteristics and traits, this information could be displayed as a web, with yarn connecting individuals with similar characteristics or interests.

Characteristic Chart Example for Hair Color

	Black	Brown	Blond	Red	Other
Student A	X				
Student B			X		
Student C			X		
Student D		X			
Student E			X		
Student F	X				
Student G					X
Student H		X			
Student I	X				
Student J	X				
Student K				X	
Student L	X				

Characteristics Web Example

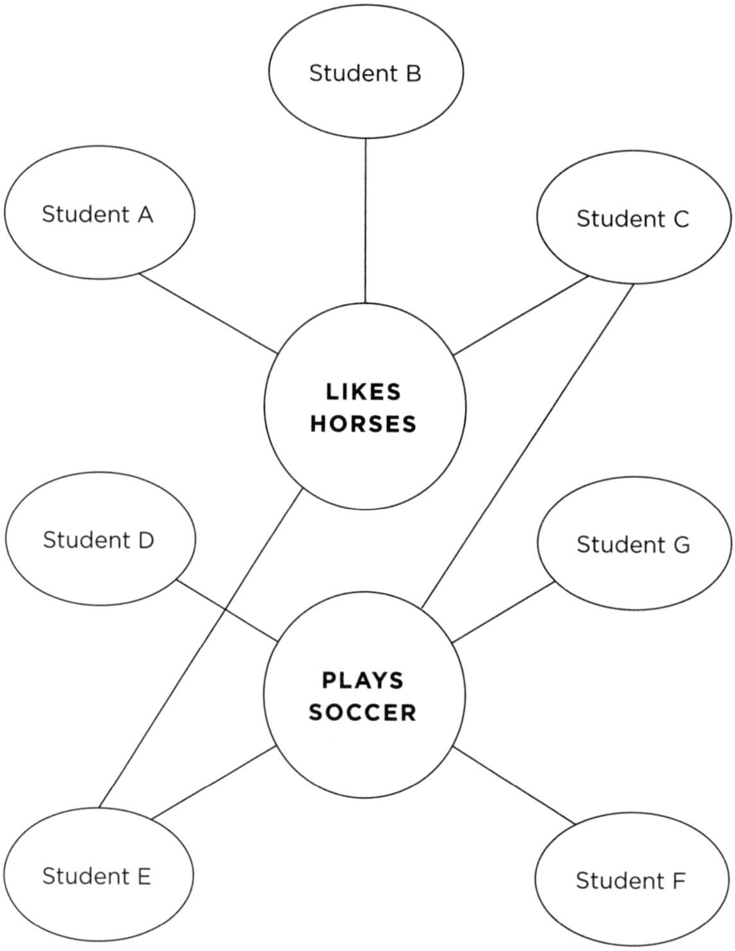

TOOL 2: INDIVIDUAL INTEREST INVENTORY

Purpose

Get to know your students as kids—*as young humans*. To generate (or surface) motivation and engagement, ask the following questions (ideally, one on one) and use their responses to craft meaningful, relevant experiences.

Elementary

Part 1: About You

1. Something I am really good at: ____________________
2. Something I like to do after school: ____________________
3. Something special about me: ____________________
4. Someone I look up to: ____________________
5. If you could teach the class something fun, what would it be? ____________________

   ____

Part 2: How School Feels

6. School usually feels: happy / OK / hard / boring / ____________________
7. My favorite part of school: ____________________
8. The hardest part of school for me: ____________________
9. School feels important when: ____________________
10. School feels frustrating when: ____________________
11. If school were an animal, what animal would it be? Why? ____________________

    ____

Part 3: Learning and Trying

12. I try my best in class when: ____________________
13. It's hard for me to pay attention when: ____________________
14. When work feels too hard, I usually: ____________________
15. One thing that helps me want to learn: ____________________
16. When my energy runs out at school, it feels like: ____________________

Part 4: Help and Feelings

17. Things that make learning hard for me: ____________________
18. When I need help, I: ask / wait / feel shy / don't know how / ____________________
19. Asking for help is hard because: ____________________
20. When school feels tough, my body feels: tired / wiggly / upset / quiet /

    ____

Part 5: Friends and Belonging

21. I feel like I belong in this class: yes / sometimes / no / ____________________
22. I feel happy at school when: ____________________
23. I feel left out at school when: ____________________
24. There is an adult at school who helps me feel safe: yes / maybe / no / ____________________
25. In our class, I feel like I am a: helper / learner / leader / quiet observer / ____________________

Part 6: Looking Ahead

26. One thing my teacher could do to help me: ____________________
27. One thing I want my teacher to know about me: ____________________
28. One goal I want to work on: ____________________
29. Is there anything else you want to tell your teacher? ____________________
30. If school were just right for you, what would it look like? ____________________

Teacher Reflection Questions

What does this kid enjoy and feel confident about?

Where does the kid seem frustrated, confused, or disconnected?

What helps this kid feel safe and successful?

What is one simple change I can try this week?

How will I check back in with this kid?

Secondary

Part 1: About You

1. Something I'm good at (in or out of school): ____________________
2. Something I enjoy doing outside of school: ____________________
3. One thing people might be surprised to know about me: ____________________
____
4. Someone I respect or look up to: ____________________
5. If you could teach the class anything at all, what would you teach? ________
____

Part 2: How School Feels to You

6. In general, school feels: enjoyable / OK / stressful / boring / frustrating / mixed / ____________________
7. The parts of school that feel easiest for me: ____________________
8. The parts of school that feel hardest for me: ____________________
9. School feels meaningful to me when: ____________________
10. School feels pointless or frustrating when: ____________________
11. If school were a movie or TV show, what genre would it be for you right now? Why? ____________________

Part 3: Engagement and Motivation

12. I feel most motivated in a class when: ____________________
13. It's hardest for me to stay engaged when: ____________________
14. When I don't try or shut down in class, it's usually because: ____________________
____
15. One thing that makes a class feel worth my effort: ____________________
16. If your motivation were a battery, when does it drain or recharge? ________
____

Part 4: Barriers and Support

17. Things that sometimes get in the way of my learning: ____________________
____
18. When I need help, I usually: ask / wait / avoid / feel unsure /____________
19. What makes it hard to ask for help? ____________________
20. When school feels overwhelming, what does it feel like in your body? _____
____

Part 5: Belonging and Relationships

21. I feel like I belong in this class: yes / sometimes / not really / Why? ________
____
22. I feel noticed and valued at school when: ________________________
23. I feel invisible at school when: ____________________________
24. There is at least one adult at school who understands me: yes / maybe / no / Who? ________________________________
25. If this class were a team, what role do you feel like you play? __________
____

Part 6: Looking Forward

26. One thing my teacher could do to help me more: ________________
____
27. One thing I want my teacher to understand about me: ____________
____
28. A small goal I'd like to work toward right now: ________________
____
29. Is there anything else you want to share? ____________________
____
30. If school worked perfectly for you, what would be different? __________
____

Teacher Reflection Questions

What patterns or themes do I notice in the kid's responses?

What type of disengagement might be present (boredom, fear, confusion, belonging)?

What strengths or interests can I build on?

What is one small change I can make based on this feedback?

How will I follow up with the kid and check for progress?

TOOL 3: NAME THAT EMOTION

Purpose

This tool helps young people identify, recognize, and name various emotions. This builds self-awareness (which leads to the development of self-control, healthy expression of feelings, and greater resilience) and empathy (which leads to stronger connections with others, positive peer relationships, and healthier conflict resolution).

Directions

Using an emoji chart or an emotion wheel for reference, engage kids in any of the following activities during transition times, while lining up, during morning meetings, or intermittently in class to make connections to content, curriculum, or current learning (see examples of an emoji chart and emotion wheel following the list).

- **Charades:** Act out the emotion while classmates try to guess it.
- **Pictionary:** Draw the emotion while classmates try to guess it.
- **Connect with content:** Identify and name emotions that a character in a story, a figure in history, or an individual in a current event may be feeling. Discuss why those emotions may be present and how they impact the person involved.
- **Connect with the moment:** Identify and name emotions that a kid may be feeling at any time during the class period or school day. Discuss what may have prompted that emotion, how it impacted the kid, and how the kid responded to that feeling.
- **Conduct emotional check-ins:** Use nine-grid graphics (see the example following the list) to help students connect with their current status. Discuss the realities of experiencing different emotions at different moments during the day.

Emoji Chart Example

Emotion Wheel Example

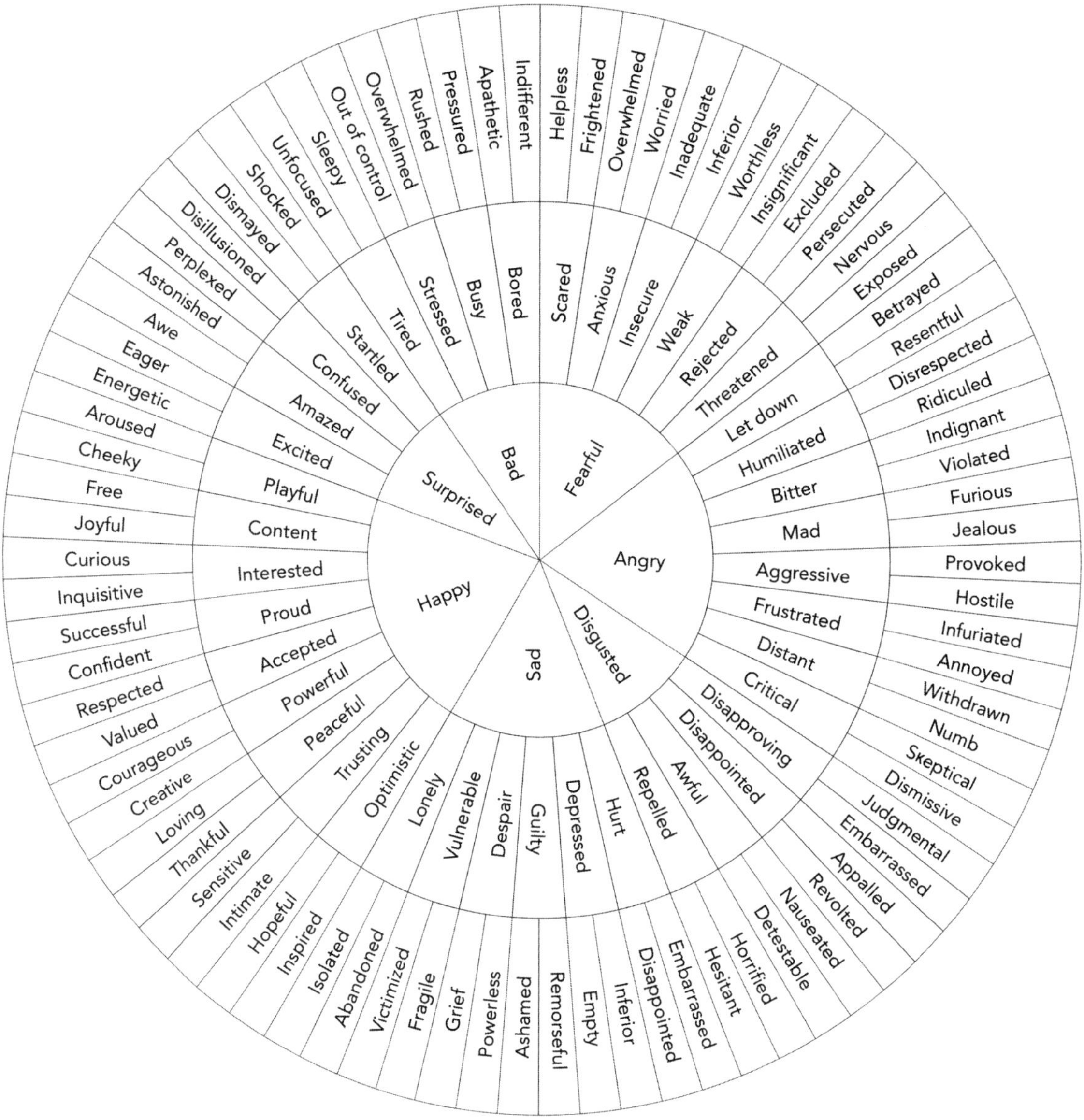

Source for wheel: Froehlich, M. (2025). The reignited educator: Rediscovering emotional engagement and purpose in your profession. *Solution Tree Press.*

Nine-Grid Graphic Example

TOOL 4: HERO INTERVIEW

Purpose

This tool enhances kids' self-worth by highlighting the uniqueness of every young person in a given setting and by sharing what makes you *you*.

Directions

After completing a characteristics web (tool 1, page 151), individual interest inventory (tool 2, page 153), strengths assessment, or another similar process for identifying strengths, characteristics, traits, and interests, ask your kids, one at a time, to prepare to introduce themselves to the class (or to a small group or a partner, depending on comfort) in the hero interview format.

- Place a chair in front of the class, group, or partner.
- Standing behind the empty chair, individuals will introduce themselves as if they were sitting in the chair, using third-person language. "This is LaMont. LaMont is in sixth grade at Cheldelin Middle School. He really likes baseball . . ." (Use third-person language, a practice called *illeism*, because it helps kids remain emotionally distanced and objective while increasing psychological safety and enhancing honesty.)
- The introduction will include an overview of a few key characteristics that describe them, including those that are unique, special, and worthy of celebration (hint: everything's worthy of celebration). If you wish, individual kids can go into greater detail about one of their key characteristics and how it shows up in their lives.

For a fun twist, you could engage in this activity as *two truths and a lie*, *Would you rather . . . ?*, or even charades, in which kids act out their skills and strengths.

The following questions may help get your kids' wheels turning.

- What is something you feel is unique about you?
- What hobby do you really enjoy?
- When are you most successful?
- What's something you do well that others ask you to help them with?
- What's a dream you had recently?
- What are three words you use to describe yourself?
- What are three words you'd like other people to use to describe you?

TOOL 5: STUDENT ATTENDANCE REFLECTION QUESTIONNAIRE

Purpose

This tool assists educators and parents in identifying and addressing attendance concerns. It enhances transparency, partnership, and communication in meeting the kid's needs and reaching the goal of consistent attendance.

Directions

As a team, including parents (and, as appropriate, the kid), engage in an open, robust conversation and complete the following form to identify root causes and underlying issues of attendance concerns. Work together to create a plan to resolve the concerns.

Part 1: Basic Information

Kid's Name: ______________________________

Grade: ______________________ Date: ______________

Completed by: ☐ Family member ☐ Teacher ☐ Both

Part 2: Attendance Patterns

1. How many days of school has the kid missed in the past month?
   ☐ 0–2 ☐ 3–5 ☐ 6–10 ☐ More than 10
2. Are absences typically:
   ☐ Consecutive (several in a row)
   ☐ Scattered (one here and there)
   ☐ Mostly partial days (arriving late or leaving early)
3. When the kid is absent, what reasons are usually given?
   ☐ Illness ☐ Family needs ☐ Transportation issues ☐ Anxiety or stress
   ☐ Other: ______________
4. When the kid is absent, what day or days of the week is it? (Fill in the number of absences on that particular weekday.)
   Mon: ______ Tue: ______ Wed: ______ Thu: ______ Fri: ______

Part 3: Kid Factors

5. How does the kid feel about school?
   ☐ Enjoys it ☐ Neutral ☐ Often dislikes it ☐ Refuses to attend
6. Does the kid talk about challenges with:
   ☐ Friends or peers ☐ Teachers or classes ☐ Academic pressure
   ☐ Safety concerns ☐ Bullying or harassment ☐ None known
7. Does the kid show signs of stress, worry, or physical complaints (headaches, stomachaches) on school mornings?
   ☐ Often ☐ Sometimes ☐ Rarely ☐ Never

Part 4: Family and Home Factors

8. Is there a consistent morning routine for getting ready and getting to school on time?
   ☐ Yes ☐ Sometimes ☐ No
9. Are there transportation challenges (such as car, bus, distance, or schedule)?
   ☐ Yes ☐ Sometimes ☐ No
10. Has anything changed recently in the home or family that might affect attendance (for example, move, new job, family stress, or health)?
    ☐ Yes ☐ No
    If yes, please describe (optional): ____________________

Part 5: School Factors

11. To what extent does the kid feel a sense of belonging at school?
    ☐ Very ☐ Somewhat ☐ Not very ☐ Not at all
12. Does the kid have at least one trusted adult at school?
    ☐ Yes ☐ Not sure ☐ No
    If yes, who is one trusted adult? ____
13. Are there academic struggles or gaps making school more difficult?
    ☐ Yes ☐ Somewhat ☐ No
14. Are there disciplinary or behavioral issues making school more difficult?
    ☐ Yes ☐ Somewhat ☐ No

Part 6: Solutions and Supports

15. What has helped the kid attend more regularly in the past?

16. What might make it easier for the kid to come to school consistently?

17. What support can the school or family provide to improve attendance?

TOOL 6: MY GOALS THAT MATTER GOAL-SETTING TEMPLATE

Purpose

This tool assists educators and parents in eliciting meaningful, self-concordant goals from kids, coupling them with clear, direct action plans. As the saying goes, "Life without goals is like a race without a finish line."

Directions

Sit down with the kid (and parents, as appropriate); ask the following questions; and engage in an open, honest, judgment-free conversation. Adapt the questions as needed for the kid's age and developmental readiness. Together, create a clear goal statement and a plan for accomplishing it, set benchmarks for monitoring progress, and revise the plan along the way.

Name of kid: ______________________________ Date: ____________

Part 1: Self-Reflection

- Awareness
    - What are some things you feel confident about in school and life right now?
    - What feels challenging, difficult, or frustrating for you?
    - How would you honestly describe your effort and focus lately?
- Analysis
    - What patterns do you notice when things go well for you?
    - What patterns do you notice when things don't go as well?
    - Who or what influences your habits and choices the most?
- Alternatives or options
    - What strategies, habits, or changes might help you grow?
    - Who could support you as you make these changes?
- Action
    - Choose one main area you want to work on improving.

Area of Focus:

Part 2: Goal Setting (Academic and Life Goals)

Write down an academic or curricular goal. (Tip: Write this goal in the form of a question that you want to answer.)

- Goal: ______________________________
- Why this goal matters to me: ______________________________
- Steps I will take to work toward this goal:
    - ______________________________
    - ______________________________
    - ______________________________
- How I will track my progress: ______________________________
- What support I need and from whom: ______________________________

Write down a personal or life goal. (This can be based on your character, habits, health, passions, relationships, and so on. Tip: Write this goal in the form of a question that you want to answer.)

- Goal: ______________________________
- Why this goal matters to me: ______________________________
- Steps I will take to work toward this goal:
    - ______________________________
    - ______________________________
    - ______________________________
- How I will track my progress: ______________________________
- What support I need and from whom: ______________________________

Part 3: Check-In and Reflection

- How will I know I am improving?
- What signs, results, or feelings will show progress?

Check-In Date: ____________________

- What went well? How do I know? Why did it go well?
- What didn't go well? How can I tell? Why didn't it go well?
- What will I adjust moving forward?

Part 4: Commitment

Kid's Signature: ______________________________ Date: ______________

Teacher/Advisor/Mentor Signature: ____________________ Date: ______________

TOOL 7: COMMUNICATION AUDIT

Purpose

This tool assists educators in assessing and analyzing their communication approaches and effectiveness with parents. Information gleaned from this audit can help streamline future communication for stronger partnerships and greater impact.

Directions

As a team, discuss portions (or all) of the following questions. Seek and supply evidence to support your responses. When appropriate, utilize quantitative data (such as numbers, facts, and dates) as opposed to relying solely on qualitative input (such as stories, examples, and comments). Use the reflective questions at the end of the audit to strategically plan for stronger future communication.

School-Home Communication Audit

1. Goal (outcome or why)
    a. What is the primary purpose of our communication with families?
    b. Is the purpose clear in the message we send?
    c. Are we communicating to inform, build partnership, celebrate, problem solve, conduct a survey, or request support?
    d. Do families understand why this communication matters for their child?
2. Method (how—and how many)
    a. What communication methods are we currently using? (Examples: email, text, calls, app, newsletters, and in-person)
    b. Are we using multiple modes so that families have more than one path to receive information?
    c. Are our communication methods accessible (language, tech, timing, and tone)?
    d. Do we proactively ask parents which methods work best for them?
3. Frequency (when—multiple touches over time)
    a. How regularly do we communicate with families?
    b. Is our communication predictable or only in response to problems?
    c. Do we balance positive outreach with informative and corrective messages?
    d. Do families receive enough repetition to remember key information without being overloaded?

4. Call to action (what families are being asked to do)
    a. In each message, is it clear what we are asking families to do, if anything?
    b. Is the request specific, reasonable, and achievable?
    c. Do we explain how the action supports kids' success?
    d. Do we communicate next steps in a way that reduces confusion or hesitation?
5. Invitation (input, voice, and partnership)
    a. Do we provide opportunities for families to respond, ask questions, or offer input?
    b. Do we signal that we welcome feedback or ideas?
    c. Do we create opportunities for families to share what they know about their child?
    d. Are family voices incorporated into goals, plans, celebrations, and problem solving?
6. Response to the response (engagement in return)
    a. When families do respond, how do we reply?
    b. Do we follow up promptly, respectfully, and personally?
    c. Do we close the loop (that is, confirming receipt, thanking them, and updating next steps)?
    d. Are family responses used to inform decisions, adjustments, or next communications?

Summary Reflection Questions

- Which of the six elements are we doing best right now?
- Which element needs the most immediate attention?
- What is one improvement we could implement this month that would strengthen partnership with families?

TOOL 8: AUTHENTIC SCHOOL-HOME PARTNERSHIP TIPS

Purpose

This tool assists educators in building and curating strong, kid-centered partnerships with parents and families.

Directions

Together with staff and families (and kids, as appropriate), read through the following core principles for school-home partnerships. Together, decide on a handful of strategies, approaches, and agreements that will foster a sense of shared purpose and support the healthy development of each kid.

1. Lead With Respect and Assumption of Positive Intent

Family members care deeply about their children, even if it doesn't always show in the ways schools might expect.

- Start from: "We're on the same team."

This mindset softens tone, increases trust, and reduces defensiveness.

2. Prioritize Listening Before Advising

Family members are more open when they feel heard.

- Ask questions like "What are your hopes?," "What are your concerns?," and "What do you see at home?"
- Listen without interrupting or preparing your response.
- Reflect what you heard before offering your guidance.

This builds collaboration rather than compliance.

3. Communicate Frequently, Proactively, and Specifically

Don't wait for problems to arise before reaching out.

- Keep interactions short, warm, and concrete: "Today, Melissa showed real persistence when solving a tough word problem. She stuck with it!"
- Avoid vague praise: "Melissa did great today!" is too generic to build trust.

Positive contact before any concerns makes future conversations easier.

4. Value Family Members as Experts on Their Children

Family members know:

- Their child's stress signals
- What motivates them
- Cultural context and community realities

Say it explicitly: "You know your child best. I'd love to learn from you." This statement is powerful.

5. Be Culturally Responsive Without Making Assumptions

- Avoid requiring parents to change to match school norms.
- Instead, adapt communication and involvement to what works for them.

Example: If a family member doesn't attend evening meetings, ask, "What's the easiest way for us to stay connected?"

6. Use Strengths-Based Language

- Start every conversation with what is going well. This communicates belief in the child, which sets the emotional tone.
- Instead of saying, "He's behind in reading and needs more focus," try saying, "He is curious and asks great questions. If we help build reading stamina, his curiosity can really shine."

Strengths-first messaging improves engagement and strengthens partnership.

7. Be Transparent and Explain the Why Behind Decisions

Family members trust what they understand. Explain:

- What the school is trying to accomplish
- Why a strategy is being used
- What improvement looks like

Clear expectations reduce misunderstandings.

8. Share Data in Small, Understandable Pieces

Avoid large data dumps. Use:

- Plain language
- Visuals when possible
- Concrete next steps family members can try at home (simple, not time intensive)

Instead of saying, "Work on reading at home," try saying, "Read with your child for five minutes tonight. You read one page, and they read the next."

Small wins build momentum, which increases confidence.

9. Invite Collaboration in Problem Solving

Use "we" language when asking questions.

- "What could we try together?"
- "How might we support him when frustration comes up?"

Collaboration increases commitment and reduces defensiveness.

10. Close the Loop

Always follow up.

- Send a short text or note about progress.
- Celebrate small successes.

This communicates: "I see your child. I see you. I care."

Tone and Phrasing That Helps

Use:

- "Let's plan together."
- "I want to make sure your child feels successful."
- "What's working well at home that we can bring into school?"

Avoid:

- "You need to . . ."
- "He always/never . . ."
- "We've already tried that."

The Most Important Mindset

Families are partners, not clients, obstacles, or spectators. The relationship is the intervention. Strong partnerships don't just support a child's learning; they amplify it.

TOOL 9: COGNITIVE INTEREST CUES

Purpose

This tool assists educators in hooking kids' interest in an upcoming activity, lesson, unit, or even an entire course, priming their brains for learning.

Directions

When planning a learning hook, take the following key characteristics and success steps into consideration. Refer to the examples in the chart as needed.

Key Characteristics of Effective Cognitive Interest Cues

1. **They relate directly to the learning outcomes:** Effective cognitive interest cues go beyond simple attention-getters by connecting our kids' curiosity to the topic and learning at hand.
2. **They're hands-on . . . which leads to minds-on:** Incorporating movement, manipulatives, or something tangible creates an opportunity for kids to apply their mental focus to the cognitive interest cue.
3. **They help kids make personal connections:** Learning is all about connections, and momentum builds when we can use cognitive interest cues to connect the *learning* to the *learner* in a personal way (tapping into interests, strengths, or relevance).
4. **They're cognitively challenging:** Effective cognitive interest cues cause our kids' brains to fire and for the wheels to turn. We want to position our kids in the Zone of Proximal Development.

Success Steps for Building Effective Cognitive Interest Cues

Step 1: Activate prior learning to create a knowledge gap.

- You know ___________, but did you know ___________?

Here are some examples.

Language Arts	Have you ever finished reading something and realized you didn't absorb much of it? How can we read closely so this doesn't happen?	Have you noticed how people can view the same event quite differently? During this unit, we'll learn to appreciate how writers' different cultures and experiences influence their views.
Mathematics	We've used linear equations to depict consistent proportional relationships. But what if relationships aren't consistently proportional?	How can we use what we've learned about mathematical modeling to predict the amount of water needed to support population growth in arid areas, like the western United States?

Science	You've all seen living things grow. What do you think may be going on deep inside them to make them grow?	If you've been near a beach in the summer, you've likely experienced daytime sea breezes and nighttime land breezes. What scientific principles might explain this phenomenon?
Social Science	Have you heard people criticize the president and other elected leaders? Did you know that in many nations such criticism is illegal? How did we get this right?	We've seen how Rome struggled to maintain an empire spread across vast bodies of water, land areas, and distinctly different cultures. What might be different for an empire, such as China, as they spread into more geographically and culturally cohesive regions?
Arts	We've learned about the rules of minor chords and scales. What would it sound like if we broke those rules with additional chromatic notes called *blue notes*?	Based on what you've learned about modern dance in the United States, in what ways does it reflect the unique culture, heritage, and people of this country?

Step 2: Spark curiosity through the following.

Mysteries

- What caused the woolly mammoth to go extinct?
- How could the vastly outnumbered Continental Army have defeated the British Empire?
- How did people know what time it was before clocks were invented?

Controversy

- Are we victims of fate like the "star-crossed lovers" Romeo and Juliet, or do we have control over our circumstances?
- One way to reduce greenhouse gases would be to build nuclear power plants. After exploring the pros and cons of this energy source, what do you think?
- Is there another way to calculate the area of this irregular shape? Which is better and why?
- "Social media does young people more harm than good." How would you respond to this statement, using facts and logic to support your argument?

Riddles and Suspense

- We've seen that Ralph and Jack have very different personalities. They're both leaders, yet tension is brewing between them. What do you think will happen now that the boys are alone on the island?
- We know that mixing baking soda and vinegar together creates carbon dioxide. What will happen when we pour this mixture into a jar with a lit candle?

- We've seen complex alliances formed across Europe in the early 20th century. What might happen if a leader of one of these nations is assassinated?
- At what point does a square become a rectangle?
- How do scientists measure the distance to faraway planets?

Cognitive Conflict

- When players make several shots in a row in a basketball game, do they really have a "hot hand" (like many people think), or does that streak of successful shots just reflect random mathematical probability?
- A lot of students think the best way to study is to reread a chapter many times. As it turns out, that's not true. Today, we'll learn a better strategy.
- When a smaller nation encounters a larger one in a military conflict, does the larger nation always prevail? Not always!
- Which is cooler, the metal part of your chair or the fabric part? As it turns out, they're both the same temperature. The metal part feels cooler to the touch because of something we'll learn about today called *heat transfer*.

Step 3: Make it relevant by asking the following questions.

- How will kids use what they learn?
- How will kids use this outside of school?
- How does this relate to their lives?
- How might kids use this to help others?

Source: © 2025 by McREL Institute. Based on Goodwin, B., & Rouleau, K. (2022). The new classroom instruction that works: The best research-based strategies for increasing student achievement. *ASCD. Used with permission.*

TOOL 10: BLOOM'S REVISED TAXONOMY TASKS

Purpose

This tool assists educators in creating a mix of questions, activities, and assessments that address varying levels of cognitive complexity.

Directions

Use the following chart (based on Bloom's revised taxonomy) to identify learning objectives, curate tasks, and stimulate thinking. While there is no set formula for which level or levels to use with what frequency, the ideal application would be to incorporate higher-order-thinking skills (those farther to the right on this chart) that elicit the *just-right* amount of cognitive challenge.

Source for table: © 2025 by TeachThought. Used with permission.

Source for levels: Anderson, L. W., & Krathwohl, D. R. (Eds.). (2001). A taxonomy for learning, teaching, and assessing: A revision of Bloom's taxonomy of educational objectives. *Allyn & Bacon.*

Remembering	Understanding	Applying	Analyzing	Evaluating	Creating
Copying	Annotating	Acting out	Calculating	Arguing	Blogging
Defining	Posting	Articulating	Categorizing	Validating	Building
Finding	Associating	Reenacting	Breaking down	Testing	Animating
Locating	Tagging	Loading	Correlating	Scoring	Adapting
Quoting	Summarizing	Choosing	Deconstructing	Assessing	Collaborating
Listening	Relating	Determining	Linking	Criticizing	Composing
Googling	Categorizing	Displaying	Mashing	Commenting	Directing
Repeating	Paraphrasing	Judging	Mind-mapping	Debating	Devising
Retrieving	Predicting	Executing	Organizing	Defending	Podcasting
Outlining	Comparing	Examining	Appraising	Detecting	Wiki building
Highlighting	Contrasting	Implementing	Advertising	Experimenting	Writing
Memorizing	Commenting	Sketching	Dividing	Grading	Filming
Networking	Journaling	Experimenting	Deducing	Hypothesizing	Programming
Searching	Interpreting	Hacking	Distinguishing	Measuring	Simulating
Identifying	Grouping	Interviewing	Illustrating	Moderating	Role playing
Selecting	Inferring	Painting	Questioning	Posting	Solving
Tabulating	Estimating	Preparing	Structuring	Predicting	Mixing
Duplicating	Extending	Playing	Integrating	Rating	Facilitating
Matching	Gathering	Integrating	Attributing	Reflecting	Managing
Bookmarking	Exemplifying	Presenting	Estimating	Reviewing	Negotiating
Bullet pointing	Expressing	Charting	Explaining	Editorializing	Leading

TOOL 11: MOTIVATIONAL INTERVIEWING GUIDELINES

Purpose

This tool guides educators through a conversation with a kid to explore un- or underutilized motivation to engage or to make a change.

Directions

Use the essential mindframes to maintain the proper headspace and engagement with the kid while proceeding through the following nine steps.

Essential Mindframes

- Motivational interviewing is a guiding style of communication. We don't tell kids what to do.
- Motivational interviewing is designed to empower people to change. We don't force the change.
- Motivational interviewing is based on respect and curiosity. We don't pass judgments on kids.

Nine Steps for Motivational Interviewing

Step 1: Ask permission to discuss the important issue.

- "Do you mind if we talk about [insert behavior]?"

Step 2: Ask about the positive aspects (good things) of the target behavior.

- "What are some of the good things about [insert behavior]?"
- "People usually [insert behavior] because it has benefited them in some way. How has [insert behavior] benefited you?"

Step 3: Ask about the negative aspects (not as good things) of the target behavior.

After hearing the responses, summarize the negatives for the kid.

- "Can you tell me about the downside to [insert behavior]?"
- "What are some aspects you are not so happy about?"
- "What are some of the things you would not miss if you stopped [insert behavior]?"

Step 4: Use change rulers.

Ask open-ended questions and use a 1–10 scale.

- "On a scale where 1 is not at all important and 10 is extremely important, how important is it to you to change [insert behavior]?"
- "Why are you at a ________ and not [insert lower number]?"
- "What might happen that could move you from a ________ to a [insert higher number]?"

- "On a 1–10 scale, how confident are you that you could change [insert behavior]?"
- "On a 1–10 scale, how ready are you to change [insert behavior]?"

Step 5: Explore life goals.

These goals will be the pivotal point against which costs and benefits are weighed. Use affirmations to support positive goals and values. Point out ways in which current behaviors are not in line with goals and values.

- "What sorts of things are important to you?"
- "What sort of person would you like to be?"
- "What do you value most in life?"
- "If things worked out in the best possible way for you, what would you be doing a year from now?"

Step 6: Ask evocative questions.

- Looking forward: "Where would you like to be in ________ years? What do you hope will be different? And how does [insert behavior] fit into that?"
- Looking back: "Remembering a time when things were better, what were you doing differently?"
- Querying extremes: "What is the best (or worst) thing that could happen if you tried to change [insert behavior]?"

Step 7: Elicit statements supporting self-efficacy (finding exceptions).

- "Last week you were not sure you could go one day without [insert behavior]. How were you able to be successful the entire week?"

Step 8: Give advice and feedback—with permission only.

- "Do you mind if we spend a few minutes talking about [insert replacement behavior]?"
- "What do you know about [insert replacement behavior]?"
- "Are you interested in learning more about [insert replacement behavior]?"
- "What do you think about that?"

Step 9: Ask for a decision.

- "Are you more clear about what you would like to do?"
- "On a 1–10 scale, what are the chances you will take your next step?"
- If there is no decision, empathize with the difficulty of ambivalence. "It can be hard to make a decision. What do you think would help you make a decision?"
- If the decision is to continue the behavior, return to step 1 at a future time.

TOOL 12: STUDENT VOICE SCALES

Purpose

This tool assists educators in assessing their student voice practices. It includes an eleven-item survey for school-level strategies and a seventeen-item survey for classroom-level approaches.

Directions

Use one or both of the surveys on pages 2 and 3 of this tool to collect data about the perception of student voice in your setting. Analyze the data to create a plan to increase or enhance your setting's student voice practices.

Survey 1: School-Level Strategies

Themes:

Questions 1–3: Opportunities—Seeking input and collaborative decision making

Questions 4–6: Participation

Questions 7–11: Responsiveness

Survey 1: School-Level Strategies	Strongly Disagree	Disagree	Agree	Strongly Agree
1. Students give ideas about how to improve our school.				
2. Students help identify what needs to be improved in our school.				
3. Students partner with adults to make decisions about how to improve our school.				
4. I have participated in at least one of the opportunities available at school to share my ideas about how to improve our school.				
5. I give ideas to school leaders about how to improve the school when I am asked.				
6. I give ideas to school leaders about how to improve the school, even when I am not asked.				
7. My school has opportunities to hear from all students about how to improve our school.				
8. My school seeks out the ideas of the students who are having the hardest time in school about how to improve our school.				
9. School leaders listen to students' ideas about how to improve our school.				
10. School leaders take action based on students' ideas about how to improve our school.				
11. School leaders tell us how students' ideas were used to improve our school.				

Survey 2: Classroom-Level Strategies

Themes:

Questions 1–8: Opportunities—Seeking input and feedback

Questions 9–13: Opportunities—Collaborative decision making

Questions 14–17: Responsiveness

Survey 2: Classroom-Level Strategies	Strongly Disagree	Disagree	Agree	Strongly Agree
1. My teacher asks students how they learn best.				
2. My teacher asks whether they should slow down or speed up their teaching.				
3. My teacher asks students what they want to learn about in the class.				
4. My teacher asks for students' ideas about how to make the classroom better.				
5. My teacher asks for students' suggestions about how they can get better at teaching.				
6. My teacher asks students what kinds of classroom activities they want more or less of.				
7. My teacher asks students what kinds of assignments they want more or less of.				
8. My teacher asks for students' ideas about how to create a classroom where everyone feels like they belong.				
9. My teacher invites students to come up with classroom rules.				
10. My teacher gives students opportunities to teach with them.				
11. My teacher works with students to plan lessons.				

	Strongly Disagree	Disagree	Agree	Strongly Agree
12. My teacher works with students to decide what to learn as a class (for example, which topics to study or which books to use).				
13. My teacher works with students to decide how students' work should be graded.				
14. My teacher actually listens to students' answers.				
15. My teacher takes students' answers and uses them.				
16. My teacher uses students' answers to make the classroom better.				
17. My teacher tells us how students' answers were used to make the classroom better.				

Source for surveys: This material is originally published by Sage Journals and is licensed under a Creative Commons Attribution 4.0 International License (https://creativecommons.org/licenses/by/4.0/). Adapted from Conner, J., Holquist, S. E., Mitra, D. L., & Boat, A. (2025). Measuring student voice practices: Development and validation of school and classroom scales. AERA Open, 11. *https://doi.org/10.1177/23328584251326893*

TOOL 13: CHOICE BOARDS

Purpose

This tool assists educators in offering options for kids to choose a topic, engage with an activity, demonstrate learning, or otherwise exhibit autonomy in a given educational experience or setting.

Directions

Use a grid (like the following) to provide options from which your kids can choose.

Hints for Successful Implementation

- Focus on the learning outcome first. Only include options that achieve the intended outcome.
- Invite students to contribute to the choices displayed.
- Make the choice board thematic and related to current events or interests.
- Include items with varying degrees of difficulty that require higher-order-thinking skills and provide scaffolding.
- Rotate the options regularly.
- Consider structured choices (Tic-Tac-Toe, pick three, bingo, and so on).
- Encourage kids to challenge themselves and each other.

Sample Choice Board

Project Choice Board Select a method to demonstrate your learning in this unit.		
Create a slideshow to accompany a presentation for the class. 	Record a news segment in which you deliver important information in real time. 	Perform a sock puppet reenactment of the events. 
Write a report (scholarly) that provides important details and historical context. 	Create a poster or infographic that summarizes the main points. 	Role-play an interview with a classmate (partner) of characters from the event. 

TOOL 14: TEN WAYS TO HELP YOUR KIDS STAY ACTIVE IN SCHOOL

Purpose

This tool assists educators in implementing strategies that incorporate movement and activity throughout the school day, untethering from desks, tables, and other sedentary methods, while keeping learning the priority.

Directions

Select a strategy from the list to weave body movement into a preplanned lesson or activity. The key is to maintain the integrity of the learning outcomes; learning is the priority, and these strategies can help accomplish the learning goals. As you learn and include more movement-based strategies, add them to the list.

1. **Stand and share:** This isn't law school; however, standing while answering a question or sharing information beats remaining seated any day.
2. **Vote with your feet:** Whenever you have to make a decision or ask a question with multiple choices, designate corners of the room for each option, and kids self-select the corner that matches their choice. This leads to great conversations, too.
3. **Gallery walk:** As kids complete projects or display learning on chart paper, post them around the room. Then, everyone moves about the room to view each other's work and offer feedback as appropriate.
4. **Charades:** Kids act out, gesture, or move to represent topics, vocabulary, events, or other curricular staples. This can be done in teams, as a whole class, or with partners. You can also consider Pictionary, Taboo, Password, Pyramid, Jeopardy!, or other games that include actions and interactions.
5. **Walk and talk:** Instead of simply turning to a partner to talk, how about a walkabout the room? Down the hallway? Across the courtyard? Some of our best conversations occur when we're shoulder to shoulder, moving in sync.
6. **Field trip:** You don't need a bus to gather your class and head outside, to the office, to the gym, or to a common area to continue a project or conversation. Sometimes a simple change of location can make a world of difference.
7. **Wall stations:** Post problems, questions, or tasks on the walls of the classroom. The kids must move about the room to address each of the postings in a designated amount of time.
8. **Find someone who . . . :** Got the same answer as you. Solved the problem differently than you. Has a different perspective than you. Agrees with you. Has a question. Needs help. The sky's the limit as this strategy encourages kids to get up, interact, and support each other.

9. **Scavenger hunt:** Kids have to find examples, synonyms, or solutions in their real-life settings. If needed, hide items or clues and consider it an Easter egg hunt.
10. **Use sign language:** The cognitive and communication benefits of using sign language for vocabulary, key concepts, and visual representation of learning are numerous, not to mention it includes movement, thought, and self-awareness. Start with one word and build from there!

Add your own ideas here:

TOOL 15: PLANNING FOR LEARNING ROAD MAP

Purpose

This tool guides educators as they construct activities, lessons, and units that follow the six phases of learning. This ensures focus, alignment, and a neuroscience-backed structure for ensuring the capture and retention of critical learning objectives.

Directions

With your collaborative team, discuss your students' learning goals and utilize the following frame (and related reflective prompts) to build a learning progression based on the six phases of learning.

1. **Become interested:** Because our brains ignore most of the stimuli they encounter, to learn anything, students must become interested in it—finding it personally relevant, meaningful, or intellectually stimulating.
2. **Commit to learning:** Learning takes mental effort, so students must commit to it—convincing their brains to stay "switched on" to learning.
3. **Focus on new learning:** To learn anything, students must focus on it in their short-term working memory. They do this best when material is both visual and verbal, and they can translate complex ideas into concrete examples and vocabulary terms.
4. **Make sense of learning:** Students' short-term working memories can juggle only small amounts of information at once. So, we must provide them with regular opportunities to pause and process new learning by connecting it to prior learning, thinking about the learning, and discussing it with peers.
5. **Practice and reflect:** Repetition is the key to long-term memory. To commit new learning to memory, students must practice it, attempt to recall it, think about it, or apply it multiple times.
6. **Extend and apply:** Ultimately, for new learning to stick, students must return to it in multiple ways—applying it, thinking about it, and using it to engage in personal and creative expression. So, to support deeper learning, we need to give students opportunities to extend and apply their learning.

Learning Plan Road Map

Use the following three-step process and accompanying questions to design the road map.

1. Identify how to hook and sustain student interest in learning. This is where you frame or anchor learning to help interest students using standards and benchmarks.

   Framing or anchoring learning so that students become interested

   - What's the goal (big idea, enduring understanding, or similar) of the unit?
   - Why do students need to learn it (what's their "What's in it for me" that compels them to focus)?
   - How will this hook student interest in learning?

   Ensuring students commit to learning

   - What are the learning intentions for students in this lesson or unit? (We will learn ________ so that ________)
   - What are the success criteria for this lesson or unit?
   - How will I involve students in identifying or developing their goals for learning?

2. Identify how to support active learning and help students consolidate learning.

   Directly teaching key concepts, knowledge, and skills during the unit

   - What knowledge and skills should students *visualize*?
   - What skills and processes will I model and demonstrate (such as with worked-out examples)?
   - What concepts will I show and illustrate (such as with graphics or illustrations)?
   - What knowledge should they *verbalize*?
   - What concepts do they need to be able to explain?
   - What vocabulary do they need to be able to use?

   Including opportunities for students to make sense of their learning

   - What skills do they need to practice in class?

- What questions will I ask to stimulate students' thinking about learning?

- When and how will I provide initial feedback?

- What opportunities will I give students to pause and process their learning?

3. Give students ample opportunities to practice, reflect, and deepen new learning.

   Helping students commit foundational knowledge and skills to memory

   - How will I use in-class quizzes ("quizzing to learn") to strengthen retention of learning?

   - How will I engage students in multiple independent practice sessions spread over time?

   - How and when will I engage students (especially those who struggle) in relearning to achieve mastery?

Helping students extend and apply foundational knowledge to engage in deeper learning

- What learning task (such as investigation, problem solving, or extended writing) will tap into student interests and challenge them to apply new knowledge and skills?

- What do students need to be thinking about during the learning task (in what way will it be hands-on and minds-on)?

- How will students demonstrate deep understanding of and ability to apply new learning (that is, what performance assessment or artifact of learning will they create)?

Source: © 2025 by McREL International and EducationHall, LLC. Used with permission.

TOOL 16: PERSONALIZED SUCCESS PLAN

Purpose

This tool helps educators create a personalized plan for kids to experience success in the school setting. This can be concentrated in a single course or expanded to a student's entire educational experience.

Directions

With your teammates (and the kid and family members, as appropriate), consider the following questions to identify a goal (short term, long term, or both) for a kid who's struggling. This work will provide a frame for building the kid's motivation and drive to engage in purposeful learning.

1. Student Information

- Kid's name: ____________________
- Grade or year: ____________________
- Date of plan: ____________________
- School or program: ____________________
- Team members: ____________________
- Review date: ____________________

2. Strengths and Interests

(List academic, personal, and social strengths; include interests, hobbies, and motivators. Examples: "Strong verbal skills," "Enjoys technology," "Good with hands-on activities," "Curious about science.")

3. Areas of Challenge or Concern

(Identify areas where the kid is struggling—academic, behavioral, social-emotional, organizational, and so on.)

4. Student Goals

(Create two to four specific, measurable goals. Use the SMART format when possible—specific, measurable, achievable, relevant, time bound.)

Goal	Goal Description	Success Criteria	Timeline	Responsible Party
1				
2				
3				
4				

5. Targeted Supports and Strategies

(List accommodations, strategies, and interventions that will help the kid reach the goals. These can be classroom based, behavioral, or social-emotional.)

A. Academic Supports

- ☐ Extended time on assignments and tests
- ☐ Graphic organizers or outlines
- ☐ Frequent check-ins with teacher
- ☐ Reduced workload or chunked tasks
- ☐ Alternative ways to show learning (such as oral, visual, or project-based)
- ☐ Tutoring or peer mentoring

B. Behavioral and Social-Emotional Supports

- ☐ Daily or weekly check-in/checkout system
- ☐ Positive behavior reinforcement plan
- ☐ Social skills coaching or counseling
- ☐ Calm-down or break area
- ☐ Journaling or reflection prompts

C. Organizational Supports

- ☐ Assignment planner or digital calendar
- ☐ Color-coded folders or binders
- ☐ Regular progress-monitoring meetings
- ☐ Home communication log

(Add or remove supports as needed.)

6. Student Voice and Self-Advocacy

(Ask the kid to describe how they feel about their learning and what helps them succeed.)

- What helps you do your best in school?

- What makes learning harder for you?

- What goals do you want to work on?

7. Progress Monitoring and Review

- Progress review dates: ____________________
- Data collection methods (grades, teacher feedback, self-assessments, observations, and so on): ____________________
- Adjustments needed: ____________________

8. Signatures

By signing the following, all parties agree to collaborate and support the student's success through the strategies outlined in this plan.

Role	Name	Signature	Date
Kid			
Family Member(s)			
Teacher			
Counselor or Support Staff			

Notes or Additional Comments:

TOOL 17: TARGETED INTERVENTION PLANNER

Purpose

This tool assists educators in maintaining a laser-like focus on the key learning goals during intervention periods, focusing support for student growth and mastery.

Directions

Individually or with your collaborative team, consider the following questions to clarify the intended outcome of the proposed intervention for your kid. Then ensure that every moment of the intervention period is aligned toward that outcome and leads unilaterally to your kid's success.

1. Student and Session Information

- Kid's name: ______________________________
- Grade or subject area: ______________________________
- Date of session: ______________________________
- Teacher or interventionist: ______________________________
- Plan period: ______________________________

2. Focus Area or Skill Target

Identify one specific skill or concept that the session will address. Examples: "Multiplying fractions with unlike denominators," "Reading fluency and expression," or "Organizing multistep writing tasks."

3. Data Source or Evidence of Need

Specify how you identified this skill as a priority. Use assessment data, classroom performance, or teacher observation.

Data Sources:

- ☐ Benchmark assessment
- ☐ Classroom observation
- ☐ Quiz or test
- ☐ Progress-monitoring data
- ☐ Writing sample
- ☐ Other: ______________________________

Brief description of data evidence:

4. Goal for Session or Series

Make it clear and measurable. What will the kid be able to do by the end of the session or series?

Goal:

Success criteria:

5. Instructional Strategies and Supports

List the methods and tools you'll use to teach or reinforce the target skill.

- ☐ Explicit modeling and guided practice
- ☐ Scaffolded steps or gradual release ("I do, we do, you do")
- ☐ Visuals or manipulatives
- ☐ Graphic organizers or anchor charts
- ☐ Alt-teaching in small group
- ☐ Use of technology tool or app: ______________________________
- ☐ Peer tutoring or partner work
- ☐ Corrective feedback and error analysis
- ☐ Real-world connection or applied example

Other strategy notes:

6. Student Practice or Application

Describe how the kid will demonstrate the skill during the session.

Practice activity:

Expected output or product:

7. Observation and Progress Monitoring

Document what you observed during or after the session.

Kid's engagement level:

- ☐ High
- ☐ Moderate
- ☐ Low

Accuracy or independence:

- ☐ Independent
- ☐ With prompts
- ☐ With full support

Evidence of progress:

Next steps or adjustments:

8. Reflection and Follow-Up

Summarize what worked and what will be targeted next time.

Educator reflection:

Kid reflection (optional):

Next session focus:

TOOL 18: FOUR STEPS TO SETTING UP AN EMPATHETIC CLASSROOM

Purpose

This tool assists educators in establishing a classroom environment characterized by empathy, social-emotional awareness, kindness, and compassion. It encourages educators to consider themselves as humans first, so kids and learning can flourish together.

Directions

Take the following four big ideas into consideration as you prepare to set up (or redefine) your classroom environment (or other instructional setting). Use the checklist to assess your curation of this empathetic environment on a weekly basis.

Four Big Ideas to Cultivate an Empathetic Classroom

Big Idea 1: Take Stock of Yourself

- Identify small daily practices that help you feel grounded, rested, and joyful.
- Intentionally incorporate one or two of these practices into your classroom routine.

Big Idea 2: Listen to Your Kids

- Ask kids (through conversation or writing) what helps them feel calm, energized, or supported.
- Observe their patterns throughout the day to understand how their needs show up in action.

Big Idea 3: Step Back for a Second

- Take a moment each day to observe your kids without directing them.
- Notice your own emotional state and adjust expectations or plans when beneficial.

Big Idea 4: Respond With Awareness

- Notice your tone, posture, and reactions, especially in moments of stress.
- When missteps occur, repair by acknowledging your part and naming how you will adjust.

Weekly Empathetic Classroom Checklist

1	I entered the classroom each day with at least one intentional self-care practice in place.	Yes	Sometimes	No
2	I observed my kids with curiosity rather than judgment.	Yes	Sometimes	No
3	I asked at least one kid what they needed or how they were feeling this week.	Yes	Sometimes	No
4	I adjusted expectations or routines in response to kids' observed needs.	Yes	Sometimes	No
5	I paused before reacting in emotionally charged moments.	Yes	Sometimes	No
6	I monitored my facial expressions, tone of voice, and body language when interacting.	Yes	Sometimes	No
7	I made a repair when I recognized that I caused harm or was incorrectly attuned to a kid's emotions.	Yes	Sometimes	No
8	I ended the week with reflection on what supported empathy and what needs attention next week.	Yes	Sometimes	No

Source: © 2026 by Maria Munro-Schuster. Adapted with permission.

TOOL 19: DAILY CHECKLIST FOR EFFECTIVE PRAISE

Purpose

This checklist assists educators in assessing (and refining) their language practices to build kids' self-esteem, self-confidence, intrinsic motivation, grit, and the mindset of success.

Directions

Scan the tip list (page 132) for opportunities to acknowledge your language, adapt or adjust your strategies, incorporate new tactics, or understand the rationale behind different approaches. Use the following daily checklist to reflect on your application and impact of effective praising practices.

Quick Daily Checklist for Teachers

Question	Examples	Notes
Did I notice specific effort or strategy today?	"I noticed how carefully you planned each step before starting—that shows great strategy." "You kept trying different ways until it worked. That perseverance really paid off."	
Did I provide descriptive feedback rather than generic praise?	"You summarized the main ideas in your own words and checked for accuracy—excellent attention to detail." "You asked clarifying questions when you weren't sure. That curiosity is how you learn best."	
Did I link success to controllable factors (effort, persistence, strategy)?	"Your careful proofreading shows you're developing strong habits." "You improved your score because you practiced consistently—that's real progress."	

Did I highlight progress or improvement, not just top performance?	"I can see how much better your paragraph structure is compared to last week." "Even though it was challenging, you didn't give up, and that persistence is paying off."	
Did I encourage reflection and self-awareness?	"You solved that problem using a method you developed yourself. What made it effective?" "You checked your answers carefully—how did that strategy help you succeed?"	
Was praise authentic and timely?	"I'm impressed by how focused you were during that group discussion—it made a big difference." "I noticed the effort you put into explaining your reasoning. That clarity helped everyone understand the concept."	
Did I support autonomy and intrinsic motivation?	"You chose a creative approach that reflects your own thinking—great decision!" "You decided to revise your draft before submitting, and it really improved your work."	
Did I balance praise across all students, not just high achievers?	"Your progress on this assignment shows that your consistent effort is paying off." "Even though this was tricky, you stayed with it—well done!"	

TOOL 20: 101 SELF-REGULATION STRATEGIES

Purpose

This tool assists educators in supporting kids' self-regulation by offering a variety of options and co-selecting strategies that work well.

Directions

Consider this list the buffet of self-regulation strategies. They've been divided into seven subcategories. Choose a strategy, and then, together with your kids, discuss it, practice it, assess it, and either add it to the go-to list (if it's helpful and accessible), adapt it (if there's a portion of it that might work better if changed), or discard it (if it's aggravating, distracting, or otherwise doesn't help). In a perfect world, each kid would have a go-to list of three to five effective, handy, quick, easy, calming strategies to use proactively to maintain self-regulation and responsively to self-regulate.

101 Self-Regulation Strategies

Physical Regulation Strategies

1. Take five slow deep breaths.
2. Do wall push-ups.
3. Squeeze a stress ball.
4. Walk to get a drink of water.
5. Stretch your arms overhead for ten seconds.
6. Do chair yoga poses.
7. Use hand fidgets or putty.
8. Take a short walk in the hallway.
9. Do a quick run (playground or gym).
10. Sit on a wobble cushion or therapy ball.
11. Lay on the floor for body pressure support.
12. Push your feet into the floor and hold.
13. Do slow neck rolls.
14. Practice "balloon belly" breathing.
15. Use a weighted lap pad.
16. Trace your hand while breathing (five-finger breathing).
17. Do jumping jacks for thirty seconds.
18. Use a "body sock" for compression.
19. Dance to a favorite song for thirty seconds.
20. Sit in a beanbag or soft chair.
21. Wrap up in a blanket like a burrito.
22. Blow on a pinwheel.
23. Do chair dips, holding onto the seat.

24. Blow bubbles (long, slow breaths).
25. Do windmill stretches or other cross-body movements.

Sensory Regulation Strategies

26. Chew crunchy or chewy snacks or gum (if allowed).
27. Listen to quiet music or nature sounds.
28. Smell calming scents (such as lavender or peppermint).
29. Use noise-canceling headphones.
30. Look at a calming visual (such as an aquarium video or lava lamp).
31. Hold something soft (such as a plushie or fabric square).
32. Keep a fidget drawer with options.
33. Sit in a low-light calming corner.
34. Dim the lights or use lamp lighting.
35. Use sunglasses or a brimmed hat indoors (for light sensitivity).
36. Tap fingers rhythmically on the desk.
37. Trace patterns or doodle.
38. Run hands under warm or cool water.
39. Hum or whistle.
40. Keep a smooth stone or "worry rock" in pocket.

Emotional Awareness Strategies

41. Name the feeling out loud (such as "I feel frustrated").
42. Use a mood meter or feelings chart.
43. Draw your emotion as a character.
44. Journal or write a quick feeling sentence.
45. Match your emotion as an emoji.
46. Identify where the emotion is in your body.
47. Hold your heart and take breaths.
48. Say, "This feeling will pass."
49. Use positive self-talk phrases.
50. Say, "I can handle this."
51. Practice "STOP" skills: Stop, Take a breath, Observe, Proceed.
52. Use a calming script (teacher or self-directed).
53. Share feelings with a trusted adult.
54. Play *emotion detective* by asking, "What cued this?"
55. Imagine your feeling as a wave that's rising and falling.

Focus and Attention Strategies

56. Use timers for work periods.
57. Break tasks into small steps.

58. Use a checklist to guide steps.
59. Highlight key instructions.
60. Have a "When I'm stuck . . ." routine.
61. Use visual schedules.
62. Work with a buddy for accountability.
63. Move seats or change your workspace.
64. Use screen blockers or folders to reduce visual distractions.
65. Color-code materials.
66. Take a sixty-second reset break between tasks.
67. Do one minute of silent breathing before tests.
68. Use finger tracking while reading.
69. Repeat instructions back to the teacher.
70. Practice whisper reading to stay on task.

Cognitive Regulation Strategies

71. Use "I wonder what will happen if . . ." curiosity prompts.
72. Think of three possible solutions to a problem.
73. Ask yourself, "Is this a small, medium, or big problem?"
74. Visualize your best outcome before starting.
75. Use "If . . . then . . ." plans (for example, "If I get frustrated, then I take a break").
76. Practice mental rehearsal of routines.
77. Make a plan A and a backup plan B.
78. Role-play common school challenges.
79. Identify unhelpful thoughts and rephrase them.
80. Use humor to reframe stress.
81. Practice gratitude by naming three things.
82. Set a tiny goal and achieve it.
83. Reflect on past success: "When else did I handle this?"

Social Regulation Strategies

84. Request a peer helper.
85. Ask for help before frustration peaks.
86. Practice tone of voice with a recording device.
87. Use sentence starters (such as "I need . . .," "Please wait . . .," and "I feel . . .").
88. Practice facial expressions and body language in a mirror.
89. Use a "time-in" with a caring adult.
90. Work in a smaller group for a short time.
91. Practice active listening (eyes, ears, and still body).
92. Learn a few key calming phrases to say to others.
93. Use kind humor to ease tension.

Mindfulness and Calm Thinking Strategies

94. Use guided visualization ("Imagine a calm place . . .").
95. Body scan from head to toes.
96. Count backward slowly from twenty.
97. Look around and name five things you can see.
98. Repeat a calming mantra (such as "I am safe" or "I'm doing my best").
99. Trace patterns or shapes slowly.
100. Sit quietly and notice sounds around you.
101. Do *nothing* for sixty seconds, engaging in stillness practice.

TOOL 21: TIPS FOR A MULTI-AGE ADVISORY PROGRAM

Purpose

This tool assists educators in building a multi-age advisory program that strengthens relationships, enhances culture, boosts belonging, and smooths transitions.

Directions

Consider the following tips when cocreating a multi-age advisory program in your school or district.

1. **Define Clear Goals**
    a. Decide what the program should achieve—academic mentoring, social-emotional learning, leadership development, or a mix.
    b. Cocreate a vivid, common vision of success together with all stakeholders.
    c. Align the advisory goals with the school's mission and student support priorities.

2. **Consider Thoughtful Group Composition**
    a. Mix ages intentionally, usually spanning two to three grade levels.
    b. Consider personality, academic strengths, and social-emotional needs to create balanced groups.
    c. Keep groups small enough (eight to twelve kids) for meaningful interaction.

3. **Train Advisers Thoroughly**
    a. Provide training on mentoring, conflict resolution, and facilitating reflective discussions.
    b. Encourage advisers to model empathy, active listening, and collaborative problem solving.

4. **Create Consistent Meeting Structures**
    a. Set a regular schedule (for example, one to two times per week for thirty to forty-five minutes).
    b. Have a flexible agenda with time for check-ins, goal setting, skill building, and informal social connection.

5. **Foster Leadership and Peer Mentoring**
    a. Encourage older kids to mentor younger peers academically and socially.
    b. Rotate leadership roles so every kid develops responsibility and ownership in the group.

6. **Integrate Social-Emotional Learning**
    a. Include activities that build self-awareness, empathy, resilience, and communication.
    b. Provide structured opportunities for reflection and discussion of real-life challenges.

7. **Encourage Long-Term Relationships**
    a. Keep kids in the same advisory for multiple years, if possible, to deepen trust and peer connections.
    b. Track kids' growth over time to measure the program's impact.

8. **Involve Families and the Community**
    a. Inform families about the purpose and benefits of multi-age advisories.
    b. Invite guest speakers or community members to contribute mentorship and enrichment experiences.

9. **Allow for Flexibility and Adaptation**
    a. Be ready to adjust group composition, meeting formats, or activities based on feedback.
    b. Regularly solicit input from kids, advisers, and families.

10. **Assess and Celebrate Growth**
    a. Use surveys, reflections, and anecdotal observations to assess social, emotional, and academic outcomes.
    b. Celebrate achievements and milestones to reinforce the value of the program.

TOOL 22: TIPS FOR A DIGITAL DETOX

Purpose

This tool assists educators—in partnership with kids, families, and other stakeholders—in creating a positive, community-building digital detox (cell phone ban) policy schoolwide.

Directions

Read through the following list together with staff, kids, families, and other stakeholders. Brainstorm strategies for implementing action steps that will create positive momentum and strengthen the school community while simultaneously removing cell phones from the educational environment.

1. Frame It as a Well-Being Initiative, *Not* a Restriction

Don't say, "We're banning phones."
Say, "We're reclaiming our attention, our relationships, and our learning."
Use language like the following.

- "We want students to feel more connected and less stressed."
- "We want recess and lunch to be social again."

Make it about *what students will gain*, not what they're losing.

2. Build the Vision *With* Students (Not *for* Them)

Create a *student advisory team* to codesign rollout messaging, posters, slogans, and celebrations.

Let students lead the movement.

- Student video testimonies: "Life without my phone at school actually helped me . . ."
- Peer-led assemblies or advisory conversations
- Student-designed murals or bulletin boards about "Being here. Actually here."

When students help shape the message, *commitment skyrockets*.

3. Clearly Define *When* Phones Are Put Away and *How*

Simplicity is key. Examples:

- "Off and away from bell to bell."
- Phones stored in one of the following.
    - Lockable classroom pouches
    - A homeroom "tech valet"
    - Personal lockers

Avoid exceptions that require ongoing negotiations. Clarity = consistency = less conflict

4. Pair It With Meaningful Positive Alternatives

Students need something *to do*—especially at recess, lunch, and break times. Stock up or launch the following.

- Yard games (cornhole, four square, spikeball, or giant chess)
- Conversation benches
- Art and coloring lounge spaces
- Music at lunch (student playlists!)
- Board games in common areas
- Staff who play too (major culture booster)

If we want students to interact, we have to create spaces and opportunities for interaction.

5. Train Adults to Model the Same Behavior

Students will watch what adults do. If teachers check phones constantly, students will resent the policy.

Possible staff commitment pledge:

> *"While students are here, I will be present with them. I will not use my phone during instructional time or student-facing supervision unless necessary."*

This builds trust, fairness, and culture.

6. Launch It Like a Celebration

Make the rollout *fun*, not heavy.

Ideas include the following.

- Human Connection Kickoff Week
- Spirit day themes (for example, "Talk to Someone New Tuesday")
- Raffles for participating in phone-free challenges
- Photo booth at lunch: "Be Here + Be Seen"
- Advisory conversation starters and games

The goal is a *positive vibe*, not compliance pressure.

7. Communicate Early, Often, and With Consistency

For families:
Share the *why*—better focus, less social pressure, more real relationships, healthier sleep cycles.

Send home the following.

- A one-page visual summary of the policy
- A short FAQ
- Research highlights (keep it brief and relatable)

Hold a community webinar titled: "Raising Tech-Healthy Kids in a Tech-Heavy World."

Families feel respected when they feel invited, not instructed.

8. Collect Feedback and Celebrate Wins

Two weeks in, ask the following questions.

- Students: "What's better? What's still hard?"
- Teachers: "Where are we consistent?"
- Families: "What changes have you noticed?"

Then, share stories.

- More talking at lunch
- Fewer hallway conflicts
- Better focus in class
- Students actually making eye contact again

Tell the success story out loud. Often.

9. Keep It Human, Not Perfect

There will be hiccups. Respond with calm consistency, not frustration.

The message is, "We're becoming a school that values presence and people," not "We're catching you doing something wrong."

Example School Motto: *"Phones Away, People Engaged: We're Better Together."*

Put it on posters, newsletters, announcements, t-shirts, and hallway displays.

REFERENCES AND RESOURCES

Abrahamsson, S. (2026). Smartphone bans, student outcomes and mental health. *Journal of Human Resources, 61*(2).

Accardo, A. L., Pontes, N. M. H., & Pontes, M. C. F. (2024). Heightened anxiety and depression among autistic adolescents with ADHD: Findings from the National Survey of Children's Health 2016–2019. *Journal of Autism and Developmental Disorders, 54*(2), 563–576.

Allen, K., Kern, M. L., Vella-Brodrick, D., Hattie, J., & Waters, L. (2018). What schools need to know about fostering school belonging: A meta-analysis. *Educational Psychology Review, 30*(1), 1–34.

Ambroso, E., Dunn, L., & Fox, P. (2021, September). *Research in brief: Engaging and empowering diverse and underserved families in schools.* WestEd. Accessed at https://ies.ed.gov/rel-west/2025/01/family-engagement-and-empowerment-brief on November 16, 2025.

American Psychological Association. (2018, April 19). *Anxiety.* Accessed at https://dictionary.apa.org/anxiety on November 16, 2025.

American Psychological Association. (2023, November 15). *Self-esteem.* Accessed at https://dictionary.apa.org/self-esteem on November 16, 2025.

Anderson, L. W., & Krathwohl, D. R. (Eds.). (2001). *A taxonomy for learning, teaching, and assessing: A revision of Bloom's taxonomy of educational objectives.* Allyn & Bacon.

Anderson, M. (2019). *What we say and how we say it matter: Teacher talk that improves student learning and behavior.* ASCD.

Ansari, A., & Gottfried, M. A. (2021). The grade-level and cumulative outcomes of absenteeism. *Child Development, 92*(4), e548–e564.

Ansari, A., Hofkens, T. L., & Pianta, R. C. (2020). Absenteeism in the first decade of education forecasts civic engagement and educational and socioeconomic prospects in young adulthood. *Journal of Youth and Adolescence, 49*(9), 1835–1848.

Arnold, L., & Croxford, J. (2025). Is it time to stop talking about authentic assessment? *Teaching in Higher Education, 30*(3), 735–743.

Attarha, M., de Figueiredo Pelegrino, A., Ouellet, L., Toussaint, P.-J., Grant, S.-J., Van Vleet, T., et al. (2025). Effects of computerized cognitive training on vesicular acetylcholine transporter levels using [18f]fluoroethoxybenzovesamicol positron emission tomography in healthy older adults: Results from the Improving Neurological Health in Aging via Neuroplasticity-based Computerized Exercise (INHANCE) randomized clinical trial. *JMIR Serious Games, 13*, Article e75161.

Axelrod, M. I., & Hupp, S. (Eds.). (2024). *Investigating school psychology: Pseudoscience, fringe science, and controversies.* Routledge.

Badcock, J. C., Holt-Lunstad, J., Garcia, E., Bombaci, P., & Lim, M. H. (2022). *Position statement: Addressing social isolation and loneliness and the power of human connection.* Global Initiative on Loneliness and Connection. Accessed at www.gilc.global/_files/ugd/410bdf_62e236db3a7146cd9f2654877a87dbc6.pdf on April 13, 2026.

Bailey, J. R., & Rehman, S. (2022). Don't underestimate the power of self-reflection. *Harvard Business Review.* Accessed at https://hbr.org/2022/03/dont-underestimate-the-power-of-self-reflection on November 16, 2025.

Balconi, M., Angioletti, L., & Acconito, C. (2023). Self-Awareness of Goals Task (SAGT) and planning skills: The neuroscience of decision making. *Brain Sciences, 13*(8), Article 1163.

Barshay, J. (2025, August 26). Students are missing a lot more school. Why chronic absenteeism may be here to stay. *Los Angeles Times.* Accessed at www.yahoo.com/news/articles/students-missing-lot-more-school-100000332.html on November 16, 2025.

Baumer, N., & Frueh, J. (2021, November 23). *What is neurodiversity?* [Blog post]. Harvard Health Publishing. Accessed at www.health.harvard.edu/blog/what-is-neurodiversity-202111232645 on November 16, 2025.

Beckner, V. L. (2023, September 26). The key we still rarely learn: How to feel your feelings [Blog post]. *Psychology Today.* Accessed at www.psychologytoday.com/us/blog/harnessing-principles-of-change/202010/the-key-skill-we-rarely-learn-how-to-feel-your-feelings on November 16, 2025.

Bernhard, R., McDermott, T., Hasenhüttl, C., Burn, K., & Sammons, P. (2024). A focus on quality of teaching in schools increases students' progress of attainment: Evidence from English secondary schools. *School Effectiveness and School Improvement, 35*(4), 506–530.

Blume, H. (1998, September). Neurodiversity: On the neurological underpinnings of geekdom. *The Atlantic.* Accessed at www.theatlantic.com/magazine/archive/1998/09/neurodiversity/305909 on April 13, 2026.

Borowski, T. (2019). *Search Institute's developmental assets framework.* Assessment Work Group. Accessed at https://searchinstitute.org/resources-hub/developmental-assets-framework on November 16, 2025.

Britannica. (2026, March 31). *Education in the earliest civilizations.* Accessed at www.britannica.com/topic/education/Education-in-the-earliest-civilizations on April 13, 2026.

Buch, E. R., Claudino, L., Quentin, R., Bönstrup, M., & Cohen, L. G. (2021). Consolidation of human skill linked to waking hippocampo-neocortical replay. *Cell Reports, 35*(10), Article 109193.

Burton, S., Raposa, E. B., Poon, C. Y. S., Stams, G. J. J. M., & Rhodes, J. (2022). Cross-age peer mentoring for youth: A meta-analysis. *American Journal of Community Psychology, 70*(1–2), 211–227.

Bushaw, W. J., & Lopez, S. J. (2012). Highlights of the 2012 PDK/Gallup poll: What Americans said about the public schools. *Phi Delta Kappan, 94*(1), 8–25.

Bushweller, K. (2019, January 8). The kids are right: School is boring. *Education Week.* Accessed at www.edweek.org/teaching-learning/the-kids-are-right-school-is-boring/2019/01 on November 16, 2025.

Busteed, B. (2013, January 7). *The school cliff: Student engagement drops with each school year* [Blog post]. Gallup. Accessed at https://news.gallup.com/opinion/gallup/170525/school-cliff-student-engagement-drops-school-year.aspx on November 16, 2025.

Buzzai, C., Sorrenti, L., Tripiciano, F., Orecchio, S., & Filippello, P. (2021). School alienation and academic achievement: The role of learned helplessness and mastery orientation. *School Psychology, 36*(1), 17–23.

Calderon-Villarreal, A., Garcia-Hernandez, A., Olvera-Gonzalez, R., & Elizondo-Garcia, J. (2025). Parental involvement barriers and their influence on student self-regulation in primary education. *Education and Urban Society, 57*(4), 327–346.

Centers for Disease Control and Prevention. (2025, June 5). *Data and statistics on children's mental health.* Accessed at www.cdc.gov/children-mental-health/data-research/index.html on April 21, 2026.

Chaarani, B., Ortigara, J., Yuan, D., Loso, H., Potter, A., & Garavan, H. P. (2022). Association of video gaming with cognitive performance among children. *JAMA Network Open, 5*(10), Article e2235721.

Chow, H. M., Knöll, J., Madsen, M., & Spering, M. (2021). Look where you go: Characterizing eye movements toward optic flow. *Journal of Vision, 21*(3), Article 19.

Clifton-Sprigg, J., & James, J. (2025). The "Friday Effect": School attendance over the week. *British Educational Research Journal, 51*(1), 73–92.

Coffin, C., & Mason, H. (2025, October 14). *Patterns and predictors of chronic absenteeism in D.C.'s middle and high schools.* D.C. Policy Center. Accessed at www.dcpolicycenter.org/publications/patterns-and-predictors-chronic-absenteeism-dc-middle-and-high-schools on November 16, 2025.

Cohen, G. L. (2022). *Belonging: The science of creating connection and bridging divides.* Norton.

Collie, R. J., & Martin, A. J. (2024). Students' perceived competence across academic and social-emotional domains: Unique roles in relation to autonomy-supportive teaching, academic engagement, and well-being. *Learning and Individual Differences, 116,* Article 102563.

Conner, J., Holquist, S. E., Mitra, D. L., & Boat, A. (2025). Measuring student voice practices: Development and validation of school and classroom scales. *AERA Open, 11.* https://doi.org/10.1177/23328584251326893

Conner, J., Mitra, D. L., Holquist, S. E., & Boat, A. (2025). How teachers' student voice practices affect student engagement and achievement: Exploring choice, receptivity, and responsiveness to student voice as moderators. *Journal of Educational Change, 26*(1), 89–118.

Crispin, L. M. (2017). Extracurricular participation, "at-risk" status, and the high school dropout decision. *Education Finance and Policy, 12*(2), 166–196.

Davis, B. (2021, December 6). *Holding students back—An inequitable and ineffective response to unfinished learning.* EdTrust. Accessed at https://edtrust.org/rti/holding-students-back-an-inequitable-and-ineffective-response-to-unfinished-learning on November 16, 2025.

Demsas, J. (Host). (2025, February 18). The dark history behind public education [Audio podcast episode]. In *Good on Paper*. Accessed at www.theatlantic.com/podcasts/archive/2025/02/the-real-origins-of-public-education/681709 on November 16, 2025.

den Heijer, A. (2018). *Nothing you don't already know: Remarkable reminders about meaning, purpose and self-realization.* Author.

Dharani, B., Witbooi, E., & April, K. (2024). Self-talk valence and motivational orientation for entrepreneurship: An exploratory study. *Small Enterprise Research, 31*(2), 163–179.

DiMarco, B. (2025, March 9). *Tracking state trends in chronic absenteeism.* FutureEd. Accessed at www.future-ed.org/tracking-state-trends-in-chronic-absenteeism on November 16, 2025.

Dodd, H. F., Nesbit, R. J., & FitzGibbon, L. (2023). Child's play: Examining the association between time spent playing and child mental health. *Child Psychiatry and Human Development, 54*(6), 1678–1686.

DuFour, R. (2012, Summer). [Keynote address]. PLC at Work Institute, San Diego, California.

DuFour, R., & Marzano, R. J. (2011). *Leaders of learning: How district, school, and classroom leaders improve student achievement.* Solution Tree Press.

Dweck, C. (2006). *Mindset: The new psychology of success.* Random House.

Eastwood, J. D., Frischen, A., Fenske, M. J., & Smilek, D. (2012). The unengaged mind: Defining boredom in terms of attention. *Perspectives on Psychological Science, 7*(5), 482–495.

Enoch, J., McDonald, L., Jones, L., Jones, P. R., & Crabb, D. P. (2019). Evaluating whether sight is the most valued sense. *JAMA Ophthalmology, 137*(11), 1317–1320.

Erkenbrack, M. (2026). School-based parental involvement: Community and student outcomes. *The Sociological Quarterly, 67*(1), 181–205.

Every Student Succeeds Act of 2015, Pub. L. No. 114-95, 20 U.S.C. § 1177 (2015).

Felitti, V. J., Anda, R. F., Nordenberg, D., Williamson, D. F., Spitz, A. M., Edwards, V., et al. (1998). Relationship of childhood abuse and household dysfunction to many of the leading causes of death in adults: The Adverse Childhood Experiences (ACE) study. *American Journal of Preventive Medicine, 14*(4), 245–258.

Figlio, D. N., & Özek, U. (2025). *The impact of cellphone bans in schools on student outcomes: Evidence from Florida* [NBER Working Paper 34388]. https://doi.org/10.3386/w34388

Flora, S. R. (2000). Praise's magic reinforcement ratio: Five to one gets the job done. *The Behavior Analyst Today, 1*(4), 64–69.

Froehlich, M. (2025). *The reignited educator: Rediscovering emotional engagement and purpose in your profession.* Solution Tree Press.

Gambone, M. (2024). The advisory program: A space for nurturing student-teacher relationships to strengthen student advocacy in a progressive secondary school. *International Journal of Progressive Education, 20*(1), 48–62.

Gardner, D. P., Larsen, Y. W., Baker, W. O., & Campbell, A. (1983). *A nation at risk: The imperative for educational reform.* National Commission on Excellence in Education. Accessed at https://files.eric.ed.gov/fulltext/ED226006.pdf on November 16, 2025.

Goodwin, B., & Hall, P. (2023). *A reflective teacher's guide to planning for learning.* McREL.

Goodwin, B., & Rouleau, K. (2022). *The new classroom instruction that works: The best research-based strategies for increasing student achievement.* ASCD.

Grose, J. (2025, September 17). The unexpected upside of phone bans in school. *The New York Times.* Accessed at www.nytimes.com/2025/09/17/opinion/phone-bans-schools-kids.html on November 16, 2025.

Haidt, J. (2024). *The anxious generation: How the great rewiring of childhood is causing an epidemic of mental illness.* Penguin Press.

Haines, J. E., & Schutte, N. S. (2023). Parental conditional regard: A meta-analysis. *Journal of Adolescence, 95*(2), 195–223.

Hall, P. (2023). *Always strive to be a better you: How ordinary people can live extraordinary lives.* Authors Place Press.

Hall, P., & Simeral, A. (2017). *Creating a culture of reflective practice: Capacity-building for schoolwide success.* ASCD.

Harris, A., & Jones, M. (2023). The importance of school leadership? What we know. *School Leadership and Management, 43*(5), 449–453.

Harvard University. (n.d.). *Toxic stress.* Accessed at https://developingchild.harvard.edu/key-concept/toxic-stress on November 16, 2025.

Hascher, T., & Hadjar, A. (2018). School alienation: Theoretical approaches and educational research. *Educational Research, 60*(2), 171–188.

Hattie, J. (2009). *Visible learning: A synthesis of over 800 meta-analyses relating to achievement.* Routledge.

Havis, A. (2023). The impact of bad teachers on education: A detrimental force in the classroom. *Journal of Educational Sciences Research, 13*(3).

Heidrich, C. V., Cardozo, P., & Chiviacowsky, S. (2025). Stereotype threat effects on motor performance and learning: A systematic review of 30 years. *Learning and Motivation, 91,* Article 102155.

Hernández, L. E., Darling-Hammond, L., & Nielson, N. (2024, November 21). *Cultivating relationships in secondary schools: Structures that matter* [Brief]. Learning Policy Institute. Accessed at https://learningpolicyinstitute.org/product/cultivating-relationships-secondary-schools-brief on November 16, 2025.

Hill, K. (2025). Creating community with multi-age looping advisory at community school. *Middle School Journal, 56*(2), 6–8.

Hoang, A., Hepburn, S.-J., Morawska, A., & Sanders, M. R. (2025). The effect of self-reflection on the outcomes of online clinical skills training: A comparative study. *Advances in Health Sciences Education, 30*(5), 1621–1639.

Holt-Lunstad, J. (2024). Social connection as a critical factor for mental and physical health: Evidence, trends, challenges, and future implications. *World Psychiatry, 23*(3), 312–332.

Hosker, D. K., Elkins, R. M., & Potter, M. P. (2019). Promoting mental health and wellness in youth through physical activity, nutrition, and sleep. *Child and Adolescent Psychiatric Clinics of North America, 28*(2), 171–193.

The Imagineers. (2003). *The imagineering way: Ideas to ignite your creativity.* Disney.

Imran, S., & Jackson, S. (2022). Attachment relationships and psychological distress in young adults: The mediating role of self-esteem. *Journal of Affective Disorders Reports, 8*, Article 100328.

Isaacs, J. B. (2012, March). *Starting school at a disadvantage: The school readiness of poor children.* Brookings Institution. Accessed at www.brookings.edu/wp-content/uploads/2016/06/0319_school_disadvantage_isaacs.pdf on April 13, 2026.

Ivanović, I. (2021). Psychiatric comorbidities in children with ASD: Autism Centre experience. *Frontiers in Psychiatry, 12*, Article 673169.

Jackson, R. R. (2011). *How to plan rigorous instruction.* ASCD.

Jadhav, B. N., Azeez, E. P. A., Sharma, J., Yadav, A., Athreya, V. S., & Mathew, M. (2025). The association of adverse and benevolent childhood experiences with grit among Gen Z: The mediating role of emotional regulation. *Psychological Reports.* https://doi.org/10.1177/00332941251363891

Jenner, E., Lass, K., Walsh, S., Demby, H., Leger, R., & Falk, G. (2021, March). *Effects of cross-age peer mentoring program within a randomized controlled trial.* The Policy and Research Group. Accessed at https://policyandresearch.com/wp-content/uploads/2021/03/i3_CSS_Evaluation_Manuscript_forWebsite_21Mar19.pdf on November 16, 2025.

Jiang, Z., & Hussain, Y. (2023). The effectiveness of nature-based learning in promoting physical, cognitive, and emotional development in young children: A case study in China. *International Journal of Education and Technology, 1*(3), 56–66.

Kang, J. C. (2024, June 14). We're all tiger moms now. *The New Yorker.* Accessed at www.newyorker.com/news/fault-lines/were-all-tiger-moms-now on November 16, 2025.

Kantova, K. (2024). Parental involvement and education outcomes of their children. *Applied Economics, 56*(48), 5683–5698.

Kappi, A. A., El-Etreby, R. R., Badawy, G. G., Ebrahem, G., & Hamed, W. E. S. (2024). Effects of memory and attention on the association between video game addiction and cognitive/learning skills in children: Mediational analysis. *BMC Psychology, 12*(1), Article 364.

Kearney, C. A., Benoit, L., Gonzálvez, C., & Keppens, G. (2022). School attendance and school absenteeism: A primer for the past, present, and theory of change for the future. *Frontiers in Education, 7.*

Keefer, E. (2023, October 10). *Classroom or courtroom? Problems and solutions to the school-to-prison pipeline.* Center for Public Justice. Accessed at https://cpjustice.org/classroom-or-courtroom-problems-solutions-to-the-school-to-prison-pipeline on November 16, 2025.

Kiadarbandsari, A., & Fa'alau, F. (2025). A demographic analysis of developmental assets, misconduct behaviours, and depression among New Zealand youth in mentoring relationships. *Journal of the Royal Society of New Zealand, 55*(6), 1639–1662.

Killen, M., Burkholder, A. R., Sims, R. N., Yee, K. M., Glidden, J., Luken Raz, K. V., et al. (2024). Does intergroup contact increase children's desire to play with diverse peers and reduce experiences of social exclusion? *Peace and Conflict, 30*(3), 413–425. https://doi.org/10.1037/pac0000713

Labokas, J. (2024). Students' alienation from learning activity: Some insights from high-school seniors' study in Lithuania. *Journal of Education Culture and Society, 15*(1), 549–555.

Lanaj, K., Foulk, T. A., & Jennings, R. E. (2022). Improving the lives of leaders: The beneficial effects of positive leader self-reflection. *Journal of Management, 49*(8), 2595–2628.

Lane, K. S., Buckman, M. M., Iovino, E. A., & Lane, K. L. (2023). Incorporating choice: Empowering teachers and families to support students in varied learning contexts. *Preventing School Failure, 67*(2), 106–114.

Lanteri, L., & Coley, R. L. (2024). School connectedness and social exclusion: Can school contexts ameliorate parental depression risks for early adolescent behavior problems? *Children and Youth Services Review, 164,* Article 107848.

Lawson, G. M., Owens, J. S., Mandell, D. S., Tavlin, S., Rufe, S., Depa, A., et al. (2024). A community-partnered research process for implementation strategy design: Developing resources to support behavioral classroom interventions. *School Mental Health, 16,* 710–726.

Learning Policy Institute. (2025, April 8). *How money matters: Education funding and student outcomes.* Accessed at https://learningpolicyinstitute.org/product/how-money-matters-factsheet on November 16, 2025.

Leung-Gagné, M., McCombs, J., Scott, C., & Losen, D. J. (2022, September). *Pushed out: Trends and disparities in out-of-school suspension.* Learning Policy Institute. Accessed at https://learningpolicyinstitute.org/media/3885/download?inline&file=CRDC_School_Suspension_REPORT.pdf on November 16, 2025.

Levin, S. (2024, November 27). *Brain power revealed: The neuroscience of human behavior.* Columbia School of Professional Studies. Accessed at https://sps.columbia.edu/news/brain-power-revealed-neuroscience-human-behavior on November 16, 2025.

Li, H., Liang, L., Zheng, C., Yuan, T., Zhang, J., Liu, K., et al. (2024). Correlation between perceived supportive parenting and adolescent cognitive performance: The mediating role of achievement attribution and depressive symptoms. *Children and Youth Services Review, 163,* Article 107815.

Lopez, I. (2024). *The EQ way: How emotionally intelligent school leaders navigate turbulent times.* ASCD.

López-Martín, E., Gutiérrez-de-Rozas, B., González-Benito, A. M., & Expósito-Casas, E. (2023). Why do teachers matter? A meta-analytic review of how teacher characteristics and competencies affect students' academic achievement. *International Journal of Educational Research, 120,* Article 102199.

Makori, A., O'Neal, D., Uka, A., McGee, T., & Jones, K. (2025). *Combating chronic absenteeism: Examining California's strategies for addressing a longstanding national crisis.* Expanding Criminal Justice Reform Critical Policy Research. Accessed at www.cjrpolicylab.com/policy-reports/combating-chronic-absenteeism on November 16, 2025.

Malkus, N. (2025, May 30). *Addressing the attendance crisis: New research on chronic absenteeism since the pandemic* [Conference presentation]. American Enterprise Institute symposium, Washington, DC.

Manno, B. (2025, February 17). Revisiting the K–12 student engagement cliff. *Forbes.* Accessed at www.forbes.com/sites/brunomanno/2025/02/17/revisiting-the-student-engagement-cliff on November 16, 2025.

Maroun, J., & Tienken, C. H. (2024). The pernicious predictability of state-mandated tests of academic achievement in the United States. *Education Sciences, 14*(2), Article 129.

Martinez-Yarza, N., Solaberrieta-Eizaguirre, J., & Santibáñez-Gruber, R. (2024). The impact of family involvement on students' social-emotional development: The mediational role of school engagement. *European Journal of Psychology of Education, 39*, 4297–4327.

May, H., Bailes, L. P., & Riser, D. M. (2025). Absenteeism and achievement in early elementary grades: A multilevel organizational analysis. *Journal of Education for Students Placed at Risk, 30*(4), 311–336.

Mayes, S. D., Gorman, A. A., Hillwig-Garcia, J., & Syed, E. (2013). Suicide ideation and attempts in children with autism. *Research in Autism Spectrum Disorders, 7*(1), 109–119.

McCabe, E. M., Kaskoun, J., Bennett, S., Meadows-Oliver, M., & Schroeder, K. (2024). Addressing school connectedness, belonging, and culturally appropriate care for newly immigrated students and families. *Journal of Pediatric Health Care, 38*(2), 233–239.

Medina, J. (2008). *Brain rules: 12 principles for surviving and thriving at work, home, and school.* Pear Press.

Miller, P., Betancur, L., Coulanges, L., Kammerzell, J., Libertus, M., Bachman, H. J., et al. (2022). Time spent playing predicts early reading and math skills through associations with self-regulation. *Journal of Applied Developmental Psychology, 83*, Article 101470.

Miller, W. R., & Rollnick, S. (2013). *Motivational interviewing: Helping people change* (3rd ed.). Guilford Press.

Min, M. O., Yoon, M., Minnes, S., & Singer, L. T. (2025). Internal assets in low-income urban adolescents from 12 to 17 years: Gender variation. *Journal of Research on Adolescence, 35*(1), Article e70018.

Mincu, M. (2022). Why is school leadership key to transforming education? Structural and cultural assumptions for quality education in diverse contexts. *Prospects, 52*(3–4), 231–242.

Moeller, J., Brackett, M. A., Ivcevic, Z., & White, A. E. (2020). High school students' feelings: Discoveries from a large national survey and an experience sampling study. *Learning and Instruction, 66*, Article 101301.

Munro-Schuster, M. (2025). *The empathetic classroom: How a mental health mindset supports your students—and you.* Free Spirit Publishing.

N., K. (2025, September). *Navigating academic rigor: What it means and why it matters* [Blog post]. Crimson Education. Accessed at www.crimsoneducation.org/us/blog/navigating-academic-rigor on November 16, 2025.

Nagata, J. M., Wong, J. H., Kim, K. E., Richardson, R. A., Nayak, S., Potes, C., et al. (2025). Social media use trajectories and cognitive performance in adolescents. *JAMA, 334*(21), 1948–1950.

National Assessment Governing Board. (n.d.). *10 takeaways from the 2024 NAEP results.* Accessed at www.nagb.gov/powered-by-naep/the-2024-nations-report-card/10-takeaways-from-2024-naep-results.html on April 27, 2026.

No Child Left Behind (NCLB) Act of 2001, Pub. L. No. 107-110, § 115, Stat. 1425 (2002).

Nurius, P. S., Prince, D. M., & Rocha, A. (2015). Cumulative disadvantage and youth well-being: A multi-domain examination with life course implications. *Child and Adolescent Social Work Journal*, *32*(6), 567–576.

NVision. (n.d.). *Best senses.* Accessed at www.nvisioncenters.com/eye-health/best-senses on November 16, 2025.

Olson, L. S. (2014). *Why September matters: Improving student attendance* [Policy brief]. Baltimore Education Research Consortium. Accessed at https://files.eric.ed.gov/fulltext/ED553161.pdf on November 16, 2025.

Orchard, K. (2025, April 18). *Motivational interviewing for educators* [Conference presentation]. Idaho Prevention and Support Conference, Sun Valley, ID.

Organisation for Economic Co-operation and Development. (2023). *PISA 2022 results: The state of learning and equity in education* (Vol. 1). Author.

Orth, U., & Robins, R. W. (2022). Is high self-esteem beneficial? Revisiting a classic question. *American Psychologist*, *77*(1), 5–17.

Passarello, N., Tarantino, V., Chirico, A., Menghini, D., Costanzo, F., Sorrentino, P., et al. (2022). Sensory processing disorders in children and adolescents: Taking stock of assessment and novel therapeutic tools. *Brain Sciences*, *12*(11), Article 1478.

Patall, E. A. (2024). Agentic engagement: Transcending passive motivation. *Motivation Science*, *10*(3), 222–233. https://doi.10.1037/mot0000332

Patall, E. A., Vite, A., Lee, D. J., & Zambrano, J. (2024). Teacher support for students' psychological needs and student engagement: Differences across school levels based on a national teacher survey. *Teaching and Teacher Education*, *137*, Article 104400. https://doi.org/10.1016/j.tate.2023.104400

Pegram, J., Watkins, R. C., Hoerger, M., & Hughes, J. C. (2022). Assessing the range and evidence-base of interventions in a cluster of schools. *Review of Education*, *10*(1), Article e3336. https://doi.org/10.1002/rev3.3336

Physical Activity Alliance. (2024, August 26). *The 2024 United States report card on physical activity for children and youth.* Author. Accessed at https://paamovewithus.org/resource/full-report-2024-us-report-card-on-physical-activity-for-children-and-youth on November 16, 2025.

Pietsch, S., Riddell, H., Semmler, C., Ntoumanis, N., & Gucciardi, D. F. (2024). SMART goals are no more effective for creative performance than do-your-best goals or non-specific, exploratory "open goals". *Educational Psychology*, *44*(9–10), 946–962.

Plato. (2007). *The republic.* (D. Lee, Trans.; 2nd ed.). Penguin. (Original work published ca. 380 B.C.E.).

Poisson, C. L., Engel, L., & Saunders, B. T. (2021). Dopamine circuit mechanisms of addiction-like behaviors. *Frontiers in Neural Circuits*, *15*, Article 752420.

Quadt, L., Csecs, J., Bond, R., Harrison, N. A., Critchley, H. D., Davies, K. A., et al. (2024). Childhood neurodivergent traits, inflammation and chronic disabling fatigue in adolescence: A longitudinal case-control study. *BMJ Open*, *14*(7), Article e084203.

Roos, L. L., Wall-Wieler, E., & Lee, J. B. (2019). Poverty and early childhood outcomes. *Pediatrics*, *143*(6), Article e20183426.

Rose, I. D., Lesesne, C. A., Sun, J., Johns, M. M., Zhang, X., & Hertz, M. (2024). The relationship of school connectedness to adolescents' engagement in co-occurring health risks: A meta-analytic review. *Journal of School Nursing, 40*(1), 58–73.

Saenz, A. L. (2020). *The EQ intervention: Shaping a self-aware generation through social and emotional learning.* Greenleaf Book Group Press.

Sakellariou, C. (2025). Reciprocal longitudinal effects between sense of school belonging and academic achievement: Quasi-experimental estimates using United States primary school data. *Frontiers in Psychology, 15,* Article 1478320.

Saks, K. (2024). The effect of self-efficacy and self-set grade goals on academic outcomes. *Frontiers in Psychology, 15,* Article 1324007.

Sandoval-Reyes, J., Idrovo-Carlier, S., & Duque-Oliva, E. J. (2021). Remote work, work stress, and work-life during pandemic times: A Latin America situation. *International Journal of Environmental Research and Public Health, 18*(13), Article 7069.

Sanganeria, V. (2025, June 5). *Through comedy, students can take "big swings" for mental health.* EdSource. Accessed at https://edsource.org/2025/through-comedy-students-can-take-big-swings-for-mental-health/733916 on November 16, 2025.

Santibañez, L., & Guarino, C. (2020, October). *The effects of absenteeism on academic and social-emotional outcomes.* PACE. Accessed at https://edpolicyinca.org/publications/effects-absenteeism-academic-and-social-emotional-outcomes on November 16, 2025.

Scales, P. C., & Leffert, N. (2004). *Developmental assets: A synthesis of the scientific research on adolescent development* (2nd ed.). Search Institute.

Scales, P. C., Redmond, N., & Benson, P. L. (2023). Thriving and sparks. In R. J. Levesque (Ed.), *Encyclopedia of adolescence.* Springer.

Schlechty, P. C. (2002). *Working on the work: An action plan for teachers, principals, and superintendents.* Jossey-Bass.

Search Institute. (2024). *State of developmental assets.* Accessed at https://d2pck61xhq74q6.cloudfront.net/State_of_Developmental_Assets-Download.pdf on November 16, 2025.

Sheehan, K., Bhatti, P. K., Yousuf, S., Rosenow, W., Roehler, D. R., Hazekamp, C., et al. (2022). Long-term effects of a community-based positive youth development program for Black youth: Health, education, and financial well-being in adulthood. *BMC Public Health, 22*(1), Article 593.

Slade, S. (2022). *Questioning education: Moving from what and how to why and who.* Routledge.

Smith, E. (1981). *Aviatrix.* Thorndike Press.

Souers, K., & Hall, P. (2016). *Fostering resilient learners: Strategies for creating a trauma-sensitive classroom.* ASCD.

Stanford, L. (2025). *Connecticut superintendents see positive outcomes after phone bans.* Government Technology. Accessed at www.govtech.com/education/k-12/conn-superintendents-see-positive-outcomes-after-phone-bans on November 16, 2025.

Stults-Kolehmainen, M. A. (2023). Humans have a basic physical and psychological need to move the body: Physical activity as a primary drive. *Frontiers in Psychology, 14,* Article 1134049.

Substance Abuse and Mental Health Services Administration. (n.d.). *Trauma and violence.* Accessed at www.samhsa.gov/mental-health/trauma-violence on November 16, 2025.

Swedo, E. A., Niolon, P. H., Anderson, K. N., Li, J., Brener, N., Mpofu, J., et al. (2024). Prevalence of adverse childhood experiences among adolescents. *Pediatrics, 154*(5), Article e2024066633.

Tajfel, H., & Turner, J. (1979). An integrative theory of social identity. In W. G. Austin & S. Worchel (Eds.), *The social psychology of intergroup relations* (pp. 33–47). Brooks/Cole.

Thompson, R. A. (1991). Emotional regulation and emotional development. *Educational Psychology Review, 3*(4), 269–307.

Thouin, É., Dupéré, V., Dion, E., McCabe, J., Denault, A.-S., Archambault, I., et al. (2022). School-based extracurricular activity involvement and high school dropout among at-risk students: Consistency matters. *Applied Developmental Science, 26*(2), 303–316.

Tomlinson, C. A. (1995). *How to differentiate instruction in mixed-ability classrooms*. ASCD.

Topor, D. R., Keane, S. P., Shelton, T. L., & Calkins, S. D. (2010). Parent involvement and student academic performance: A multiple mediational analysis. *Journal of Prevention and Intervention in the Community, 38*(3), 183–197.

Turner, W. (2024). *Embracing adult SEL: An educator's guide to personal social emotional learning success*. Routledge.

U.S. Department of Education. (2023). *2020–21 Civil Rights Data Collection: Student discipline and school climate in U.S. public schools*. Author. Accessed at www.ed.gov/media/document/crdc-discipline-school-climate-reportpdf-21409.pdf on November 16, 2025.

U.S. Department of Education. (2025, January). *Parent and family engagement: Title I, Part A of the Elementary and Secondary Education Act of 1965 Act*. Accessed at www.ed.gov/media/document/parent-and-family-engagement-guidance-2025-109202.pdf on November 16, 2025.

Utami, A. Y. (2022). The role of parental involvement in student academic outcomes. *Journal of Education Review Provision, 2*(1), 17–21.

van den Toren, S. J., van Grieken, A., Mulder, W. C., Vanneste, Y. T., Lugtenberg, M., de Kroon, M. L. A., et al. (2019). School absenteeism, Health-Related Quality of Life [HRQOL] and happiness among young adults aged 16–26 years. *International Journal of Environmental Research and Public Health, 16*(18), Article 3321.

van Jaarsveld, G., Wong, J., Baars, M., Specht, M., & Paas, F. (2024). Goal setting in higher education: How, why, and when are students prompted to set goals? A systematic review. *Frontiers in Education, 9*, Article 1511605.

Van Marter Souers, K., Orchard, K., & Hall, P. (2025). *The fostering resilience workbook: Strategies and steps to support our learners*. ASCD.

Vygotsky, L. S. (1978). *Mind in society: The development of higher psychological processes*. Harvard University Press.

Wallace Foundation. (2021, February). *How principals affect students and schools*. Accessed at https://wallacefoundation.org/report/how-principals-affect-students-and-schools-systematic-synthesis-two-decades-research on November 16, 2025.

Walton, G. M., & Cohen, G. L. (2007). A question of belonging: Race, social fit, and achievement. *Journal of Personality and Social Psychology, 92*(1), 82–96.

Warren, H. (2024). *Are you a helicopter parent?* Accessed at www.bcm.edu/news/are-you-a-helicopter-parent on November 16, 2025.

Winthrop, R., Shoukry, Y., & Nitkin, D. (2025, January). *The disengagement gap: Why student engagement isn't what parents expect.* The Brookings Institution. Accessed at www.brookings.edu/wp-content/uploads/2025/01/REPORT_The-Disengagement-Gap_FINAL.pdf on November 16, 2025.

Wolf, S., Magnuson, K. A., & Kimbro, R. T. (2017). Family poverty and neighborhood poverty: Links with children's school readiness before and after the Great Recession. *Children and Youth Services Review, 79,* 368–384.

Young, E., McCain, J. L., Mercado, M. C., Ballesteros, M. F., Moore, S., Licitis, L., et al. (2024). Frequent social media use and experiences with bullying victimization, persistent feelings of sadness or hopelessness, and suicide risk among high school students—Youth Risk Behavior Survey, United States, 2023. *Morbidity and Mortality Weekly Report, 73*(4), 23–30.

Yu, X., Du, H., Li, D., Sun, P., & Pi, S. (2023). The influence of social exclusion on high school students' depression: A moderated mediation model. *Psychology Research and Behavior Management, 16,* 4725–4735.

Zhang, X., Li, J., Xie, F., Chen, X., Xu, W., & Hudson, N. W. (2022). The relationship between adult attachment and mental health: A meta-analysis. *Journal of Personality and Social Psychology, 123*(5), 1089–1137.

INDEX

T

V

W

Z

Agents of Impact

G. Williamson McDiarmid, Ronald A. Beghetto, and Yong Zhao

Help students take charge of their learning and impact the world around them. This resource reveals how schools can guide students to discover their potential, set meaningful goals, and prepare for an ever-changing future.

BKG140

Tough but Worth It

Christopher L. Van Loan and Justin D. Garwood

Authors Christopher L. Van Loan and Justin D. Garwood present a powerful, relationship-focused model for supporting students with emotional and behavioral challenges. Grounded in self-awareness and connection, this approach helps educators prevent crises, strengthen trust, and reduce burnout by transforming how they understand themselves and their students.

BKG220

Flip the Script

Rebecca A. Knighton and Jessica R. May

Gain strategies for impactful teacher-student relationships founded on trust, authenticity, and mutual respect. This book arms teachers with research, transformative personal reflections, and strategy examples from five highly effective teachers. Educators will break down internal barriers for themselves and their students.

BKG266

Heroes Within

Aaron Hansen

Empower students to break free from attitudes of disengagement, apathy, or passive compliance. Detailing the hero-maker framework, this book speaks directly to overcoming the student motivation challenges teachers face as they work to empower students with purpose, ownership, and self-efficacy to face challenges.

BKF805